D1565865

GAME OF
MY LIFE

CHICAGO

CUBS

GAME OF MY LIFE

CHICAGO

CUBS

MEMORABLE STORIES OF CUBS BASEBALL

LEW FREEDMAN
WITH STUART SHEA

SPORTS
PUBLISHING

Sports Publishing books may be purchased in bulk at special discounts for
sales promotion, corporate gifts, fund-raising, or educational purposes. Special
editions can also be created to specifications. For details, contact the Special Sales
Department, Sports Publishing, 307 West 36th Street, 11th Floor, New York, NY
10018 or sportspubbooks@skyhorsepublishing.com.

Sports Publishing® is a registered trademark of Skyhorse Publishing, Inc.®,
a Delaware corporation.

Visit our website at www.sportspubbooks.com

10 9 8 7 6 5 4 3 2 1

Library of Congress Cataloging-in-Publication Data is available on file.

ISBN: 978-1-61321-069-7

Printed in the United States of America

CONTENTS

INTRODUCTION

There is no explaining the Cubs. They defy the law of averages. They defy the law of common sense. One would think that they would've won a pennant by accident just once since 1945. One would think that they would win a World Series by accident just once since 1908.

Nah.

The mystique surrounding this National League franchise dates back to its foundings in 1876. So many of the players who passed through the clubhouse over the years remain smitten with the team, the town, the ballpark, the experience. Relatively few of those players (the ones still living, anyway) enjoyed the type of success that most Major League players hunger for, dream about, reflect on in their old age, yet they remain Cubs to the core.

There is something unique about the Cubs, a kind of tradition that cannot be duplicated in the modern world, a sense of belonging to an organization that has been around since long before automobiles clogged the neighborhood around its park. Wrigley Field, an architectural gem and shrine, is worthy of pilgrimmage for the long-distance fan. It is both ancient marvel and trendy gathering place, a must-see and a must-be-seen-there structure.

The lack of institutional success, dating back a century, makes it more difficult for Cubs players to highlight a game of their career that took place while wearing the big 'C' on their chests. No former living Cub can describe the emotion of bringing the World Series title home to the North Side. Only a few Cubs are alive who can describe what it meant to bring a pennant home to the North Side.

That does not mean, however, that we have been devoid of glorious and exciting Cub baseball moments in recent decades. From no-hitters to division championships, players have created memories they—and fans—cherish.

From Andy Pafko and Lennie Merullo, who are among the very few living Cubs who participated in the 1945 World Series, to the players of the 1950s, 1960s, 1970s, 1980s, 1990s, and 2000s who hit home runs, drove in key runs, pitched big games, there are many special occasions to remember. The Cubs have provided enough entertainment to amuse, delight, and thrill their remarkably loyal fans (who came out 3.2 million strong in 2006 to watch a team that finished 30 games under .500).

Although there has been a shortage of championship moments to celebrate, there have been an abundance of great players to toast. Ernie Banks, Ron Santo, Billy Williams, Ferguson Jenkins, Ryne Sandberg, Mark Grace, Don Kessinger, Glenn Beckert, Bruce Sutter, and several other Cubs greats always put on a show worth the price of admission.

—Lew Freedman

GAME OF MY LIFE

CHICAGO

CUBS

Chapter 1

ANDY PAFKO

THE EARLY LIFE OF
ANDY PAFKO

Born into a Polish family, Andrew Pruschka grew up on a farm that grew primarily corn in Northwest Wisconsin, closer to the Minnesota twin cities of Minneapolis and St. Paul and closer still to the city of Eau Claire than to Chicago.

"There were cold winters up there," said Pafko, whose name was Americanized from the one written on his birth certificate.

Pafko was a talented athlete as a youth, but Boyceville was a little community that offered few opportunities in organized high school sports. Pafko played amateur baseball on Sundays with a local team, but his high school fielded a softball team, not a baseball team. He liked basketball, but there was no school hoop squad, either. Pafko was muscular and played some football, but compared to post–World War II America—with the startup of Little League and other organized baseball leagues for teens—Pafko was a novice in the sport even by the end of high school.

Given the limited background, Pafko was surprised and flattered when a local coach encouraged him to pursue the game.

"He says, 'Andy, you've got some ability,'" Pafko recalled. "'Why don't you try out for professional baseball?'"

The baseball landscape differed substantially in the 1930s from the 2000s. Minor league clubs all over the United States ranked from Class

AAA down to Class D. Nearby Eau Claire had a Class D team. For Pafko, it was like trying to walk on to the junior varsity. He showed up for an open tryout and flashed some raw talent, but not enough polish to be retained. The manager took Pafko aside and delivered a mixed message of hope and disappointment. Manager I.B. Griffin told Pafko he was going to be a good ballplayer, but that there was no room for him on the roster. He suggested Pafko return to the farm and wait for an opening—that some player was bound to get hurt once the season began, and Pafko might get a spot.

"I'll remember you," Griffin promised.

Pafko took the news like a youngster after a dose of vile cough medicine. He never believed that Griffin would ever retrieve him for the Eau Claire Bears. As he glumly returned to Boyceville, Pafko thought, "Well, there goes the career."

Time passed. The corn sprouted on the Pruschka farm. It was harvest time when a big, shiny automobile rolled into the family driveway. Pafko was wearing overalls and sitting atop a stack of straw some distance away, and thought, "Oh, my goodness, who's that?'"

The man stepped from the vehicle and asked, "Where's Andy Pafko?" He was pointed out sitting on the straw. When he recognized Griffin, Pafko said, "'Oh, my God," and climbed down. "He remembered me and said, 'One of my boys got hurt. I want you to come back and finish the season for me.'"

Pafko changed from overalls to traveling clothes about as swiftly as Clark Kent changing to Superman, making it to Eau Claire to play the last dozen or so games of the season. Pafko was no miracle story who lit up

NAME: Andrew Pruschka
BORN: February 25, 1921 in Boyceville, Wisconsin
HOMETOWN: Boyceville, Wisconsin
CURRENT RESIDENCE: Mount Prospect, Illinois
OCCUPATION: Retired major league baseball player; former major league coach and scout; former minor league manager
POSITION: Outfielder, third base
HEIGHT: 6 feet
PLAYING WEIGHT: 190 pounds
ACCOMPLISHMENTS: Played 17 major league seasons with the Chicago Cubs, Brooklyn Dodgers, and Milwaukee Braves, appearing in 1,852 games with a lifetime average of .285; five-time All-Star; played in the World Series with all three of his major league teams.
THE GAME: Chicago Cubs versus Detroit Tigers in the first game of the World Series—October 3, 1945

A 17-year major leaguer, Andy Pafko began his career with the Cubs in 1943. He played a key role in the outfield for the 1945 team that advanced to the World Series—the last time the Cubs reached the Fall Classic. Although Pafko also participated in the Series with the Dodgers and Braves, he chooses to wear his Cubs World Series ring. *Brace Photo*

the pitchers, but his appearance in the games put his name into public view.

"That was my start," Pafko said. "The next year, I went to spring training with the Milwaukee Brewers."

In those days, the Brewers were an independent AAA farm club, not to be confused with the Major League Brewers who came into the majors much later as an expansion team. Pafko was excited, but the caliber of play was over his head. No argument from him on that—he didn't have the depth of experience of most other players. He needed seasoning, time in the field. Pafko spent the summer playing in Green Bay in the Wisconsin State League, and when the Brewers again brought him to spring training, he pictured himself cracking the lineup of the best-known team in his home state.

Yet, Pafko's minor-league days took a turn. Instead, he was shipped to Macon, Georgia, and when he was sold to the Cubs and promoted to AAA, he was sent cross-country to the Los Angeles Angels in 1943. Like the big club itself, the Angels played in a stadium called Wrigley Field. Pafko matured as a player. He found his batting stroke and became a slick center fielder. Demonstrating readiness for the majors, Pafko led the Pacific Coast in hitting. However, that was not his greatest thrill with the Angels.

"Joe DiMaggio was stationed in California during the war, and he got himself together a club of former big leaguers," Pafko said. "They came over and played our club in Los Angeles. I'll never forget it because Joe DiMaggio was my hero, my idol. They arranged a photo session for the two of us, and when I saw him coming toward me, oh God, I thought I'd died and gone to heaven. Here comes my idol. And I'll never forget, he put his arm around me and said, 'Kid, I'll see you in the big leagues.' Oh, coming from him, what an endorsement that was for me."

THE SETTING

Pafko made his major league debut in 1943, appearing in 13 games and making a good impression with a .379 average. It was apparent he would be patrolling the outfield at the real Wrigley Field the next season; and in 1944, he became a full-time big leaguer.

In fact, from the moment DiMaggio uttered his stamp of approval, mentally Pafko had made the last leap. "Oh boy, I felt like a big leaguer then and there," Pafko recalled.

Before Pafko rooted himself in the outfield, he was thrust into a variety of infield positions, particularly third base. Glib manager Charlie Grimm nicknamed Pafko "Handy Andy."

"Charlie Grimm had names for everybody," Pafko said. "So it was just naturally, 'Handy Andy,' because I could play so many different positions."

Lennie Merullo, a Cubs shortstop of the era who also played on the 1945 World Series team, said that Grimm "called him (Pafko) 'Pushka.'"

Pafko said his favorite position was center field "because I think it's the easiest place to play in the outfield. You're right behind the pitcher, and you get to see where the ball is, inside or outside, and you get a better jump than you do in left or right. You've got more ground to cover, but it's still the easiest of the outfield positions in my opinion."

By 1945, Pafko had established himself in the Cubs outfield. He batted .298 that season and drove in 110 runs. His .995 fielding average led National League outfielders. Guided by Grimm, the Cubs won 98 games.

Things happened quickly in Pafko's career. Being from the adjacent state of Wisconsin, Chicago fans adopted him as a local. He was in just his second full season when the team threw an "Andy Pafko Day" in celebration.

"Before we even won the pennant," Pafko said. "My friends got together and bought me a couple of items, a couple of suitcases, some small things. I really appreciated it. It was a big thrill."

Pafko's mother, Susan, had never seen him play baseball, so she attended one game during the 1945 season, too. The team brought her to Chicago.

"I came up to the plate the first time, the bases were loaded, and I struck out," Pafko said. "I thought, 'What a beginning this is.' Later in the same game, I hit a home run, and it helped win the game. My poor mom didn't know too much about baseball. As I was rounding second base headed for third, everybody was standing up. My mom was sitting down because she didn't understand what happened. Finally, she got up, and I looked up at her; and she was smiling. Somebody must have told her that the best thing a guy could do in baseball was hit a home run. That was a big moment in my life. It was the one and only game she saw me play. The following year, she passed away."

When the Cubs captured the NL pennant, the city was happy, but not overwhelmed. The perception of the team differed markedly from the way the franchise is viewed today. Chicago was not seen as a woebegone team, with longtime baseball observers shaking their heads because nearly a century had passed without a World Series crown. Not that fans were spoiled—it had been almost 40 years since the 1908 World Series championship—but the Cubs had won three pennants in the 1930s, and the 1945 World Series against the Detroit Tigers was the tenth in team history.

"The fans were revved up about it, I know that," Pafko said. "It had been a long enough time since 1938."

The Cubs were not expected to contend in 1945. They improved by 23 games in the standings and needed most of those wins to fend off the St. Louis Cardinals, who finished three games back. America was still at war when the season began. With Pafko, Bill Nicholson, Stan Hack, and Phil Cavaretta—who batted .355 that year and won the National League Most Valuable Player award—the Cubs had more top-flight talent than other clubs whose rosters had been depleted.

Germany surrendered on May 7, ending the war in Europe. Japan surrendered on August 14, ending World War II. The Cubs solidified their chances of winning a pennant by purchasing pitcher Hank Borowy from the Yankees. Borowy had fallen into the doghouse of New York owner Larry MacPhail, who called him a "seven-inning" pitcher. (In 2007, that qualifies as a compliment. In 1945, that was an insult.) Pafko said the Borowy trade in late July was the difference maker for the Cubs.

"Without him, we wouldn't have won the pennant," Pafko said. "He stabilized that pitching staff, and that's why we won it."

Borowy went 11-2 for the Cubs in August and September. The Cubs clinched their first pennant in a decade on September 29 by beating the Pittsburgh Pirates, 4-3, in the first game of a doubleheader. Pafko drove in the game-winner, and Borowy collected the win.

And then the party began.

"That was the first time I'd ever tasted champagne," Pafko said.

Just like eating a hot dog in the stands, drinking champagne in the clubhouse has a distinct, memorable flavor.

THE GAME OF MY LIFE

BY ANDY PAFKO

I went to the World Series with three different teams—and I was on the winning team with the Milwaukee Braves. Yet, the World Series ring that I wear is from the Cubs' World Series in 1945. It means the most to me—probably because it was my first World Series and because I still live in the Chicago area.

We won the first game of the World Series in Detroit (9-0) before more than 54,000 people, and that was a huge thrill. They were throwing Hal Newhouser, who was a great pitcher. He won 25 games that year; and for the second year in a row, he won the Most Valuable Player award. He was their big gun, but we had everything going for us that day. We clobbered him. We scored four runs in the first inning, so we felt pretty good about ourselves. And then we scored three more runs in the third.

That was a great game for me. I had two singles and a double, and I scored three runs. I also threw out Hank Greenberg (the Tiger first baseman on his way to the Hall of Fame) sliding into third. He was on first base, and there was a line drive to left-center. I got the ball, whirled around, and threw to Stan Hack at third. I think I had Greenberg by about five steps or so. I always had a great arm. I led the league one year in assists, threw out 26 base runners.

It was something. Here I was in my second full year in the big leagues, already in the World Series. I'll never forget the first game of the World Series. I think it was the greatest game of all.

I was nervous before the start. I'm in the World Series and there's all this attention. And I knew all of the people back home in Wisconsin were listening for me on the radio. I knew they were nervous for me, too. But I had a big game with those three hits off Newhouser (a future Hall of Famer, too). He was a big man at the time. He had great control, a fastball, curveball. Of course, he was a left-hander, but I didn't mind hitting against lefties. I was very proud that I got three hits off one of the great left-handers of all time.

The Tigers won the second game, but we won the third game (3-0) when Claude Passau pitched a one-hitter. The fourth game, we were back in Chicago at Wrigley Field—that was the game when the guy (Chicago restaurant operator Billy Sianis) tried to bring the goat into the game. They didn't let him, and that's where they get this stuff on "The Curse of the Billy Goat." I don't know if the goat is a curse or not, but we never would have thought we would be the last Cubs team to make the World Series.

GAME RESULTS

The Cubs won the first game of the Series with a dominating performance, but the Tigers took the championship in seven games. At the start of the 2007 season, it had been 62 years since the Cubs won a pennant and advanced to the World Series; and it had been 99 years since the Cubs won a World Series.

Pafko was traded to the Dodgers during the 1951 season and played in another World Series with Brooklyn in 1952, then played for the championship Braves in 1957.

"I think of some of these former great Cubs players like Ron Santo and Ernie Banks, and they played all those years and never had the opportunity to play in even one World Series game," Pafko said. "And here I was with three clubs and always in the World Series. I was a very fortunate person."

After the 1945 Series, Pafko was invited home for some festivities.

"When the World Series was over they honored me at the high school in my hometown of Boyceville, so I came back a hero," Pafko said. "I'll never forget that. I had several thrills in baseball, but playing in that first World Series topped them all.

"For years after I retired, around the Chicago area, people always wanted me to talk about winning the pennant in 1945. Now when they see me it's, 'Andy, when are they going to win another pennant?' Of course the saying around Chicago is, 'Wait 'til next year.' I changed that to, 'Wait 'til the next century.' And it already is the next century."

REFLECTING ON BASEBALL

Pafko retired after the 1959 season, satisfied with his unlikely baseball career. He then coached three seasons for the Milwaukee Braves, managed in the minors, and scouted. In all, Pafko spent about 40 years in professional baseball, but the off-field work couldn't compare to the on-field play.

"It's nothing like playing," he said.

Pafko does not hesitate to compare playing the game then and how he sees it played now.

"I took pride in my outfield play," Pafko said. "That's the trouble with baseball today. They don't hit the cutoff man. It's the little things. They say a home-run hitter drives a Cadillac and a singles hitter drives a Ford. They all want to drive a Cadillac. Sure, the home run is exciting, but there's more to baseball than a home run. It's the little things—you need to execute, hit and run, bunt, but today everybody just wants to hit home runs. It's the little things that win ballgames.

"Guys want to hit this and that, but defense is important, too. I played hurt many times. Today, a guy has something wrong with his fingernail, and he's on the disabled list. One year, I ran into the wall at Wrigley Field catching a line drive—I ran into the ivy. I hurt my arm, but I didn't say anything. I didn't tell the manager. I played the whole game with my arm hurt. Afterwards, the trainer said I had better go to the doctor. I played the whole game with a bone chipped in my elbow."

After Pafko retired, Boyceville named a local ballpark "Andy Pafko Park" after him. A plaque was placed on site with the highlights of his career etched on it, and the writing included a quote from Pafko suggesting he loved the game so much he would have played for free. Pafko's late wife Ellen often teased him, "You did, honey."

When Pafko started playing in the majors he was paid $500 a month. His top salary was $30,000 a year. Pafko said when he sees that someone playing today makes a million dollars while hitting just .220 he can't believe it.

"My God, in my day if I had that number, I'd be in the minors so far down they couldn't find me," he said. "If I was playing today—I had a batting average of almost .290 for 17 years—I would make millions."

Pafko said he only saved a smattering of memorabilia from his playing days; a Cubs shirt, and the World Series rings that he treasures.

He has sold autographs at sports memorabilia conventions and said he wears the Cubs ring as a conversation piece.

"It's not only a World Series ring, but it's an antique," he said. "I don't know what it takes to be an antique; but in my opinion, it's an antique."

A Cubs World Series ring? That must qualify.

Most of the players from the 1945 World Series team have died and the few survivors are in their 80s and live far apart. A few years ago, however, shortstop Lennie Merullo was invited to an autograph session in Chicago. He had no idea who else would appear. He had not seen Pafko for years, and after the session began, Merullo nudged another athlete near him and asked, "Who's the fellow next to me?" The man said, "See what he signed?" It was Pafko.

"I didn't even recognize him!" Merullo said. "Then I saw the sign, and it said, 'Andy Pafko.' I elbowed him and said, 'You son of a gun! I didn't even recognize you.'"

Pafko said he gets most of his baseball from television these days, but tries to attend a half-dozen Cubs games a season. He attends the annual winter Cubs convention and stays in touch with team president John McDonough. The team treats him royally, Pafko said, and the Cubs are still No. 1 in his heart.

"I consider myself a Cub," Pafko said. "Chicago is a great town with great fans. I played in a bunch of great towns with great players, but people remember me as a Cub because I live here, I make my home here. If anybody deserves a pennant, it's the wonderful Chicago Cubs fans. They come out daily to fill the ballpark, but unfortunately they haven't had a winner since 1945. I hope they win one before I leave this earth. To play in one World Series for the Cubs and then to see one in person as a spectator, my life would be complete."

Chapter 2

LENNIE MERULLO

THE EARLY LIFE OF LENNIE MERULLO

The accent is as pronounced as comedian Dennis Leary's. You know you are talking to a Bostonian when you talk to Lennie Merullo. He is all Boston down to his cuticles—except for one thing. His entire major league career was spent as an infielder for the Chicago Cubs. Merullo was born in East Boston, across Boston Harbor from downtown. He attended East Boston High School and St. John's Prep school in Danvers, a private school that stressed education, sports, and Catholicism—an avenue that led him to Villanova University on Philadelphia's Main Line.

One of 12 brothers and sisters, Merullo grew up in an Italian family competitive in sports. He was sensational at baseball, the primary team sport of the era, and was highly regarded by a local figure named Ralph Wheeler. Wheeler was a sportswriter for the *Boston Herald*, ran his own team, and funded the Suburban Baseball League. He was nicknamed "Mr. Baseball" in the Boston area for his commitment to the game.

Although Wheeler operated in a town that then served as home to the American League Red Sox and the National League Braves, he had connections with the Chicago Cubs. He was so tight with the team that, when the Cubs visited Boston, they allowed Wheeler to put on a uniform and work out with the club. They also allowed some of his prize players to mingle with the major leaguers.

Wheeler brought Merullo to Braves Field and turned him over to the Cubs trainer, who outfitted him with a uniform and told him to sit on the bench in the team dugout.

"So that's how I loved the Chicago Cubs from way back," Merullo said. "I loved that infield they had—Stan Hack, Billy Jurges, Billy Herman, and Charlie Grimm. Later they had Phil Cavaretta, whom I roomed with for years on the road."

Unlike young Cubs fans of today, Merullo grew up watching a team that won the pennant in 1932, 1935, and 1938.

"They had a rhythm of it," he said. "Every three years. They had a fine club in those days, and they had a good infield. People would go out there early just to watch the Cubs have infield practice. They don't do that today."

Merullo earned a B.S. in education from Villanova in 1948 and thought that he would become a teacher and a high school coach (which he would after he finished his major league career). When the Japanese bombed Pearl Harbor in December of 1941, Merullo expected to be drafted. There were nine boys in his family, and several of them were close in age. He was just waiting his turn to go into the Army when he got the chance to join the personnel-diminished Cubs.

The draft board took one Merullo brother at a time, but kept postponing the service of others by six months each time.

"They would give me another six months, and then another six months, because I had brothers in the service," Merullo said. "And before you know it, the war was over. So I got a really good chance to play because it was the war years. Hey, I was the best they could get at the time."

Merullo broke into the majors in 1941 and got into seven games. He moved into the infield

---

NAME: Leonard Richard Merullo
BORN: May 5, 1917, in Boston, Massachusetts
HOMETOWN: East Boston, Massachusetts
CURRENT RESIDENCE: Reading, Massachusetts
OCCUPATION: Retired major league player and scout
POSITION: Shortstop
HEIGHT: 5-foot-11
PLAYING WEIGHT: 168 pounds
ACCOMPLISHMENTS: Seven-year major league player with the Chicago Cubs; a regular on the 1945 pennant-winning team; attended Villanova University; grandson Matt played six years in the majors.
THE GAME: Chicago Cubs versus New York Giants—August 20, 1944

Personable Lennie Merullo is one of the last living members of the 1945
Cubs World Series team. Although he lives in his native Boston, Merullo—
who had a grandson play in the majors as well—still roots for Cubs success.
Brace Photo

more permanently in 1942 and batted .256, though his main strength was always fielding. Merullo might have made the majors sooner, but during spring training of 1939, he came up with a sore arm.

"I could run and throw," he said. "I could throw with anybody. I never gave the sore arm a chance to heal. I never did play at all that year. I had to take the whole year off. In 1940, the Cubs sent me to Tulsa in the Texas League. Roy Johnson, who later became a coach with the Cubs, was the manager. In 1941, I was in Los Angeles, but Los Angeles made a deal for me with the Toronto ball club because they needed a shortstop. They lent me to them, and that was the A's organization. And then it was up to the Cubs."

Merullo had no value to the Cubs if he couldn't make the throw from the hole. The right-hander injuring his throwing arm was almost as incapacitating as an injured wing on a bird. He did not carry a big stick, but rather a toothpick, to the plate. Merullo hit home runs about as often as people celebrate birthdays. Both occasions came around roughly once a year and were hailed equally.

THE SETTING

Merullo hit only .240 in his career and stroked just 12 home runs in his seven major-league seasons. With few exceptions, until the 1980s or so, it was a rare shortstop who registered with the opposing pitching staff as a home-run threat. The Cubs' own Ernie Banks was the major exception of the 1950s.

During his cup-of-coffee, seven-game 1941 season, Merullo did not hit a home run. In 142 games during the 1942 season, Merullo hit two home runs. In 129 games during the 1943 season, Merullo hit one home run. While only playing in 66 games during the 1944 season, Merullo hit just one homer. He was hardly the first batter who opposing managers considered when they thought about intentional walks. If Merullo was going to beat a team, it was as a table-setter, a man who walked ahead of the big sluggers. The odds against Merullo smashing a game-winning home run seemed as remote as breaking a casino in Las Vegas.

"I wasn't a power hitter," Merullo said in a bit of understatement. "I think, when I was a rookie, my first major-league hit was a base-hit through the hole against the New York Giants. That's how I hit. What a thrill that was."

No one—not Merullo, fans, or sportswriters who chronicled Cub doings—was prepared for any sign of Merullo slugging prowess during the third week in August of 1944. They had all seen enough of Merullo against big-league pitching to know better.

THE GAME OF MY LIFE

BY LENNIE MERULLO

The game of my life was really the hit of my life more than a whole game. We were playing the Giants in Wrigley Field. Wrigley Field was a good ballpark—the brick wall, the ivy, all of that. Hitters liked it, but, of course, I wasn't that much of a hitter.

We had the bases loaded in the fourth inning against the Giants. The pitcher was Harry Feldman. He was a right-hander who was in the National League just about the whole time I was. I think he may have been another player who benefited from the rosters being short because of World War II.

I can remember hitting the ball. I hit it well, and I saw it take off. Right away, I thought I might have a two-base hit. I never thought about home runs. When I saw the ball go into the stands, though, I jumped so high in the air that I tripped and fell flat on my face. I jumped so danged high that I really went down.

It was the first game of a doubleheader, and we won 7-4. Then we won the second game, too. I never hit home runs. That's why I went kind of crazy on the basepaths. It was pretty funny.

We were already near the end of the season, and that was my first home run that year. There was a sportswriter with one of the Chicago newspapers, the *Chicago American*, who always had a lot of fun when he wrote about the games, and he was always kidding me. In the next day's paper, above his write-up was the headline, "Merullo Hits Annual Homer."

That was a good one. I always remember that.

GAME RESULTS

The game-winning grand-slam home run was a memory-maker for Merullo, but that was a brief moment of personal glory. The Cubs finished only 75-79 that season, fourth in the National League, so the results of individual games didn't mean so much.

That changed suddenly the next season, and Merullo was right in the mix when the Cubs turned things around to win their first pennant in seven years and appear in their last World Series for at least 62 years.

Merullo crushed a double in the pennant-clincher, a 4-3 victory over the Pirates. The team stayed in a hotel across the street from Forbes Field that offered a beautiful view, and that Merullo said also had the best food in the league. The victory party got a little bit out of hand when Cubs pitcher Paul Derringer, who had a grudge against Pirates owner William Benswagner, gave him a shove.

"Some of that shouldn't have happened," Merullo said. "But they squelched it. The celebration wasn't completely what I had hoped."

Merullo was a low-key man, so it wasn't clear if the arrangement for him to room with Phil Cavaretta on the road was because they were both Italian or because they were temperamentally compatible. Cavaretta, who won the National League batting title and was the MVP that season, was known to lose his temper often.

"If you got me mad, I wasn't worth a damn," Merullo said. "But he would fly off the handle at the waiters, and he had to find something wrong with everything. I would calm him down, talk to him. I kept him more on an even keel. He was very fortunate to have a fellow like me. He was MVP and had a great year. I always gave myself credit for helping Phil become the MVP. He needed a guy like me to keep him on an even keel."

It took four years with the Cubs for Merullo to reach a World Series. He had grown up with the pattern of the every-three-years visits, so he was overdue. Little could he or his teammates imagine that this would be the last Cubs World Series for decades.

"We had a veteran club that could win it every year," Merullo said. "No doubt, you get the feel that, if you win one pennant, you can do it again. But then many changes come along in baseball. I wish we could have won again. Just being in that World Series, hey, the excitement was something."

There was also more than one kind of disappointment. Merullo had been the Cubs starter at short almost the entire season, but at the start of the Series, Charlie Grimm used backup Roy Hughes.

"I was very excited to be in the World Series, and then Charlie Grimm decided to start Hughes at shortstop to give us a little offensive potential at the beginning of the game. He (Grimm) talked to me. He was very, very good about it. He made me understand. He said he would get me in as soon as he possibly could."

Merullo did see action in the Series, starting some and filling in as a pinch runner or late-inning defensive replacement in other games. He entered Game 6 in the late innings of the Cubs' 8-7 12-inning victory and was guarding second base on an attempted steal by Tigers backup shortstop Joe Hoover in the tenth.

Merullo did not get souvenir World Series championship items from 1945, but he did take home another permanent souvenir—a scar on his left arm from the collision.

"It was my fault," Merullo said. "He came in hard stealing a base. I just wanted to be sure I tagged him out. I tried what we called a quick-drop tag. You catch the ball and just drop the glove and let him slide in. You get your hand out of the way. He pinned my arm up right against the bag. He slid into it very, very hard; and instead of me giving the quick tag and pulling out of there, I stayed on the bag. He swiped me in the left arm. The scar is about three inches long. I had to be taken out of that ballgame.

"I still carry that scar. Every time it started to heal, I would scratch off the scab. It's a World Series scar."

During the 1945 World Series, Billy Goat Tavern owner Billy Sianis tried to bring his pet goat into Wrigley Field and was turned away at the gate. He supposedly put a curse on the Cubs saying they would never win the World Series again. They haven't yet. Merullo said the ballplayers didn't know about the incident at the time, but he has heard about it many times since. Sportswriters call periodically to ask about "the hex," as Merullo calls it.

New Cubs managers come along every few years and downplay the curse, and players always pooh-pooh it, but former player Merullo thinks the curse is real. Do you really believe there's a hex on the Cubs, Lennie?

"Yes, I do," he said. "I don't know a ballplayer who wasn't superstitious."

REFLECTIONS ON BASEBALL

Not every game Merullo played was worth remembering, though there was one he couldn't forget no matter how hard he tried. If the grand slam was the hit of his career, the September 13, 1942 Cubs game against the Braves was the worst game of his life.

During the second game of a doubleheader that the Cubs managed to win 12-8, Merullo committed a major league record-tying four errors in one inning. He made four errors within six batters in the second inning, bobbling three grounders and dropping one throw.

There were mitigating circumstances. On the morning of the games Merullo dropped off his pregnant wife, Mary Eugenia, better known as Jean, at a Boston hospital. She was expecting at any time, and Merullo was more nervous in a game than he ever had been. Right after the game, Merullo joined Jean at the hospital.

"My baby was born the next morning at 5:30 or six o'clock, and I was right there," Merullo said.

The next day's headline discussed how Merullo had booted four balls in the infield and so he named his son Boots. Boots had his own baby boy years later, and he followed in his grandfather's footsteps. Matt Merullo spent six seasons in the majors, mostly with the White Sox, between 1989 and 1995.

"It was a thrill to watch him play," Merullo said of his grandson. "I used to kid him. He's a big, red-haired, freckle-faced, blue-eyed kid, who is 6-foot-2 and 215 pounds. I'd say, 'What the hell are you doing with the name Merullo?'"

Merullo's Cubs career ended in 1947, and he played a year with the AAA club in Los Angeles. Merullo planned to settle in California, but as soon as he retired, Cubs management called, asking him to become an East Coast scout. Merullo thought he would try it for a while before he used that Villanova degree for teaching and coaching.

"Full-time scouting was very little money, but it was a great opportunity; and I grabbed it," Merullo said. "I never got out of baseball."

Merullo spent the next 55 years scouting for the Cubs until he retired in 2002. His favorite signing was of one-time Cubs pitcher Moe Drabowsky, who came up with the Cubs in 1956 and spent 17 years in the majors. Drabowsky, who died at age 70 in June of 2006, was playing in a summer college league in Nova Scotia.

In the weeks leading up to Drabowsky's 21st birthday, Merullo babysat him so he would not sign a contract with another club. Drabowsky didn't own a car, so Merullo enticed him into the Cubs' lair by lending him a car regularly in exchange for a promise that when he turned 21 he would sign.

"He kept his promise, and we flew from Nova Scotia into Boston, picked up his mother and father, and went to Chicago and signed that day," Merullo said.

Merullo possesses split rooting allegiances. He played his entire major-league career with the Cubs, so he cheers for them. He has lived most of his life in the Boston area, so he cheers for the Red Sox. In 2003, when both teams seemed on the verge of winning their respective league championship series' and advancing to the World Series, local television stations parked trucks in front of his house waiting to capture Merullo's reaction.

"They had this all planned," he said. "It would have been a dream come true."

With only a handful of outs standing between them and the World Series, both teams faltered at the end. Who would Merullo have rooted for in a showdown World Series?

"Both of them!" he said. "I'm an old-time Red Sox boy, but I'm still a Cub at heart. If they get in the Series, I'll be there. I'd be there before they invited me."

Chapter 3

GEORGE ALTMAN

THE EARLY LIFE OF GEORGE ALTMAN

When George Altman was a youngster during the Depression in Goldsboro, North Carolina—a community of about 20,000 people—Little League Baseball had not yet been founded. Altman's introduction to baseball came through his local grade school. The three elementary schools in the area played a handful of games against one another.

His team was called White Oak. Altman believes it was named after the trees so, prevalent in the area. As a youth, he experimented with all positions, even catcher. There was one drawback to filling that role, however.

"We played without adequate equipment," Altman recalled. "I had to catch with no mask. It was dangerous, but I was the catcher because I didn't have any older brothers to look out for me. If I wanted to play, I had to catch. They made me. After that, though, I grew fast and started playing shortstop. When you grow a little bit bigger you can kind of dictate what you want to play."

That first team was run more by bullying than by meritocracy. Altman, who reached his full height of 6-foot-4 by the time he reached high school, was the anomaly in his family. The sports gene did not run through his parents, but alighted on him. He came from a family of auto mechanics. There were no older athletes in the clan to mentor him, but Altman was good at most sports.

By the time he enrolled at Diller High School in Goldsboro, Altman alternated between third base and the outfield in baseball. By his sophomore year, he had become a forward and center on the basketball team.

"I was just taller than most guys," Altman said. "There wasn't any formal center position because we played more or less a scramble game running."

Altman was lean and fast, had quick feet, and developed his reflexes playing baseball. Goldsboro was home to Seymour Johnson Field, an Air Force Base, and a man stationed there married a local girl. He observed many of the local athletes, and when he spotted someone who looked like a good college prospect, he would contact his old coach serving as football coach and athletic director at Tennessee State in Nashville. That convoluted pipeline produced a basketball scholarship for Altman in 1951, and he majored in education and minored in biology.

Like the more famous Grambling, Tennessee State was a traditionally African-American college that turned out winning football teams. But the basketball team was pretty good, too. There was a national black high school basketball tournament held in Nashville, and teams from all over participated. Tennessee State picked up a handful of players from Chicago to join Altman.

"They had dibs on all the best players around the Midwest to the East Coast at that time," Altman said. "When I went down they had about 55 guys trying out. It was quite a circus."

Altman provided a mix of scoring, rebounding, and passing for a squad that won collegiate championships three of the four years he played

NAME: George Lee Altman
BORN: March 20, 1933, in Goldsboro, North Carolina
HOMETOWN: Goldsboro, North Carolina
CURRENT RESIDENCE: O'Fallon, Missouri
OCCUPATION: Retired baseball player; retired stockbroker
POSITION: Outfielder
HEIGHT: 6-foot-4
PLAYING WEIGHT: 200 pounds
ACCOMPLISHMENTS: Spent nine years in the major leagues, mostly with the Chicago Cubs, compiling a lifetime average of .269; two-time All-Star; led the National League in triples with 12 in 1961 and twice batted over .300; played winter ball in Cuba and played eight seasons professionally in Japan after his major-league stint.
THE GAME: Chicago Cubs versus Los Angeles Dodgers—April 11, 1959

A two-time Cubs All-Star in the early 1960s during his nine-year major-league career, hard-hitting outfielder George Altman had one of the most colorful baseball careers of all time. He played in the Negro Leagues and in Japan, in addition to his time in the National League. *Brace Photo*

for Tennessee State. The school did not have a baseball team until Altman's junior year. After earning his degree, Altman spent a year coaching the junior varsity basketball team at Des Moines College, but he had played baseball so well that a contact at Tennessee State put a good word in for him with the Kansas City Monarchs.

Jackie Robinson integrated Major League Baseball with his Brooklyn Dodgers breakthrough in 1947. Gradually, over the ensuing years, the old Negro Leagues dried up. The Monarchs, one of the premier teams for black players for decades, was hanging on as an independent club. Buck O'Neil, the famed first baseman and manager, was about to shift over to the Chicago Cubs as a full-time scout, but 1955 was in his final season with the Monarchs.

"Buck O'Neil was my first manager," Altman said. "He made an impact on me. With that big voice, he was quite an inspirational guy. We did well under him in 1955. As a matter of fact, Satchel Paige came back to play on that team, too."

Paige, perhaps the greatest pitcher of all time, had been active as a Negro Leagues star, Caribbean winter league star, and barnstormer for roughly three decades by then. He was semi-retired, or at the least lacking top form when he joined the Monarchs in July of that summer.

"We were playing down in Birmingham, and there was all this publicity, but they told people he hadn't been pitching, and they had to take it easy on him," Altman said. "Well, the young guys on Birmingham are going like, 'Who is Satchel Paige?' And they started hitting him all over the place."

Paige was a very proud man, and he never took a pounding on the mound well. Altman said he got angry and said, "'Okay, young bucks, wait till the next time I see you.' About three weeks later, we played Birmingham again, and then he set them down."

As a black man who grew up in the 1930s and 1940s, Altman understood what kind of discrimination men like O'Neil and Paige endured to make their marks, and he felt it was a privilege to share a dugout with them.

"I felt like I was playing on hallowed ground," Altman said. "I had heard so much about those guys. To be on the same team with the legendary Satchel Paige, and to sit around listening to him tell stories, was something. He used to brag about how he could hit. He could hit a little bit, too."

Although Paige worked to keep his age a secret, baseball finally adopted 1906 as his birth year. That meant he was 49 during the 1955 season.

"And he was still hitting line drives," Altman said. "He was quite the guy."

Not long after O'Neil joined the Cubs, he urged owner P.K. Wrigley to sign Altman, Lou Johnson, who had an eight-year major-league career, though he played only briefly with the Cubs; and Stacy Hartman, who did not make the majors. Rookies did not typically earn big bonuses at the time, although there were exceptions for the so-called "bonus babies."

"Buck recommended all three of us, and we got a pack of chewing gum from Wrigley," Altman said.

A pack of chewing gum?

"I was just kidding," he said. "We didn't get anything. Not even a pack of chewing gum to sign. We were just happy to get out of (where they were) because the teams were having financial problems. We got the opportunity to go into pro ball and perhaps get the opportunity to move up the ladder."

Altman was shipped to Burlington, Iowa, for seasoning, but then he went into the Army. Altman played on a championship service team with future major league slugger Leon "Daddy Wags" Wagner. When he was released from the service in Colorado, Altman immediately joined a minor-league team in Pueblo. He worked his way back into shape by playing winter ball in Panama and then came to Cubs' Mesa, Arizona, spring training camp in 1959 ready for the jump to the majors.

That was his game plan, not the Cubs'. Altman was earmarked for a season in AAA, but he got a break. One day, practice halted for picture day. The major leaguers were shooed out of the batting cage into a lineup for the team photo. But the batting practice pitcher was still on the mound. Altman stepped in, urged him to throw, and began spraying line drives all over the desert.

"I was hitting them out," Altman said. "I got lucky. They were going all over the place. And the guys were going, 'Ooh, ooh.' They started teasing, 'That guy's going to take your job.' 'Ooh, boy.' You know how guys ride you. Finally, the manager, Bob Scheffing, kind of eased over to me and said, 'You come down a little early tomorrow and get an early workout.'"

Scheffing liked Altman's swing. He asked if Altman had played center field. Of course, Altman claimed he had, even though he hadn't. Altman raced several of the regulars and beat them, making him just about the fastest runner in camp.

"They put me in the lineup, and I did pretty well," Altman said. "I hit maybe .340 that spring, and they tore up my AAA contract."

When the 1959 season began, Altman was a member of the Chicago Cubs.

THE SETTING

George Altman had beat the odds and upset the Cubs' roster plans by emerging from spring training as a keeper. Scheduled to open the 1959 season at Wrigley Field against the Los Angeles Dodgers, the game was postponed by snow.

Altman was a southerner, and he greatly preferred warm weather. He was not a guy who thrived on playing baseball in frigid conditions and had frequently skipped winter altogether during the early years of his playing career by competing in places like Cuba and Panama while most of the United States was shivering.

Leading up to the opener, manager Bob Scheffing let the left-handed-swinging Altman know he was going to start in center field. He had been starting regularly in spring training, so he knew he had the job won. But the official word put him on edge. Spring training was off the books. A regular-season game put him in the *Baseball Encyclopedia*. It was the real thing.

"I was nervous and in awe of Wrigley Field," Altman recalled, "and the whole process. You know, there was Ernie Banks and guys like Dale Long. They had a veteran ball club. Bobby Thomson of Giants home-run fame was there. Richie Ashburn was on the team. We had veterans there."

Although Altman was an older rookie, just past his 26th birthday, he was still a rookie. The older guys were neither especially helpful nor especially hurtful. They did not nurture him or tease him much. They more or less seemed to leave him alone for his debut.

Altman had come a long way from the time he played elementary school baseball in his hometown. He was a college graduate, he had played with the venerable Kansas City Monarchs, had played in Latin

American countries, had served in the Army. He had seen more of the world than the typical wet-behind-the-ears rookie, but it still meant a lot for him to be in the Cubs starting lineup.

THE GAME OF MY LIFE

BY GEORGE ALTMAN

It's funny. The thing that I remember the absolute clearest about my first game in the majors was that it was cold. It was really cold in Wrigley Field for opening day that year. In fact, we had snowflakes.

We were playing the Dodgers, and they were starting Don Drysdale, who of course went on to the Hall of Fame. So here it is: my first game, and I've got snowflakes and Don Drysdale. That's a good start. Don Drysdale was one of the most intimidating pitchers of his time. He brushed guys back from the plate all of the time. He liked to establish his territory, and he let you know exactly where it was.

The high temperature was only 42 degrees that day, and there were only 12,288 fans at Wrigley. Can you imagine that now? So you know it was cold out there. I come up to the plate for the first time. I'm a rookie. And on the absolute first pitch of my major-league career, Drysdale hits me. I got hit by a pitch, right on the thigh. Wow! First pitch.

I wonder how many guys that has happened to. I remember that the best, but later in the game, I think I got a little bleeder for a hit. My first major-league hit traveled maybe 100 feet. I'm not sure, but I think it was an infield hit.

I know a lot of guys remember their first game very well, but it wasn't like, after it was over, I was saying, 'Oh, I'm a major leaguer now.' I was just hoping that the weather would get better. I'm glad I didn't have to play in that weather all of the time."

GAME RESULTS

The Cubs defeated the Dodgers 6-1 that day. Bob Anderson was the winning pitcher, and catcher Sammy Taylor knocked in four runs. Drysdale got beat. Taylor, who was not a power-hitting catcher, probably cherished the memory more than Altman.

During his rookie year, Altman played in 135 games and batted .245 with 12 home runs and 47 runs batted in. He was feeling his way a little bit that season, and through gradual improvement, he became an All-Star in 1961 as he smashed 27 home runs with 96 RBIs and batted .303. He hit a career-high .318 in 1962.

Altman suffered with several nagging injuries over the years, but when he was right he had the admiration of his teammates.

"He was a hell of an athlete," said catcher Cal Neeman.

When Altman was chosen for his first National League All-Star team in some ways, it was like making his rookie debut all over again. He had the same sort of butterflies.

"I really was excited and wide-eyed about playing with Willie Mays, Hank Aaron, and those guys," Altman said. "I guess it's like a dream."

The game was played on July 11 at Candlestick Park in San Francisco. This particular All-Star game was notable for the famous incident when Giants relief pitcher Stu Miller, a slightly built man, was blown off the mound by a blast of wind in notoriously gusty Candlestick. The breezy conditions blew dirt into the players' eyes and chilled the air.

Altman entered the game after some starters were removed and pitchers had changed. He faced American League pitcher Mike Fornieles, a Boston Red Sox reliever. In those days, there was no inter-league play, and players tended to stay in either the American League or the National League for most of their careers. Fornieles would have been a stranger to Altman, except that both men had played in Cuba. So Altman knew Fornieles relied heavily on his breaking ball. On Fornieles' first pitch, Altman swatted the ball into the seats.

"He threw me a curveball, and I was waiting for it," Altman said.

The National League won 5-4 in 10 innings.

REFLECTIONS ON BASEBALL

Altman played the 1963 season with the St. Louis Cardinals, the 1964 season with the New York Mets, and then he returned to the Cubs for three more seasons before going to Japan in 1968 for a satisfying, educational, eight-year run.

"I had a lot of injury problems with the Cubs," Altman said. "When I went to Japan, I got in better shape than most of my teammates. I worked out a little harder than most. They used to get on me a little bit for trying to show them up."

Altman said he took a course in Japanese to help him adjust, and he picked up other phrases and words as he went. Altman played for the Tokyo Orion team, which became the Lotte Orions. A Korean chewing gum maker bought the team. The irony of going from the Wrigley-owned Cubs to another baseball team operated by a gum manufacturer was not lost on Altman. He later played for the Hanshin Tigers. There was a quota of two Americans at a time on each team. Some other former major leaguers Altman crossed paths with were Jim Lefevbre and Arturo Lopez.

With a season high of 39 home runs, Altman powered more than 200 long-distance blows during his time in Japan, playing about 130 games each year. During Altman's time there—from the late 1950s until near the end of the 1960s—American players were welcome, but not too welcome. There are legions of stories about how Japanese players and managers conspired to prevent Americans from setting records; and Altman said he saw that side of the game.

Teams would play unusual fielding variations to favor a hitter. A favored player who hit a grounder would be allowed to reach base on routine plays.

"They'd play those kind of games," Altman said. "Later on, they kind of straightened their act out, but that was the kind of thing they'd do. And the strike zone, I won't even talk about that."

Overall, Altman said he had a terrific time in Japan and learned a lot about discipline and other lessons helpful in life. He adapted to the Japanese way of life that stressed "wa," or harmony.

"It was a great experience," he said. "It taught me humility. Very often, you know, you'd have to stand in line and wait and things like that."

Altman became a stockbroker after he retired from baseball and settled about 30 miles west of St. Louis. He needed all of the discipline he learned during his years in the sport, however, when he was diagnosed with colon cancer. He won that battle by using the same focus and determination he employed to succeed in all of his other endeavors. He has led a full and varied life. Although it is difficult to be a baseball fan who roots for both the Cubs and the Cardinals, somehow George Altman has found the harmony to balance that act.

Chapter 4

CAL NEEMAN

THE EARLY LIFE OF CAL NEEMAN

Cal Neeman was a small-town Southern Illinois boy as a youngster in the 1930s. He was born in the small community of Valmeyer, but actually spent most of his time in the unincorporated area of Cahokia. His family did not receive mail at home, but had a post office box in East St. Louis—near the Missouri state line.

It was farm country, but the Neemans did not live on a farm. Neeman's father, Amandus, who went by 'A.J.', worked for the Monsanto Chemical Company, but most of Cal Neeman's family came from a rural background. Neeman began playing baseball with local friends; and, since they were from places that hardly qualified as major population centers, they teamed together on a county squad encompassing East St. Louis.

No lightning bolt zapped Neeman, no booming voice told him that he should become a catcher. He analyzed the situation and felt playing the least popular position would allow him to get ahead.

"Originally," Neeman said, "I just wanted to play. I was kind of a little, skinny kid, and nobody else wanted to catch; so that was one way I was able to play. In the majors, I liked that catchers are always part of things. Catcher is a great spot to play. If you lose, though, when a pitcher gives up a couple of hits or a home run, you sort of feel responsible for that, too. I don't know if I buy into the idea that it's a real leadership role. I know the smartest games I ever caught were when the pitcher had a good fastball and a good curveball."

When he was young, the idea of playing in the majors did not occur to Neeman, who enrolled at Illinois Wesleyan and played baseball there his freshman year. Ray Fancher, a scout for the New York Yankees, saw Neeman play.

"He said, 'Would you like to play baseball for a week for free?'" Neeman recalled. "He told me to go to a tryout camp in Branson, Missouri. Once I went, they would pay me back for the bus trip down and then play me in games for a whole week."

It was the summer of 1948, after Neeman's freshman year in college, and he was 19 years old. Neeman followed through, and showed up in Branson—not yet a musical tourist mecca—only to face disappointment.

"The funny thing about it was, when I got there they had everyone all divided up into four teams, and I wasn't on the list," Neeman said. "There was a guy there, and he said, 'What's the matter?' I said, 'I can't find my name.'"

When the man asked Neeman who sent him, and he replied Ray Fancher, the guy said, "I've never heard of him." The camp facilitator turned out to be Burleigh Grimes, the old spitball pitcher who won 270 major league games. He was managing one of the four squads.

Neeman must have looked like the saddest young man in the Ozarks, but rather than send him away, Grimes said, "Well, you're already here. I'll put you on my team." Neeman rode the bench for almost the entire first game, but in the late

NAME: Calvin Amandus Neeman
BORN: February 18, 1929, in Valmeyer, Illinois
HOMETOWN: Cahokia, Illinois
CURRENT RESIDENCE: Lake St. Louis, Missouri
OCCUPATION: Retired baseball player; former health food store operator; former railroad switchman; former school teacher; former map supplier
POSITION: Catcher
HEIGHT: 6-foot-1
PLAYING WEIGHT: 192 pounds
ACCOMPLISHMENTS: Played seven years in the major leagues—four with the Chicago Cubs—with a lifetime batting average of .221; competed in the National League and the American League, primarily as a backup catcher; was Cubs starter his rookie year of 1957 and hit 10 home runs and batted .258.
THE GAME: Chicago Cubs versus Milwaukee Braves—April 16, 1957

The season of 1958 was Cal Neeman's rookie year as a Cubs catcher and his most productive. As a native of Illinois—and still a resident of the state—it was a thrill for Neeman to play for a Chicago team as part of his seven-year major-league career. *Brace Photo*

innings, a pitcher was due to hit with two men on. Grimes turned to Neeman and said, "Okay, kid, grab a bat. Go up there and hit."

It became a storybook scene. The pitcher laid one right down the middle, and Neeman teed off, slugging the ball over the center-field fence for a home run. Grimes' comment? "Well, now."

The home run got Neeman noticed, and he was placed in the lineup on a full-time basis. This was no run-of-the-mill tryout camp. Among other players seeking an opportunity was Al Pilarcik, who spent six years as a major-league outfielder; and pitcher Tom Sturdivant, who spent ten years in the majors and won 16 games for the Yankees one season. At that time, however, Sturdivant was a third baseman.

"He had a great arm," Neeman said of Sturdivant. "Everybody marveled about what a great arm he had, throwing from third to first. After the camp was over, I went back to Illinois Wesleyan, and I played basketball in my sophomore year. When it came time for baseball, however, I signed with the Yankees, and I went to spring training."

The Yankees were the kings of baseball in the 1950s, and the Yankee scouts sought the cream of prospects. Only it was a particularly bad time to be a catcher in the New York farm system. Not only was Yogi Berra—with the big club—the top catcher in the American League; Elston Howard, a future All-Star, was backing him up, and Johnny Blanchard, who wielded a terrific bat, was battling for playing time. In the minors, the Yanks also had Gus Triandos, who would later start for the Baltimore Orioles, as well as Lou Berberet and Hal Smith, also future major leaguers.

"They had a Yankees school, and I was invited to go to that," Neeman said. "They were loaded at the position, but I never paid attention to those things. I could run as well as any of them, better than most, and when I hit it, I hit it far. I never was as good a hitter as Elston Howard, Blanchard, or Triandos, though. They became better hitters."

After spending 1950 with Joplin in the Yankees' minor-league system, Neeman entered the Army for two years. He spent an entire year in Korea during the Korean War and said, after he was discharged and returned to baseball, that he was never quite the same.

"I just could never get going like I did before," Neeman said.

Other catchers had advanced in the Yankee system while Neeman was away and he was stuck in the minors. He was not on the Yankees' major league roster, meaning he was unprotected from teams prospecting in the draft. The Cubs swooped down and grabbed Neeman from the Yankees.

THE SETTING

Although many players of the 1950s dreamed of playing for the Yankees because they could count on making it into the World Series, Neeman never had the assurance he would make the final roster. The Chicago Cubs rescued him from the minors.

"The Cubs needed a catcher, and they drafted me," Neeman said. "Bob Scheffing (the manager) gave me a chance to play."

The Cubs were in a down period, trying to build something; and a young player with some seasoning appeared to fill one of their needs. There was no one standing in Neeman's way to assume the catcher's job full time. Scheffing made it clear to Neeman early on that he was his guy. Coming out of spring training, Neeman knew he would start, even though the largest stage Neeman had previously seen was minor-league Birmingham, Alabama; Scheffing gave him the word about a week ahead of opening day that he was going to play from the get-go.

There are certain moments every young man remembers clearly, from his first kiss to his first day on a job. Yet, if it is a special job—like getting paid to play major league baseball—his debut game is one that always stands a cut above the rest.

THE GAME OF MY LIFE

BY CAL NEEMAN

Opening Day is very special for every player that ever played.

I had spent several years in the minors, so I was a little bit excited knowing that I was going to start in my first major-league game. I didn't get so eager that I became too nervous to focus on the job. What I felt was an appreciation—an appreciation for an opportunity in life. It was more than, "Oh well, here we go." I felt the significance of it.

Bob Rush was the starting pitcher for the Cubs, and Warren Spahn started for the Braves. Of course, Spahn was headed to the Hall of Fame, but I wasn't scared of him. He threw a pitch for a strike, and I took it, but I said, "I can hit that." It wasn't that mysterious.

That was my first time at bat in the majors. Spahn retired the first 14 Cubs he faced that day, but later in the game, I got a base hit—my first hit. Bob Rush hit a double, and I scored from first. I scored a run in my first game, and I went one-for-three.

GAME RESULTS

The Braves defeated the Cubs, 4-1, that day before 23,674 fans at Wrigley Field. Spahn—the winningest left-hander of all-time who captured 20 victories in a season 13 different times—handled the Cubs routinely that day.

The game made Neeman a major leaguer. It put him in the record books and validated his rise through the minor-league ranks. He did not think of it that way because the contest against the Braves was not a solitary appearance. He was playing almost every day.

Not long after opening day, Neeman recorded his first career home run, also against the Braves. He hit the home run in the ninth inning to beat Lew Burdette, 3-2.

"We had to get them out in the last half of the ninth after that," Neeman said. "They either had the bases loaded or a couple of men on, and Hank Aaron hit a line drive right to shortstop. Jack Littrell was at short that day; Ernie Banks was playing third base. Aaron hit it right at Littrell. He hit it so hard, it spun him around; but he caught it, and we won the game."

For a rookie, and a catcher from whom little was expected at the plate, Neeman had a good season. He was 28 and had every reason to think he would be the starting catcher once again in 1958 and hold the job for a while. Yet, it didn't work that way. Neeman made it into just 76 games (though he did hit 12 homers) and platooned with Sammy Taylor. He never again caught as many games in a single season as he did as a rookie.

"Taylor was a good hitter, and I think we had a good thing going between us," Neeman said. "I was hitting left-handers, and he hit against right-handers, but I wasn't happy with that, because of course there are more right-handed pitchers. After playing a whole lot the year before, it was kind of a letdown. The manager treated me good, though, so I felt I was pretty fortunate—I felt fortunate to be a major league baseball player, without question. I don't know if I even thought of playing in the big leagues when I first went away from home. It was something that was still so far away. I had only seen the Cardinals play a few times when I was a kid."

In the late 1950s and the early 1960s, during Neeman's tenure with the Cubs, it always seemed they were about to make a move in the standings and push ahead to their first World Series title since 1908. The Cubs recruited good players, but something always went wrong. Promise went unfulfilled. Pitchers suffered sore arms.

"This organization has really been snake-bitten," Neeman said. "They had Ernie Banks, Billy Williams, Ron Santo, Lou Brock. I mean they haven't been shut out on superstars by any means, and they had a lot of other good ballplayers, but something would always happen."

REFLECTING ON BASEBALL

Whether he only played in a handful of games or played in a full season, Cal Neeman was an extraordinary fielder. The numbers next to his name in the *Baseball Encyclopedia* show that errors occurred with remarkable infrequency.

Some of his seasonal major-league fielding averages with the Cubs read as follows: .990, .992, .994, and 1.000. Accidents did not happen often around Neeman.

"I was a pretty good catcher," Neeman said. "I could throw, and I had good hands."

Neeman does not attend many major-league games these days; but when he does go, he usually sees the Cardinals, located about 40 minutes away from his home. If he has the right seat in the ballpark, he spends time studying the catcher's style and moves, and how he interacts with the pitcher.

"If I'm close enough I like to see what the pitchers are throwing," Neeman said. "I think the best thing a catcher can do is give pitchers a chance and try to keep them ahead of the hitters."

Neeman's last major-league season was 1963. He ended his campaign with the Washington Senators but never really informed the team not to count on him for 1964.

"I didn't retire," Neeman said. "I just didn't go back. I just didn't want to go back."

Efforts to establish a health food store fizzled, so Neeman worked at a few other jobs while finishing a degree at Southern-Illinois Edwardsville. Before retiring from the business world, Neeman spent 27 years supplying maps to schools. He enjoys spending time with his grandchildren, and he still roots for the Cubs—the team that gave him a chance to play in the majors.

"I'd like to see them win," he said. "They've really had a lot of bad luck. The fans definitely deserve a winner."

Chapter 5

JIM BROSNAN

THE EARLY LIFE OF JIM BROSNAN

Jim Brosnan has a variation on the story that senior citizens, with a twinkle in their eye, tell to grandchildren about how tough they had it walking uphill both ways to school through the snow in the good old days. If Brosnan wanted to attend a Cincinnati Reds baseball game when he was a youngster, he had to walk about three and a half miles to Crosley Field, and then three and a half miles back.

"Each way," Brosnan emphasized. "It was a good walk."

Brosnan was born in 1929, and during his childhood, the Reds were not exactly at the top of their game. They were usually near the bottom of the National League.

"The Reds were usually picked to finish last, and they didn't disappoint their fans," Brosnan said. "There wasn't much to talk about, except maybe Ernie Lombardi. I can remember Ernie Lombardi hitting, and Bucky Walters was my favorite pitcher. He was probably their best."

Lombardi twice led the National League in hitting, with .342 and .330 averages, virtually unheard of for a catcher. Walters won 198 games in his career, three times topping 20 victories in a season for the Reds.

There was an intriguing dichotomy in the Brosnan household. His father, John, wanted Jim to become a pitcher. His mother, Rose, wanted Jim to become a doctor. So, as a teen Brosnan worked at a local hospital taking the sick and wounded from the emergency room to the X-ray department while performing other tasks that did not directly threaten the lives of patients. At the same time, he was a star American Legion pitcher, and his fastball attracted the attention of scouts. Tony Lucadello, whose eye for spotting talent was renowned, saw Brosnan throw in his team's regional finals and in the championship series in Charleston, South Carolina. Lucadello watched Brosnan twice, and Brosnan shut out both foes. He then approached Brosnan with the same question young baseball players nationwide have dreamed of hearing since the late 1880s: "Would you like to play professional baseball?"

"I had not thought about it," Brosnan said.

Brosnan's father had played ball but was not a good hitter, so to stay involved, he shifted to umpiring semi-pro games around Ohio. He certainly had thought about his son playing pro ball, and his approval determined the outcome of the debate with Rose.

"He won," Brosnan said. "He talked my mother into allowing me to go ahead and do it, sign the contract."

Brosnan signed with the Cubs organization for a $2,500 bonus. Although he was not looking at medical schools, he did enroll at Notre Dame. Given the astronomical cost of higher education, nowadays that would pay for about two weeks of class and one textbook; but it afforded him an education, and Brosnan remained a student of sorts throughout his baseball career. He was an avid reader, questioned anything he didn't understand, and dazzled bullpen mates with his vocabulary, where he earned the nickname "Professor."

However, it took Brosnan longer to make it to the majors than it does for most students to

NAME: James Patrick Brosnan
BORN: October 24, 1929, in Cincinnati, Ohio
HOMETOWN: Cincinnati, Ohio
CURRENT RESIDENCE: Morton Grove, Illinois
OCCUPATION: Retired baseball player, author, broadcaster, magazine feature writer
POSITION: Pitcher
HEIGHT: 6-foot-4
PLAYING WEIGHT: 210 pounds
ACCOMPLISHMENTS: Nine-year major-league pitcher with the Chicago Cubs, St. Louis Cardinals, and Cincinnati Reds; won 55 games, saved 67 as a reliever; went 10-4 with 16 saves for Cincinnati's 1961 National League pennant-winner; author of two acclaimed baseball books looking at the game from a player's perspective—*The Long Season* and *Pennant Race* remain in print decades after first being issued.
THE GAME: Chicago Cubs versus St. Louis Cardinals—April 17, 1954

Jim Brosnan was one of the early high-profile relievers to compile a respected career prospering out of the bullpen 1954 and 1963. He is also remembered for pioneering insider looks at the world of baseball through his popular books *The Long Season* and *Pennant Race*. *Brace Photo*

collect undergraduate degrees. He was 19 when he signed, but spent two years between the Army and an apprenticeship in the minors. By the time he matriculated for the Cubs' Pacific Coast League affiliate, the Los Angeles Angels, in 1953, Brosnan had teammates openly telling him he and his 90-mph fastball belonged in the big time.

Steve Bilko, the slugging minor-league first baseman who would soon be anointed with a major-league call-up himself, had been a winter league teammate in the Dominican Republic. He was a vocal member of the Jim Brosnan fan club. The talent was waiting to be noticed by the Cubs' management.

THE SETTING

Jim Brosnan was 24 years old during spring training of 1954, but he still didn't figure into the Cubs' plans in a major way. There was every indication he was headed back to the minors, until an epidemic struck. One after another, Cubs starting pitchers went down or were called away, taking their arms with them. Brosnan earned his place on the roster ... well, kind of.

"It was a coincidence of a sort," he said. "Bob Rush, Dick Drott, and Moe Drabowsky were going to be starting pitchers, but Drabowsky and Drott were in the service for six months, and Rush had the measles. All of a sudden, (manager) Bob Scheffing didn't have enough pitchers. And he said, 'Looks like you're it.' And that's the way he put it."

That put Brosnan on the staff, but there was no indication he would be counted as a regular member of the rotation. Although Brosnan started two games that season, he spent most of his life in the bullpen. He made his major-league debut on April 15, 1954, in an 11-5 loss to the Reds. During the season, Brosnan made 18 appearances and finished with a 1-0 record. Winning just a single game in the majors put him way ahead of the vast majority of hopeful players who never progress to the point of signing a major-league contract.

The day Brosnan won his first major-league game was not an optimum afternoon for spending time on the mound. In a long history of bizarre games played at Wrigley Field, where the wind affects batted balls as dramatically as Gulf Coast winds, Brosnan picked up his milestone first victory.

THE GAME OF MY LIFE

BY JIM BROSNAN

I won my first game, but that wasn't the most memorable thing about that day. I think *surviving* was.

The wind was blowing out, as it often did at Wrigley, so it wasn't much of a day for pitchers. I didn't start. The Cubs won 23-13 in a game that took almost four hours to play. (There were 35 hits and five home runs.)

I don't remember a whole lot about the game itself, but I knew that being 1-0 was a lot better than I thought I was going to be. There wasn't much to remember about that game as a pitcher, but the game stood out because it was the only one I figured in that year.

When I say being 1-0 was a lot better than I thought I was going to be, it wasn't because I had rookie nerves or wasn't confident, or anything like that. It was a matter of me living up to the expectations of my old roommates, other players on the Los Angeles Angels team who had insisted I should be in the big leagues. It wasn't that I felt I had to prove myself so much, but that I was trying to live up to the expectations they had for me.

They thought I should concentrate a little harder and throw a little harder, and I would make it in the big leagues.

GAME RESULTS

It wasn't as if Brosnan knocked 'em dead in one of the many run-him-out-there relief appearances in what was the highest scoring Cubs-Cardinals game of all time.

Brosnan impressed no one enough to get extra work, but mostly performed as a mop-up man, and by the time he pitched his way through two starts and 16 other relief showings, the Cubs were convinced he needed a better curveball.

"Soon enough I was being urged by pitching coach Howie Pollet to accept a demotion," Brosnan said. "I think he put it this way: 'You know where you can go to learn how to throw breaking balls? I want to teach you. And it's not here.' It turned out to be Beaumont, Texas."

This was a double demotion for the 1955 season. From the majors down to AA ball in the Texas League, skipping right past AAA.

"It was a place where I would certainly get to pitch," Brosnan said.

Brosnan had spent a year in the minors in Macon, Georgia, and he thought he knew what hot weather was all about. Nope. If it was sweaty in Georgia, it was sizzling-pavement hot in Texas.

"It was a 100 degrees in Fort Worth when I landed there, and it stayed between 90 and 100 degrees for the next month," Brosnan said. "That was my introduction to baseball played in the Texas League. Macon was warm, and there it was hot."

By 1956, Brosnan was hot, too—hot enough to stick with the Cubs, hot enough to be considered a starting prospect. Since the team knew he was also a capable reliever, though, he kept getting the bullpen call when the need arose.

Early in the season, Brosnan was thrown into a tense situation against the Cardinals in a close game in St. Louis and with Hall of Famer Stan Musial due up. Brosnan had more confidence in his slider than either his fastball or new curve. The Cubs had a two-run lead, there were a couple of men on and a couple of men out. Musial worked the count to 3-and-2, and Brosnan ran through his options with computer-like speed.

"If he hits the ball good, we're all tied up," Brosnan said. "It occurred to me that he had never seen me throw this new curve, so I would do it. I dropped it right over the plate, and he was called out. A week later, the Cardinals were in Wrigley Field, and Musial was up with a couple of men on base. Now I'm in the same position, 3-and-2. I thought, 'Am I going to do it again?' I forgot that he's a pretty smart guy and a pretty good hitter, and he would probably look for it. He did, and he hit it.

"I saw it go by and out onto Waveland Avenue, completely out of the ballpark. Musial ran to first base and turned to the left, and he had a big smile on his face. He looked over at me and just shook his head, 'You dumb rookie. It was exactly the pitch I knew you were going to throw.'"

REFLECTING ON BASEBALL

Brosnan never did become a regular starting pitcher—his niche was relief pitching. He was a specialist, but not like the relievers of today, who are often summoned into the game for a single batter. Brosnan, a right-hander, alternated with a southpaw much of the time, but usually pitched one or two innings at a stretch.

"I had the kind of pitches that would be effective for an inning, two innings, three innings, but seldom did I have to go three innings," he said. "I was happy not to have to pitch nine innings, to tell you the truth. I did start opening day in Cincinnati once because two people who would have pitched were either sick, or something else. Relief pitching was not looked upon as a primary thing. You didn't think of the ball club dependent in great measure on how good the relief pitchers were. Not nearly so much as they do now."

Brosnan spent three seasons and part of a fourth with the Cubs. He said general manager John Holland told him he figured into the team's long-term plans and maybe even as a starter. Brosnan told Holland he was going to buy the Morton Grove house he still owns a half-century later. As soon as he began making the mortgage payments, though, he was traded to the Cardinals at the end of May of 1958. Brosnan actually started 20 games between the two teams that season, but never approached that mark again. In 1959, Brosnan was shipped to the Reds, the team he cheered for as a kid. It came at just the right time as the Reds were building their best clubs in decades. One reason Brosnan was moved was his high salary—$15,000 for a reliever—paid by P.K. Wrigley with the Cubs.

"That's not a million dollars," Brosnan said. "I still can't believe (how much current players are paid). I get shocked whenever I see the figures."

Until Brosnan's book *The Long Season* was published in 1960, baseball books were mostly as-told-to biographies. Brosnan's set a new standard for incisive commentary, flat-out honesty, and high-quality writing. It was universally praised in the literary world and panned among many baseball people. There was a feeling that locker-room behavior and talk had to stay in the locker room.

"It was getting more good publicity than bad," Brosnan said, "although Joe Garagiola, who since has become a friend, said I was a traitor to the game and shouldn't be allowed to play. There was nothing funny about that."

The irony being that the usually joking Garagiola, a retired catcher and longtime announcer, had authored his own memoir, *Baseball Is A Funny Game*.

Brosnan—whose other entertaining baseball book, *Pennant Race*, which is about the 1961 Reds—was seen as a player who established a new genre of tell-all sports journalism. In reality, his books, while informative and pleasurable to read, were mild in content compared to Jim Bouton's revolutionary *Ball Four*. Bouton's often hilarious book was far juicier and revealed far more sophomoric New York Yankee behavior—from drinking to attempted womanizing.

Later, Brosnan said Bouton told him, "You left out the most important parts about playing baseball in the big leagues."

And what was that? Having women swoon over the players and eating in fancy restaurants with others picking up the check. It just may have been that Brosnan and Bouton kept different company.

When he retired as a player in 1963—symmetrically concluding his major-league career with a partial season on the Chicago White Sox—Brosnan wrote other baseball books and stories for such magazines as *Life*. He relished being on his childhood team at the right time—when the Reds were pennant winners in the 1960s—but said he is loyal to the Cubs for giving him his big-league chance.

"I still have a shirt downstairs," said Brosnan, who said he would like to see the Cubs win a World Series in 2007—or by the time the 100th anniversary of their last triumph rolls around in 2008.

"Guess I'll have to stick around," Brosnan said. "Two-thousand seven will be heaven—is that Ernie Banks' new saying? If it's not, it should be."

Chapter 6

GLEN HOBBIE

THE EARLY LIFE OF GLEN HOBBIE

Glen Hobbie grew up in rural Southern Illinois farm country, though he did not come from a family of farmers. Corn, bean, and wheat fields surrounded the Hobbies, but Glen's father was a salesman of farm goods. He did not grow up dreaming of becoming a major-league player, a teacher, a baker, or a candlestick maker when he was hanging out with his six brothers and three sisters. At least until he was through with junior high school-level classes, Hobbie had a simple life plan.

"I just wanted to hunt and fish," Hobbie said. "We had a bayou pond on the property, and it was really stocked good with bass. I practically lived there almost all summer, every summer. I fished with neighbor kids, and I fished a lot with my brother, Ray, who has passed away since."

Hobbie's first serious baseball was played when he enrolled in high school. He had played basketball but became attracted to the baseball team. His basketball coach was the baseball coach, and Hobbie had an interest in the game and a rooting interest in the nearby St. Louis Cardinals.

"The coach looked at me and said, 'We're going to make a pitcher out of you,'" Hobbie said. "That's how it worked. I figured, as long as I get to play, I'm ticked to death. I didn't know anything about pitching.

All I knew was, you threw the ball in front of you. I didn't even know what fancy pitches there were at the time."

If his background did not suggest that Hobbie knew what he was doing, his skill level definitely contradicted the notion. He had instant success. He got people out, won some games, and, with practice, developed more of a mound presence.

"Things were getting to be more fun than I thought they would be," Hobbie said.

By his senior year in high school, Hobbie's participation was sought for a regional team of adults encompassing three counties. He was only 17, pitching against men who were in their 20s and 30s, but finished the year 22-1. Hobbie had a reputation as a tough pitcher locally, and a scout in Springfield made casual contact.

However, Hobbie's brother Roy was working at a shell refinery with a part-time scout. That man got in touch with Danny Menendez, at the time the general manager of the AAA Charleston, West Virginia team. Hobbie joined that club for spring training but was too raw to stick at such a high level of the minors. He was shipped to a Class C team that represented Duluth, Minnesota, and Superior, Wisconsin. He also discovered that spring isn't as warm all over the Midwest as it is in Southern Illinois.

"It was pretty cold there," said Hobbie laughing at the big chill of memory.

NAME: Glen Frederick Hobbie
BORN: April 24, 1936, in Witt, Illinois
HOMETOWN: Witt, Illinois
CURRENT RESIDENCE: Ramsey, Illinois
OCCUPATION: Retired major-league
    baseball player; plant manager for a
    roller-derby skating corporation
POSITION: Pitcher
HEIGHT: 6-foot-2
PLAYING WEIGHT: 195 pounds
ACCOMPLISHMENTS: Played eight seasons
    in the major leagues between 1957 and
    1964; was a regular member of the
    Chicago Cubs starting rotation and also
    pitched for the St. Louis Cardinals; twice
    won 16 games in a season.
THE GAME: Chicago Cubs versus Pittsburgh
    Pirates—July 30, 1960

Hobbie pitched well for half a season in the Upper Midwest, but suffered a back injury. A knot showed up beneath his shoulder blade. He was only 19 years old and ignorant about the threat to his pitching, just figuring it was a transitory ailment.

"If it happened today, it would scare me to death," Hobbie said decades later.

In a career cut short by injury, Glen Hobbie twice won 16 games for the Cubs as part of the starting rotation in a major-league career spanning from 1957 to 1964. In 1959, he pitched a one-hitter to beat the Cardinals, 1-0. *Brace Photo*

This was more than just a minor ache. It sounded like the type of injury that could lead to early retirement. Every four or five days, Hobbie felt well enough to pitch, but after two innings of throwing, the knot reappeared and put pressure on his shoulder blade.

"Every time I tried to throw a ball, it would hurt like the devil," he said.

So Hobbie rested for most of the second half of the season. Dozens of pitchers come and go in the minors sidelined forever by mysterious arm or shoulder ailments, but Hobbie was one of the lucky ones. When he resumed pitching for the 1956 season, he was okay. There was no monitoring by a full-time trainer, no step-by-step doctor's healing program—Hobbie performed his own rehab. For 60 days straight, he went swimming in the Mississippi River, stretching the muscles, using the muscles, rebuilding the muscles.

"That was my therapy," Hobbie said. "I've never had another problem since. I was lying on the beach and swimming in the Mississippi River while I was on the disabled list. I was worried about my future. If my back was going to ever get better, I felt I would have a future. Getting over that thing was worrisome, yeah; but at that age, you don't worry about a whole lot. You're single, things just don't worry you at that age."

Hobbie's health bounced back, and he played some Class D ball, but remained aligned with Charleston. The team went bankrupt, but Menendez, Hobbie's benefactor, surfaced as the general manager of a Memphis team and brought Hobbie with him in 1957. Ultimately, Menendez sold Hobbie to the Cubs. Before the end of that season, Hobbie made two brief appearances in Major League games.

Hobbie pitched only four and one-third innings, but it removed some of the unknown for him and set up his confidence for spring training of 1958.

"I actually felt that I could pitch," Hobbie said. "I had seen the other pitchers pitch, and I didn't see where they had anything more than I did. I felt that if I could just get my control where it belonged, that I could handle the major leagues."

THE SETTING

Glen Hobbie was in the majors to stay in 1958 and had a first-rate season, finishing 10-6 with a 3.74 earned run average, mixing starting and relieving. The next season, Hobbie was 16-13; and in 1960, he was 16-20 on a fairly weak club.

"I think I pitched better ball that year than I did the year before," Hobbie said. "Our relievers weren't as good as we had in 1959. I think someone said we had the youngest starting rotation in major-league history. There was Moe Drabowsky, Bob Anderson, Dick Drott, and myself. Everyone was under 25, I think. We should have had some great ball clubs. We had some real good personnel there. We should have won a couple of pennants. We had Ernie Banks, and he won the MVP that year."

One of Hobbie's finest games was pitched early in the season. On April 21, 1959, he fired a one-hitter at the St. Louis Cardinals. He retired the first 20 batters in a row before superstar slugger Stan Musial stroked a double in the seventh inning. Hobbie held on for a 1-0 victory.

"I thought I had the chance for the no-hitter, and then I hung a curveball up about a foot too high," Hobbie said. "I tried to throw it too hard. You think about a no-hitter and then when they get the first hit, you think about a shutout. If they get a run, you think about winning the ballgame. Those three things go through your mind every time you walk out there. No-hitters don't happen too often, I'll tell you. Guys can swing the bat."

By 1960, Hobbie was an established member of the Cubs' rotation. His arm was admired and he seemed certain to have a long future with the team. Periodically, he came through with performances that thrilled his teammates and managers.

The Cubs of 1960 finished a horrible 60-94, 35 games out of first place. But whenever manager Charlie Grimm—or his mid-season substitute Lou Boudreau, who came down from the broadcast booth in an unusual job switch—called upon one of the young hurlers, the poor-hitting Cubs had a chance to win.

Hobbie's 1959 one-hitter was a tease. In mid-June, against the Milwaukee Braves, he came almost as close to pitching a no-hitter. This game had more adventure, however. Hobbie pitched a two-hitter to beat the Braves, 3-2, at Wrigley Field, after no-hitting them for seven innings. But both of the Braves' hits were solo home runs. Catcher Del Crandall hit one in the seventh inning, and future Hall of Fame third baseman Eddie Mathews stroked a homer in the ninth.

"I think both of them were my fault because my control wasn't as good as it should have been," Hobbie said. "I'd get behind to the hitters, and they'd know what was coming."

Don Zimmer, who later managed the Cubs, played third base for the team when Hobbie was on the roster, and he provided vivid infield chatter. He shouted to Hobbie, "Throw them the cotton-pickin' ball." Only, as Hobbie said, "cotton pickin'" was not the actual phrase used. Zimmer kept agitating for Hobbie to throw the ball down the middle and just let the Braves hit it.

"I threw my best fastball down the middle, and Mathews hit it out of there," Hobbie said. "The next time I looked around for Zimmer, he was out in left field. He knew what I was going to say to him: "Next time, *you* play third base, and I'll pitch."

Unfortunate but true, that season Hobbie could rely on little help from the hitters and less help from the bullpen. If he wanted to win, he had to throw low-hit games and try to stay on the mound into the late innings. On July 20 of that summer, Hobbie once again started a game humming in his best stuff and sitting opposing batters down as quickly as they strode into the batter's box. He retired the first 21 Cincinnati Reds in order and threw a complete-game, two-hit shutout to win 4-0—on the road at Crosley Field.

THE GAME OF MY LIFE

BY GLEN HOBBIE

The best game I ever played in my whole life was on July 30, 1960. I don't remember the details of all my best games, but it's easy for me to remember this one. My son, Glen Jr., was born that day; and on the morning of the game, I took my wife, Sharon, to the hospital in Chicago. That morning, Sharon said she was having cramps and that she had better go to the hospital. It was about nine o'clock in the morning. She wasn't due. There was no reason to think she was going to have a baby that day. I figured I would drop her off at the hospital and then go back and pick her up that night after the game. That ain't the way it worked out. My son was born about six weeks premature.

We were facing the Pittsburgh Pirates, and it was the game of the week on a Saturday afternoon on national television. It was an afternoon game, and my son was born at game time, 1:30 p.m. I was already on the mound. It was my regular turn in the rotation. I pitched well that season, and I was pitching well that day.

Lou Boudreau was the manager at that point in the season. He had started the year in the broadcast booth, as Charlie Grimm was the manager, but they traded jobs. They waited until the third inning to tell me that I had a baby boy. Boudreau did it. I can't remember whether he told me on the mound or when I came in after the inning.

I was very surprised. I did not expect to have a kid that day. That's something that can affect a pitcher's concentration, but I was able to stay focused on my business. Boudreau told me that Sharon was okay and that she was watching the game on television.

I kept on pitching. I also got a double and scored a run. Bob Friend (who would win 18 games that season) was the Pirates starter. I struck out six Pirates in a complete game. That's all we had back then, complete games or else. The word 'closer' hadn't been invented yet for relief pitchers.

After the game, I went to the hospital and saw my wife and my son; and they were doing all right. And you know what? On the same day, Dick Ellsworth, one of our other pitchers, had a baby boy, too.

GAME RESULTS

The Cubs beat the Pirates 6-1 in Hobbie's most memorable game, and he continued to produce extraordinary efforts throughout the rest of the season. Less than a month after Hobbie dismantled the Pirates and his son was born, he got another shot at them.

Hobbie swatted a walk-off home run—the first of his career—to defeat the Pirates 2-1 and best Vinegar Bend Mizell at Wrigley Field. Hobbie brought Reggie Jackson brashness to the plate that day, although given his prior lack of homer production, it was hard to see why.

"I knew what I was going to do when I left the bench," Hobbie said. "Oh, I knew I could hit the ball out of the ballpark. There was no doubt in my mind that I could hit it that hard because I did it in batting practice constantly. And the first two hitters to the plate, Mizell throws them soft curveballs, and they both grounded out. Well, I knew who was catching. Smokey Burgess. I knew what I was going to get. I went up there thinking, 'Man, if it's a strike, I'm going to nail it.'"

Hobbie said his teammates expected him to take the first pitch, and that would have been a common-sense maneuver since the previous hitters did little with Mizell's openers.

"You're not supposed to swing," Hobbie said. "I'm supposed to take it. But I ain't about to take something when I know what's coming. He threw the same thing, up in the strike zone, and I nailed it. The ball landed in a catwalk in left field. It was a neat feeling when I ran around the bases."

Hobbie finished the season 16-20, harboring the notion that with a little more run support and some periodic help from the bullpen he could become a big winner down the road. He could not have imagined that the prime years of his career were behind him, and he would never win as many games in a season again.

REFLECTIONS ON BASEBALL

Cubs owner P.K. Wrigley was sick of losing, and he was game to try anything to shake his team's long-term slump. He proved it for the 1961 season when he introduced the first-and-only rotating staff of managers. His so-called "College of Coaches" featured nine leaders. Alas, it led to chaos. There were contradictory policies from one week to the next.

"They had the College of Coaches, and they hired some Olympic track coach to be our trainer," Hobbie said years later. "What they didn't understand was that a track coach trains you for one event. But you don't train that way for 154 events. Before the end of spring training, we were all worn out. They way overdid it. We were ready for the season to be over."

Worse, Hobbie injured his lower back on the right side—he believes from too much stress. Repeating exercises caused the strain, he felt, and the ache hampered the follow through in his pitching. By compensating, he ended up hurting his shoulder.

"I lost quite a bit off my fastball, and everything went downhill from there," Hobbie said.

Hobbie tumbled to a 7-13 record and never had another winning season, retiring prematurely in 1964 at age 28.

After he left baseball, Hobbie spent years working for the Roller-Derby Skate Corporation in Litchfield, Illinois. He helped manufacture roller skates, ice skates, and baseball spikes and later became plant superintendent.

On a 280-acre farm in Ramsey, in Southern Illinois, Hobbie occupies most of his time with the same passions he has carried throughout his life. He still follows baseball closely, wondering why the Cubs can't pull it all together and win a World Series, and he still indulges his hunting and fishing interests, though he has cut back.

Old knees are hampering some of Hobbie's outdoor trips. He said he would fish more, but is shaky in a boat; and he would hunt more, but fears falling on rough terrain with a shotgun on a quail hunt.

"My son lives next door, and I've got my two grandsons, who hunt and fish here," Hobbie said. "We just have a great time. We've got a bass pond, and we've got big old channel catfish that weigh anywhere from 15 to 20 pounds. We catch them, take their picture, cut the line, and turn them loose again. I think every kid in the town of Vandalia has caught them and had their picture taken with them."

Hobbie is very attached to his land and just sits back and watches the wild turkey wander through it. "I've always enjoyed the outdoors just about as much as baseball," he said.

Chapter 7

DICK ELLSWORTH

THE EARLY LIFE OF DICK ELLSWORTH

Dick Ellsworth was born in the small Wyoming town of Lusk, but only stayed there until he was a toddler. His family relocated to Fresno, the self-proclaimed "Raisin Capital of the World," and the Central California city basically has been his home ever since.

As a youngster Ellsworth played his first baseball on the community's playgrounds with friends and joined his first organized teams when he was 13. Ellsworth made the roster of a local Babe Ruth League team and played on his junior high squad at the same time. He later played on his high school team and local American Legion team as he grew older.

By then, the best baseball people around knew Ellsworth had thunder in his arm and potential in his game.

"I got noticed when I was in the ninth grade," Ellsworth said. "My baseball coach in junior high told me that a couple of scouts had contacted him and asked about me."

Such early recognition was nice, but it didn't mean too much to Ellsworth at the time. He was too young to consider what life as a professional meant. He just felt he was noticed because his team was good. When Ellsworth was in high school, though—and the time scouts came around in numbers—things began to take shape and meaning. The scouts saw Ellsworth play so often that they could have eaten raisins for breakfast, lunch, and dinner.

57

"My parents pretty much selected the Cubs," Ellsworth said. "I think it was based on the integrity and honesty of the scout—and the fact that we were told that, being a left-handed pitcher, I probably had a real good chance of being a major-league pitcher with the Cubs."

High school baseball being a spring sport, the season generally runs up to graduation, and that certainly was the situation in Ellsworth's case in 1958.

"I graduated on Wednesday, signed a contract on Friday, and I was on an airplane for Chicago on Saturday," he said.

With Dick in demand, the Ellsworths could make a demand or two of their own. The lanky pitcher had signed a major-league contract that afforded him a few visits to the Wrigley Field dugout with the big-league team before the end of the season.

Before the majors adopted inter-league play, the Cubs and White Sox played an annual series against one another for charity and alleged proof of Chicago supremacy. The young Ellsworth found himself standing on a mound facing the White Sox briefly. Soon after he made his major-league debut for real. Ellsworth started against the Cincinnati Reds, but only lasted 2 ⅓ innings. He gave up four runs and left the park with an earned run average of 15.43.

He also left the Cubs—temporarily—sent to Forth Worth, then a class AA team. Ellsworth rejoined the Cubs for the month of September during the traditional late-season call-up period of minor leaguers when rosters expand.

In 1960, Ellsworth became a full-fledged, full-time rookie pitcher for the Cubs. He was a major leaguer to stay and was part of a core group of young throwers that Cubs management hoped

NAME: Richard Clark Ellsworth
BORN: March 22, 1940, in Lusk, Wyoming
HOMETOWN: Fresno, California
CURRENT RESIDENCE: Fresno, California
OCCUPATION: Retired major-league baseball player; real estate company vice president; part-owner, minor-league baseball team
POSITION: Pitcher
HEIGHT: 6-foot-4
PLAYING WEIGHT: 195 pounds
ACCOMPLISHMENTS: Spent 13 years in the major leagues, mostly with the Cubs; won 22 games during the 1963 season, hurling 290⅔ innings and 19 complete games; excelled for the Boston Red Sox by winning 16 games during the 1968 season; won 10 or more games in a season five times.
THE GAME: Chicago Cubs versus Philadelphia Phillies—June 1, 1963

In his 13-year major-league career, one of southpaw Dick Ellsworth's season's stands out above all others. His 22-10 record in 1963 was one of the greatest by a left-hander in Cubs history. *Brace Photo*

and believed would lead the team out of the wilderness and into the pennant race. Unfortunately, the Cubs finished 60-94 that season. Ellsworth, who turned 20 right before the season opener, started 31 games that year and put up a record of 7-13.

THE SETTING

The Ellsworth family analysis was correct. Being a hard-throwing lefty did Dick no harm whatsoever. He was invited into the Cubs rotation as a rookie and stayed there for seven years.

The majors placed little premium on relief pitching in the 1960s. Many relievers were serving punishment duty in the bullpen. Many others were considered second-class pitching citizens because they couldn't pitch complete games. It was the last decade before baseball underwent a metamorphosis and truly began embracing the specialty skills of relievers.

Ellsworth was one starter who was relied on to start—and to finish what he started. In five of those years in the rotation, he topped 200 innings (with a high of 290); and in two others, he approached 200 innings. He had three seasons under his belt by the time he was just past voting age.

Ellsworth was strong-armed and young and trying to obtain the experience that a pitcher needs to succeed. The learning and growth process transformed Ellsworth from a young thrower to an extremely promising pitcher. The sweet moments were rare in 1961, when Ellsworth finished 10-11; or in 1962, when he endured a 9-20 season with a 5.09 earned run average.

But 1963 was different. That was Ellsworth's year. He put a special stamp on the Cubs' season, going from boy to man as king of the staff. On May 1, Ellsworth had taken the mound against the Pittsburgh Pirates at Wrigley Field and twirled a two-hitter, lifting the Cubs to a 3-1 victory. Pittsburgh's only safeties were singles by Donn Clendenon in the second inning and Dick Schofield in the ninth. Ellsworth was not a strikeout specialist, but when his stuff was working well, opposing batsmen beat pitches into the ground. That game Ernie Banks was playing first, and he collected a record-setting 22 putouts. Ground ball out, ground ball out, ground ball out—hitters couldn't do a thing with Ellsworth that day.

THE GAME OF MY LIFE

BY DICK ELLSWORTH

The game I remember best was against the Phillies. I pitched a one-hitter, and their outfielder Wes Covington, who was a pretty solid player, got the only hit on a drag bunt between me and the first baseman.

That was the Phillies' only hit. After the game a lot of people thought that was somewhat unprofessional, to break up a no-hitter that way. That was the only hit, and it came in the fifth inning.

It was sort of in the flow of things, and they were just trying to win the ballgame, but so was I. Some people thought he was just trying to get the hit and wasn't doing it to win the game.

My outlook on the game was the same every day. They gave you the ball every fourth day, and every fourth day you went out to try to win the best way you knew how. You wanted to complete the ballgame. It just so happened that day I pitched better than I usually did.

The game is so much different now. It's a game of specialists today. Starting pitchers are not expected to pitch more than five innings. They might even take you out after giving up one hit. It's just a different mentality. The game is set up differently today than it was when I played. The pitching staffs are much bigger and they have a relief pitcher for every occasion.

GAME RESULTS

The Cubs won the game 2-0 at Connie Mack Stadium, and it was probably the best-pitched game of Ellsworth's career during the best overall season of his career.

Ellsworth turned in his best record—22-10—and recorded a stingy 2.11 earned run average. He was one of the top pitchers in the National League that season. The Cubs actually posted a winning record, too, going 82-80.

During the early 1960s, owner P.K. Wrigley experimented with a new way to lose. Rather than entrusting his franchise to one manager who couldn't turn things around, he set up his aforementioned system of shared responsibility with nine coaches, or rotating managers, who couldn't turn things around. The plan didn't work; young players especially were confused about the lines of authority; and ultimately, Wrigley shelved the structure and returned to the one-man, one-manager way of life.

In 1963, Bob Kennedy was still called "Coach," but he ran the team, and the players were relieved.

"That year was the most fun I had, not just because I was winning the most," Ellsworth said. "We had just come out of two years of total frustration with a 'head coach.' We didn't like that. We were the laughingstock of baseball."

It was the type of strange management decision that made players grit their teeth and just hunker down and persevere.

"When we were in the middle of it, we knew it wasn't going to work," Ellsworth said. "But we came out of that. They hired Bob Kennedy, and he was a real player's manager. He had a big job in front of him because of what we had suffered through the previous two years. But he got everybody to the point where, as a team, we were believing we had the talent to do a lot better than we had been doing. It was the only year I was with the Cubs where we actually finished above .500."

In 1966, hampered by continuing tendinitis, Ellsworth endured a disappointing 8-22 season and then was traded to Philadelphia. He played one year there and then moved on to the Red Sox in 1968 where he regained his previous form and finished 16-7. Ellsworth was settling down in Boston and was shocked when he was traded to the Cleveland Indians after only two appearances in 1969.

"I felt that I had proved myself and that I may have a home there for a few years," he said. "And as it turns out I got traded right after the start of the '69 season. That was a big disappointment."

Winning 16 for the Red Sox was a last hurrah for Ellsworth. He recorded limited numbers in his final few seasons with the Indians and the Milwaukee Brewers; and when he retired after the 1971 campaign, he returned to Fresno and began a new life without baseball.

REFLECTIONS ON BASEBALL

Dick Ellsworth was not a souvenir hound. He did not pile up the memorabilia from his Cubs or baseball days in his suitcases, bring it all home, and display it.

"I imagine somewhere in a drawer I have a ball, but I don't dwell on it," Ellsworth said. "When I came home I had finished a career, and I needed to get started with the rest of my life. As a professional athlete, it comes and goes. You have a long life in front of you after professional sports, so I came home and got immersed in the business world."

Ellsworth immediately entered the real estate field and was still at it 35 years later. He picked the right place, and his business has grown with the community.

"Fresno has grown rapidly over the years and I've been fortunate to be part of it," Ellsworth said.

Fresno is equidistant from Los Angeles, 200 miles to the south; and San Francisco, 200 miles to the north, so Ellsworth does not live close to where any major-league baseball is played. He no longer roots for any specific big-league club, but worries about the health of old teammate Ron Santo, the former star third baseman who has had challenges from diabetes in recent years, and exchanges phone calls with fellow Cubs moundsman Glen Hobbie periodically.

More than anything, Ellsworth said, he probably cheers for the Atlanta Braves because manager Bobby Cox is from Fresno, and because Pat Corrales was coaching there.

"I've always had a soft spot in my heart for Bobby Cox because he's a local boy, and I played against him in high school," Ellsworth said. "And Pat Corrales was my catcher in high school. I've always wanted them to do well."

Somewhat to his own surprise, Ellsworth also became part owner of the local minor-league baseball team, the Fresno Grizzlies of the Pacific Coast League. Ellsworth got involved not because he missed baseball, but out of civic boosterism.

"I pay attention to them," Ellsworth said. "I have an ownership interest in the ball club. I thought it would be good for the community."

For decades, Ellsworth has been loyal to Fresno, remembering always that it was the place that gave him his start.

Chapter 8

DON KESSINGER

THE EARLY LIFE OF DON KESSINGER

The twang is still ripe in Don Kessinger's voice. Except for the years he spent playing professional baseball, the son of the South grew up and lived in either Arkansas or Mississippi. The slower pace of life is more agreeable to him than the frenetic bustle of a major city like Chicago. Kessinger was born during World War II in Forrest City, Arkansas, a community of about 10,000 people that believed in its youth and supported' the young people with a solid athletic program. Kessinger was a good athlete from an early age and played every sport he stumbled into, from baseball to football, from basketball to track.

"I just came through there at a great time, when there was a lot of really good athletes; so it was easy to fall in with the crowd," he said.

Formal Little League programs were spreading in the early 1950s as Kessinger turned 10, and he went right from his local sandlots into organized play and then on to American Legion ball. His older brother, Bill, led the way. Kessinger said Bill was likely capable of playing pro ball, too, but suffered a debilitating knee injury and an eye injury.

"My family loved sports," Don said of the clan that operated a small grocery store as a profession. Kessinger was actually a superior basketball player in high school and was heavily recruited by a multitude of colleges to play that sport. "I was better known for basketball in high school," he said. "I had the opportunity to go most any place I wanted in basketball. I played guard, and I shot as often as I could. If you shoot enough times, some of them go in."

One reason Kessinger chose to attend the University of Mississippi was its proximity to his home, only a three-hour drive. He also knew he could play both basketball and baseball for the school, but he knew that the baseball program, highly developed under coach Tom Swayze, might give him a boost toward fulfilling his dream of playing in the majors.

Despite three years of varsity play for the Rebels, making All-Southeastern Conference and getting some All-America notice as a senior, Kessinger turned aside queries from teams urging him to turn professional in basketball, he said, because, in his heart, he preferred baseball.

"Several clubs asked me, if they drafted me would I play basketball," Kessinger said, "but I answered them honestly, and said, 'No, I want to play baseball.' So that's what I did."

NAME: Donald Eulon Kessinger
BORN: July 17, 1942, in Forrest City, Arkansas
HOMETOWN: Forrest City, Arkansas
CURRENT RESIDENCE: Oxford, Mississippi
OCCUPATION: Retired major-league baseball player; former big-league manager; former University of Mississippi baseball coach and associate athletic director; former investment business partner; works in real estate in son Kevin's business
HEIGHT: 6-foot-1
PLAYING WEIGHT: 175 pounds
ACCOMPLISHMENTS: Sixteen-year major-league shortstop, mostly with the Chicago Cubs, playing 2,078 games; six-time National League All-Star; led league with .976 fielding average in 1969; lifetime .252 batting average; formed memorable Cubs double-play combination with second baseman Glenn Beckert; managed Chicago White Sox.
THE GAME: Chicago Cubs versus St. Louis Cardinals—June 17, 1971

Before the major-league amateur draft began in 1965, signing players was a free for all. The teams with the best scouts and the deepest pockets could sign players anywhere and everywhere in the country. Kessinger finished at Ole Miss the year before the draft started, so he was free to negotiate with any major-league team.

For decades, the St. Louis Cardinals were the majors' southernmost and westernmost team. If you grew up in a certain part of the country, the Cards

One of the slickest fielders in Cubs lore, lanky shortstop Don Kessinger was a major leaguer for 16 years between 1964 and 1979. Most of his best seasons were spent sharing Wrigley Field with the best group ever to man the infield—Glenn Beckert, Ron Santo, and Ernie Banks. The quartet stays in touch to this day. *Brace Photo*

were your team. The Southeast was one region that adopted the Cardinals.

"Where I grew up, everybody was a Cardinals fan," Kessinger said. "Because that was the one team that you could really hear on the radio all the time and follow them."

Since Mississippi went to the College World Series in Omaha, Nebraska, the Rebels' season ended late, and some teams had already spent heavily on bonus players. Kessinger thinks playing into June might have cost him money on his initial contract, but he had no shortage of suitors. The Cardinals were in the mix—so were the Phillies, Yankees, and Cubs. The offers were not far apart, and Kessinger sat down with Swayze and evaluated all of them together. He chose to sign with the Cubs.

"I think we just felt like I had the best opportunity to get there quicker with the Cubs," Kessinger said. "In the long run, it worked out fine."

The prevailing opinion among major-league teams at the time was that college players might be wasting their time and coming into pro ball too late to develop. But Kessinger was more of a ready-made guy. He jumped directly from Ole Miss to Fort Worth, a class AA team in the Texas League, but he adjusted well enough that the Cubs brought him to the majors in September with their mass minor-league call-up.

"Gosh yeah, walking into Wrigley Field was exciting, but the crowds weren't too big back then," Kessinger said. "The Cubs weren't very good; and by September, they were out of it. But it was thrilling. I know I was nervous; and I know I was excited; and I know I didn't do very good; but I don't have great recollections of what happened. The next year, I went to spring training with the big club and then went back to AA. I only played about six weeks and then was back in the big leagues."

It was a four-game appearance with the Cubs in 1964, but Kessinger got into 106 games in 1965. After that, he was the man at short. He thinks the Cubs brought him up because he was the shortstop of the future, not because he was ready. If there was an eye-opening, welcome-to-the-majors-Don moment during that '65 season, it took place near the end of the year.

On September 9, future Hall of Famer Sandy Koufax pitched a perfect game to beat the Cubs, 1-0, on a day when Chicago right-hander Bob Hendley threw a one-hitter. Koufax struck out 14 men, and

Hendley had his own perfect game going until the fifth. Koufax never wavered—in fact, he even got better at the end, striking out the last six men to face him.

"Not only was he great," Kessinger said, "but the last two innings of that game he was unhittable. Over the last two innings, it was like a great running back who just is not going to be denied the goal when he is right down there on the goal line. That's the way Sandy was to me that day. The last two innings, it was like, 'Okay, here comes my best. See if you can hit it.' And we couldn't. He was awesome. It was the greatest thing, and the thing that was really remarkable about that game was how Bob Hendley pitched for the Cubs."

Los Angeles Dodger fans long have been notorious for their late arrivals, well after the first pitch is thrown. That was one day the latecomers missed something.

"That late-arriving Dodger crowd was getting there as we were leaving," Kessinger joked. "We didn't prolong the agony, I'll say that."

THE SETTING

Very little time seemed to pass between Kessinger shuttling to the minors and his becoming entrenched in the Cubs' starting lineup, where he established a reputation for himself. Lithe and athletic with quick hands, he was always a better glove man than stick man; but his fielding was so slick that he was selected to several National League all-star teams. The first time was in 1968, and Kessinger marveled at being chosen.

"Those are certainly great memories," he said. "The first year was about the players. That is a special, special feeling to be selected by your peers as the guy they want to represent the league. I started in four of the six games I played in. Usually, the starters played about five innings."

Kessinger is not opposed to fans voting for All-Star starters, but he found it more meaningful to be chosen by fellow players. Now the fans start voting in the spring two months ahead of the game, and it seems to be more about popularity than who is having the best season.

"When the players voted then, they voted like two nights before the game, and it was truly the guys who were having the good years. So from a player's standpoint it was special," Kessinger said.

The first All-Star game was nice, but being selected for the 1969 game meant even more to Kessinger. That year's game in Washington, D.C., celebrated 100 years of professional baseball, and the Cubs' representation was its best ever.

"That was a very special deal for me that year because the whole Cubs infield was there," he said.

Kessinger was joined for the All-Star festivities by second baseman Glenn Beckert, third baseman Ron Santo, first baseman Ernie Banks, and catcher Randy Hundley. The entire starting infield and the catcher all together on the All-Star team.

"It was unbelievable," Kessinger said. "It was just unbelievable."

Kessinger and second baseman Glenn Beckert were pals on and off the field, although they are very different men. While Kessinger is low key, Beckert is a bit of a party animal. Beckert likes to describe the difference between them as being a matter of language. Kessinger, who has long been involved with the Fellowship of Christian Athletes, has a very tame vocabulary. Beckert said the harshest words his old friend might utter are "Jiminy Cricket." The Federal Communications Commission, on the other hand, could fine Beckert, who calls himself more of "a Pittsburgh type," on any given day. The opposites attracted, however. On the field, they learned each other's habits well, recognizing one another's tendencies and styles when the ball was being flipped between them for a potential double play.

"It just became instinct," Beckert said.

Kessinger made the big plays at short, going deep in the hole and firing the ball across the infield to Banks on the first-base bag. What he didn't always do was compile a high batting average. The year Kessinger made his first All-Star team he batted only .240; but once in a while Kessinger's stick outshone his mitt.

THE GAME OF MY LIFE
BY DON KESSINGER

We were playing the Cardinals, and Steve Carlton started. That day I went 6-for-6. My going 6-for-6 was unusual, but it was one of those days. The thing that was really unusual that day was, when I left home that morning; I said to my wife, Carolyn, "I'm kind of tired today." She asked, "Why don't you ask for a day off?"

Up to that point in the season, I had played every inning of every game, but when Carolyn said that, I just laughed and said, "Goodness gracious, I can't ask for a day off."

It didn't help my outlook that Steve Carlton was pitching. He won more than 300 games, and I just couldn't hit him. I think I was about 0-for-3 years against him. Then I ended up going 6-for-6 that day. Of course, by the fourth hit, I wasn't tired at all.

It was a close game, and it went into extra innings. Carlton might have given up the first four hits, and then I got a couple more against relief pitchers. It was 6-6 in the 10th inning when I came up for the last time, and I got a hit and that started a rally. We won 7-6.

I had had some four- and five-hit games, but I certainly didn't think I'd ever have a six-hit game. You just go to the park to play every day. I mean that. I don't know that I would ever go to the park thinking I was going to get six hits. But I can truly say I never went to the plate where I didn't think I was going to get a hit.

I think I convinced my wife that it would have been a bad idea to take a day off that day.

GAME RESULTS

The Cubs defeated the Cardinals that day on the way to a 83-79 record.

Rather remarkably, before the end of the summer, Kessinger had another all-time hitting game, on August 31 collecting five hits in six at-bats. That time his final hit, a single, drove in the winning run in another 7-6 game, this time against the Montreal Expos. It was another 10-inning game, too.

Even with all of those hits clustered together in just two games, Kessinger batted only .258 in 1971. He remained the Cubs' shortstop through the 1975 season, then was traded to the Cardinals, where he played less than two full seasons.

"I really thought I was only going to play a couple more years and retire," Kessinger said. "But then I moved to the White Sox and played two and a half more years. I didn't know how the fans would take to me with the White Sox after coming over from the other side (of town), but they were great to me. I went to the White Sox not knowing what was going to happen. You know, sometimes it doesn't work. The first game I played was against the Yankees, and there was a full house at Comiskey Park. They put me in as a pinch runner—I'd just gotten there late that afternoon. And the fans gave me a standing ovation. I can't tell you what a good feeling that was. The people of Chicago were always really nice to me. They just kind of adopted this little boy."

Kessinger managed the Sox for the better part of one year, but it didn't go very well, and he was finished with a 46-60 record. The next time he served as a field boss, it was running the baseball program at his alma mater.

REFLECTING ON BASEBALL

For a guy who functions around the collegiate sporting seasons of the South, looking forward to football in the fall, basketball in the winter and baseball in the spring, it was a natural fit to return as baseball coach to Mississippi, where he had excelled in two sports. Between 1991 and 1996 Kessinger led the Rebels to a 185-153 record and then became associate athletic director until 2000.

"I love college sports," Kessinger proclaimed.

By the time Kessinger assumed the coaching job, his son, Keith, had already passed through the program; and in 1993, he reached the lineup of the Cincinnati Reds for 11 games. For two seasons, though, Kessinger was able to coach his youngest son, Kevin, who then signed with the Cubs after being drafted as an outfielder in 1992. The younger Kessinger's career, however, was truncated because of injury.

"He was a really outstanding player," his father said, "but he hurt his back the first week he was playing pro ball, and he never did get to play. When he came back to Mississippi, he started the real estate company. After I got through coaching I just asked him if I could have an office. We've been working together for several years."

It has become Cubs tradition to invite former players back to lead the singing of "Take Me Out to the Ballgame" during the seventh-inning stretch at Wrigley Field. Kessinger, who is heavier around the middle and missing much of the hair that he displayed in his prime years with the Cubs, does return to Chicago periodically for autograph signings, but he does not pretend to be the Frank Sinatra of the south.

No singing.

"I love the Cubs, and I love their fans," Kessinger said. "I love all of it, but that's not part of what I do. If I come back, I'll watch the game."

Maybe he'll hum that favorite baseball tune under his breath?

"That's right," Kessinger said.

Chapter 9

GLENN BECKERT

THE EARLY LIFE OF GLENN BECKERT

Glenn Beckert grew up in the Steel City, where he developed his athletic skills. Pittsburgh was a hard-around-the-edges town when Beckert was young, much like Chicago. A guy might get in a scrap on the way to or from school, or use language to tell someone off that might offend a lady. Pittsburgh ballplayers were known as tough players, and Beckert fit the description on all counts.

"Back when I lived there, Pittsburgh was noted for football," Beckert said. "And I think everybody who was recruited for anything had to play football, too. I believe that's why the Steelers are still in business. It's a football town; and even though the Pirates won a couple of World Series, it's still a football town."

Beckert, of German descent, was born in the city, but lived on the outskirts on a 128-acre farm owned by his grandfather, George Garr. The wide-open space afforded room for a sandlot, where he first practiced the game. Besides room for baseball, they were growing crops like tomatoes and corn. The entire family canned tomatoes and made tomato juice. There were always pigs living on the farm, and the farm produced milk, as well.

"When I talk to my two kids, they don't understand how wonderful they have it in today's society," Beckert said.

Beckert was 10 years old when he went hunting for rabbits with his grandfather and used a shotgun. "He showed me how to do it and I missed the first two rabbits I shot at. Then I hit the third one. I was so excited. My grandfather said, 'Okay, be sure to take out the other shell and pick up the rabbit. I'm going to teach you how to skin it so we can have it for dinner.' That was a totally different thing for me."

Little League came along at just the right time for Beckert to participate, but the playing rules weren't as strict. Beckert said kids did not yet wear batting helmets. In the pickup games, or in organized youth games, the best athlete was chosen to play shortstop, which was Beckert's position. The lesser talents were relegated to right field. The Little League squads represented smaller neighborhoods, but as Beckert reached high school age, the American Legion teams combined groups to form a regional team. One of his teammates was future major leaguer Sam McDowell, who possessed a blinding fastball and later became the most feared strikeout pitcher of his time in the American League.

As a teenager, however, McDowell had not yet harnessed his great talent, Beckert said; and when the Pittsburgh Legion team advanced to the statewide playoffs, it finished second.

"We would have won, but Sam walked like 21 guys in a seven-inning game," Beckert said. "And he struck out 20. The guys I knew in Pittsburgh were very good athletes."

Beckert's family lived next door to Steelers owner Art Rooney and his family; and the two clans became very close, he said.

"I'm a Pittsburgh guy," Beckert said. "We talk simple. We talk in our own funny language."

After Legion ball, Beckert played at Allegheny College in Pittsburgh, but also played on high-caliber

NAME: Glenn Alfred Beckert
BORN: October 12, 1940, in Pittsburgh, Pennsylvania
HOMETOWN: Pittsburgh, Pennsylvania
CURRENT RESIDENCE: Englewood, Florida
OCCUPATION: Retired major-league baseball player; Chicago Board of Trade investor who leases his seat
POSITION: Second baseman
HEIGHT: 6-foot-1
PLAYING WEIGHT: 190 pounds
ACCOMPLISHMENTS: Eleven-year major-league player, mainly with the Chicago Cubs; four-time All-Star; led the National League in runs scored with 98 in 1968; career .973-percentage fielder; lifetime batting average was .283 in 1,320 games.
THE GAME: Chicago Cubs versus Pittsburgh Pirates—July 7, 1968

A four-time All-Star second baseman, Glenn Beckert was a cornerstone of the famous 1969 Cubs team that nearly brought the National League pennant to town after a 24-year absence. Beckert lives in Florida, but maintains close ties with the Cubs; and when he visits Chicago in the summer, he leads Wrigley Field fans in singing "Take Me Out to the Ballgame" during the seventh-inning stretch. *Brace Photo*

local semipro teams. Many of the players were former minor leaguers. There was also a catcher on the club named Mike Ditka. The future Hall of Fame football star, who led the Bears to the 1986 Super Bowl championship, was a hard-nosed plate guardian as well. Apparently, he did not have all the tools to succeed on the diamond, though.

"The worst hitter I've ever seen," Beckert said. "He was as big as he was when he went to play football at the University of Pittsburgh; and he could hit the ball over the fence once in about 20 times up. We're still friends. He's a good man, a good guy."

The team played in the North Pittsburgh League, and with the mix of young talent coming out of high school, some college players, and ex-pros, it attracted some attention. Spectators did not buy tickets to watch, but instead passed the hat to hold contributions.

"They passed the cup just like they do at churches," Beckert said. "That was the gate. They'd bring in about 2,000 people. My father, Alfred, was a farmer—and our family was farmers before us—so my father came to one or two games. He always had to be at work tomorrow. His advice to me was simple: 'Don't embarrass your mother.'"

Beckert was in college, 19 years old, when scouts first noticed him, though at the time he felt, "I had no idea what I was doing."

The raw ability shone in a tryout. The New York Yankees flew Beckert and his father to New York—in the late 1950s—and brought them into the locker room. They sat in front of Mickey Mantle's locker. Gil McDougald's locker was nearby. Phil Rizzuto had retired but was around broadcasting; and Tony Kubek was the new shortstop. The Yankees offered Beckert $25,000 to sign. Alfred Beckert asked for some time to talk things over with Glenn. Then he turned to the young player and said, 'You're not going to make this team, son. They're too good.'"

Beckert did not sign with the Yankees but returned to Pittsburgh, where the Phillies were waiting. They flew the duo to Philadelphia, but after the tryout, their offer wasn't in the same ballpark.

"They were cheap," Beckert said. "My dad said, 'This is a cheap organization.' Because we had to take a bus trip or something like that."

Back to Pittsburgh—along came the Red Sox, wooing the Beckerts with a visit to Fenway Park.

"I had a really good time," Beckert said. "But I made one tremendous mistake. I was hitting the ball good against the left-field wall, and one of their coaches said, 'Glenn, I want you to hit the next pitch and run straight to second base.'"

No problem, right? At that time, teams were first beginning to use protective screens to shield batting-practice pitchers and fielders from line drives.

"They had that thing, and I had never seen one before," Beckert said. "I ran into the damned screen at first base. Full blast. It was like a fish in a net. That is a true story. I said, 'Boy, Dad, I think I messed that one up.' But we went upstairs, and they offered me some money anyway. My dad said, "I don't think they have a good player at second base or shortstop.' So I ended up signing with the Red Sox."

Not that the Red Sox invested heavily in Beckert Futures. His bonus was just $2,500 with another $5,000 thrown in if he made the majors. The Red Sox of the early 1960s were not loaded up the middle and relied on journeymen Chuck Schilling at second and Don Buddin at short. Beckert, however, never made it to the top in Boston. The Red Sox left him off their major league roster, and the Cubs drafted him.

"My dad just thought I had a better chance to make the majors through Boston," Beckert said. "I didn't know I was better than what they had. Fortunately, the Cubs, in the other league, were the same way. They needed infielders. The Red Sox had some guys they had paid a lot of money for; so they put me on their AAA roster, and the Cubs picked me. It worked out fine for me."

It is not clear what Beckert's future would have been with the Cubs, either, except for the tragedy that befell Ken Hubbs. Hubbs was the 1962 Rookie of the Year second baseman who was killed when the small plane he was piloting crashed in February 1964.

"He was awesome," Beckert said of Hubbs' talents.

By 1965, Beckert was the Cubs' full-time second baseman.

"I was very fortunate," he said.

THE SETTING

When Glenn Beckert broke into the majors in 1965, he did it in a single leap. He went from not making the Cubs roster in 1964 to starting 154 games and going to the plate 614 times. He batted .275 that season.

From the beginning, Beckert teamed with shortstop Don Kessinger, and he became one of the core members of a stable Cubs lineup that put some of the most revered players in team history on the field year after year from the early 1960s to the early 1970s.

"They needed somebody at second base (after Hubbs died); and they brought two people in who didn't work out," Beckert said. "I ended up with the job."

The Cubs had been in a team slump for a couple of decades, and in 1966, Beckert's second season, owner P.K. Wrigley decided to make a bold statement. He hired fiery manager Leo "The Lip" Durocher to run his club. Durocher took one look at the talent assembled and announced, "This is no eighth-place club." It was supposed to be an uplifting comment. Instead, the Cubs were worse than Durocher thought. He was right. The Cubs were not an eighth-place team. They were a 10th-place team that finished 59-103.

Beckert batted .287 that year and .280 in 1967. During his first few seasons in the majors, Beckert's family and friends attended games at Forbes Field when he came to town. But Beckert wanted his mom and dad to see him play in his own habitat—at Wrigley Field. It made sense for them to see a Pirates game because that was their hometown team, and Beckert wanted their visit to be a special occasion. In 1968, Beckert's parents journeyed to Chicago to see their baby boy play in the majors.

THE GAME OF MY LIFE

BY GLENN BECKERT

My mother, Grace, had never been on an airplane, and I think the only time my father had flown is when we went to major-league tryouts together, so that alone was a pretty big deal that they were going to fly to Chicago.

I went to Leo Durocher, the manager, and I said, "Leo, I'm going to bring my parents in. They've never seen me play in Chicago." Right away, Leo said, "I'll take care of it." He set my parents up in some great box seats right next to the dugout.

We played a doubleheader against the Pirates that day, and we won both games in the bottom of the ninth inning. In the second game, I got a hit, and I came around to score. I was 1-for-3 that day, but I helped beat my hometown team. I think it was a long single off the wall.

But after I got the hit—and I was on base—I was standing pretty close to where their seats were. The fact is, I looked over at them, and my mother had tears in her eyes; and seeing that brought tears to my eyes. Later, I said to her (about the crying), "They're not that good of a team, Mom."

It wasn't winning the game that mattered, of course. And I had a lot of hits that were more important than that. But it was the fact that my mom and dad were there to see it and enjoy it. And because they were, that made me enjoy it more. It was just a nice, special time.

GAME RESULTS

The Cubs won that game, 4-3. More importantly, though, the Cubs finished 84-78 and in third place. People were beginning to look at them as a team on the move.

Beckert also had the best stretch of hitting he had sustained in the majors to that point. He batted safely in 27 straight games that season. At the time, the modern Cubs record for consecutive games hitting belonged to Beckert's close friend, Ron Santo, the third baseman. He hit in 28 straight in 1966. The buddies were roommates for years, and Santo would tease Beckert about threatening his record.

Most players of the 1960s did not make enough money to live on their baseball salaries year round and took on off-season work.

"When I got within a game of his record," Beckert said, "Ron, who had some involvement with a company that made some of Chicago's famous Italian beef said to me, 'Don't worry about this record. I'll get you another job. I don't want you getting another hit.'"

Beckert did not eclipse Santo; in 1989, Jerome Walton established the team's post-1900 record by hitting in 30 consecutive games.

REFLECTING ON BASEBALL

The 1969 Cubs were the greatest team that never was. Fans revere that team, but it failed to win a championship after holding first place for most of the season. The Mets caught the Cubs, passed them, and, in a miraculous finish, won the World Series.

That summer was magical until September. Many Cubs fans consider it the best time they ever had rooting for the team. That was the season Beckert, his shortstop partner Don Kessinger, Mr. Cub Ernie Banks, Santo, and catcher Randy Hundley were all selected for the All-Star team. The Cubs were a loose team, having fun, on a roll, and making Durocher look like a genius.

During a doubleheader just before the All-Star break—on July 20, 1969—the Cubs swept the Phillies 1-0 and 6-1. Santo hit a home run in the higher scoring game, and the Wrigley Field crowd was ecstatic. The fans went crazy. Santo ran around the bases, stepped into the dugout grinning, and announced, "I've never had a standing ovation like this." Beckert, about to bust out laughing, forced Santo to look at the video screen in center field. It was showing pictures of Neil Armstrong becoming the first man to walk on the moon.

"I go, 'Hey roomie,' take a look at the television in center field,'" Beckert said. "He thought it was for him. The cheering was for Neil Armstrong."

Beckert's most famous Ron Santo stories involve the time they shared hotel rooms. One day—coincidentally while Santo was on a hot streak—Beckert noticed Santo injecting drugs into his body. Time out, Beckert declared.

It was then that Santo let Beckert in on his secret—he suffered from Type 1 diabetes.

"He had kept it very, very quiet," Beckert said.

The teammates who shared those special times—especially in 1969—formed a bond that remains nearly 40 years later. They are still friends, call one another, follow the progress of their children, and enjoy the pleasure of one another's company when they cross paths, particularly in Chicago.

"We still talk about that year and our time together," Beckert said. "It's amazing. We still have each other's phone numbers—Ferguson Jenkins, Billy Williams, Ernie Banks, Kenny Holtzman. We're still close. You know, sometimes I see one of the players from that Mets team that won it. I saw Jerry Koosman, and I asked, 'Do you talk with the guys?' And he said, 'I don't even know where the hell they are.' I think as we get older and cross the age of 60, or 65, or 70, that we realize how important that time in our life was; that we did something special. It stays with you."

Beckert has a daughter who lives in Crystal Lake, a Chicago suburb, and when he visits her, he gets recognized in restaurants by old Cub fans. He is not shy about taking the Cubs up on their offer to lead the singing of "Take Me Out to the Ballgame" during the seventh-inning stretch at Wrigley Field, either. Beckert belted out the song in 2005 and 2006; and he'll keep it up as long as he is able.

During the summer of 2006, Beckert was diagnosed with lung cancer, but doctors caught the disease at a very early stage. He was not even expecting to need chemotherapy. "I was very lucky," Beckert said.

As it so happened, Beckert's singing opportunity came against the New York Mets. Beckert considered that slightly ironic, but he accepted the challenge. He also stopped by the Cubs broadcast booth to chat with Santo. "I got Ron upset at me," Beckert said while laughing. "He said, 'Rooms, how are you? You look really, really good.' And I said, 'You're looking fat, Ron.' I said the wrong thing." But after 40 years of friendship, after 40 years of digs, one sarcastic comment isn't going to break up the act.

Chapter 10

RON SANTO

THE EARLY LIFE OF RON SANTO

Ron Santo got his start in life and baseball in the Pacific Northwest. Growing up in Seattle during the 1940s and 1950s, he did not have the opportunity to attend major league baseball games in person, but he became an avid watcher of television's *Game of the Week*. Studying the ballplayers, teams, and stadiums of the time, Santo became an early fan of the Chicago Cubs—particularly of Wrigley Field. From afar, he developed an affinity for the team and the park. For him there was just something special about the place, even though that was well before Wrigley took on the mystical aura it has acquired today.

"For some reason I always loved the National League," Santo said. "I have no reason why, other than maybe I was just able to watch the National League more. And when I saw the Cubs and I saw Wrigley Field, right there and then it was something special. I don't know why, but there was just something I loved about that ballpark. And that was just through television. And Ernie Banks was special to me, the way he conducted himself."

Santo's parents split up when he was six, and before she remarried, his mother worked two jobs, as a waitress and in a drug store, sometimes working till 10 p.m. Santo's stepfather, whom he called "Dad," was a major influence. As he grew, Santo emerged as one of the top players in the area and established his name with his all-around skills as Seattle teams played in local and regional competition. It was more difficult for young players to get noticed in those days, especially outside of a major league town, but Santo's reputation spread and he had no shortage of suitors.

"I had all 16 major league teams after me," Santo said. "They came in one at a time, and the Cleveland Indians were the first team I saw. They offered me—and this is amazing in 1959—$50,000 to sign."

At the time Santo, his sister, mother, and stepfather were living in a duplex without, as he put it "a lot of material goods." Outwardly, the family remained calm about the offer. Inwardly, Santo said, "I couldn't even swallow."

Call it fate, but those early television impressions made a difference for Santo when scouts representing major league teams came calling and attempted to woo him for their organizations. Santo told his stepfather that he wanted to play for the Cubs, even though the team did not come close to making the best offer. Part of the reason was a reliable local scout whom he had built a rapport with; and part of it was what he had seen on television.

NAME: Ronald Edward Santo
BORN: February 25, 1940, in Seattle, Washington
HOMETOWN: Seattle, Washington
CURRENT RESIDENCE: Chicago, Illinois and Scottsdale, Arizona
OCCUPATION: Retired major league baseball player; current Chicago Cubs radio broadcaster
POSITION: Third base
HEIGHT: 6 feet
PLAYING WEIGHT: 190 pounds
ACCOMPLISHMENTS: Fifteen-year major-league baseball player, 14 years with the Chicago Cubs; nine-time All-Star; five-time winner of National League Gold Glove award; career totals of .277 average, 342 home runs, and 1,331 runs batted in; one of the most beloved Cub players of all time; prominent spokesman and fund raiser of treatment and cure for diabetes.
THE GAME: Chicago Cubs versus Pittsburgh Pirates—June 26, 1960

The Cincinnati Reds and the New York Yankees offered even more money to Santo—deals in the $75,000 range, he said. However, he took far less money—$20,000—to join the Cubs. It just felt right.

"I wanted to be a Cub," Santo said.

Even before Santo signed with the Cubs, he harbored a secret he had no desire to share with scouts. When he was 18 years old, Santo was diagnosed with Type 1 juvenile diabetes. Doctors told him he would be insulin dependent for the rest of his life. What wasn't clear—and was alarming to Santo when he did some research—was just how long he could

Ron Santo did it all for the Cubs. The slugging third baseman hit 342 career home runs and drove in 1,331 runs in his major-league career between 1960 and 1974. He was also an outstanding fielder who many believe should be in the Hall of Fame. A longtime Cubs broadcaster, he is regarded as "Everyman" in the booth, wearing his love for the team on his sleeve. *Brace Photo*

expect to live. Although the bleak analysis Santo read about is no longer accurate due to advances in treatments and medicines, reading that the life expectancy of someone in his situation was only 25 slapped him across the face.

Santo became proficient in administering his own shots in private—without telling teammates, coaches, or Cubs managers that he suffered from diabetes. He was adamant about keeping quiet about the illness. Mostly, it was pride. He did not want diabetes to play a role in whether or not he was able to reach the big leagues or in whether or not he held a roster spot. He wanted to be looked at as just another ballplayer, not a player with a handicap. He didn't want managers to take his health into consideration when they were evaluating fielding and hitting.

For years, Santo kept the story of his own diabetes out of the limelight, monitored his blood sugar levels on the QT, and self-administered the necessary shots. No one connected to the Cubs had an inkling that anything was wrong. Given Santo's rapid rise in the organization, his talent was a much larger factor.

THE SETTING

No one can predict how long it will take to make the roster or whether a hot prospect signee will ever make the major-league roster at all. And certainly, no one can predict stardom. It is all educated guesswork. Safe to say, then, few would have taken to the airwaves and declared that Santo would be the Cubs' regular third baseman by the time he was 20 years old—certainly not any senior member of the Cubs' hierarchy.

At the end of spring training, just as the 1960 season was about to start, the Cubs believed Santo needed more seasoning in the minors. That meant they had a hole in the infield at third base. The Cubs thought it was a crater-sized hole. So they traded Ron Perranoski (later a terrific relief pitcher), John Goryl, and Lee Handley, plus $25,000 to the Los Angeles Dodgers for Don Zimmer.

Zimmer, who spent a half-century in baseball and later managed the Cubs, was supposed to man the fort at third until Santo jumped to the big leagues in 1961. Two and a half months later, after seeing what Santo was capable of, the Cubs brought Santo to the majors. Zimmer was moved to second base.

Santo was ready. Although he produced many outstanding games and seasons for the Cubs—and wears his devotion to the team on his sleeve—Santo's most memorable game was the first one he ever played for the team.

THE GAME OF MY LIFE

BY RON SANTO

I joined the Cubs at Forbes Field in Pittsburgh. I had never been in a big-league park in my life. I sat there on the bench and watched the Pirates take batting practice. I watched Roberto Clemente, Dick Groat, and Bill Mazeroski all hit.

Then I went into the clubhouse to start getting dressed. Lou Boudreau was managing. He and Charlie Grimm had changed jobs, with Grimm going up to the broadcast booth. Boudreau brought me into his office and said, "You're starting today. We have a doubleheader, and you're hitting sixth."

I just said, "Okay." I hadn't known if I was going to be playing when I came out to the park. I put my uniform on, and I went out early and sat in the dugout. I was sitting there before Cubs batting practice, and Ernie Banks came out and sat next to me.

Now in those days, none of the veterans talked to you. You're a rookie, and you have to prove yourself. There are only 400 ballplayers in the major leagues, and you're taking the job of one of their friends or teammates. You had to prove you could play.

So, when Ernie sat right next to me and said, "Are you nervous, kid?" I said, "Oh yeah, Ernie." He said, "Well, look at these two guys as if they're AAA pitchers."

Guess who was pitching? It was Vernon Law and Bob Friend, who were the Pirates' two best starters, and remember: they won the World Series that year. I looked at Ernie, and I said, "That's easy for you to say."

During batting practice, I was so nervous that I didn't hit a ball out of the cage. My first time up, in the second inning, Friend threw me a curveball that buckled my knees. The catcher was Smokey Burgess, and as he threw the ball back to the mound, he said, "That's a major-league curveball, kid." I stepped back in the batter's box and hit a line drive up the middle for a base hit.

The first game, I got two hits and drove in three runs. In the second game, I got another hit and drove in two more runs. I ended up getting three hits and driving in five runs that day. It was a good way to start.

GAME RESULTS

The Cubs won both games of the doubleheader, 7-6 and 7-5, on Santo's first day in the lineup. Although he was nursed along with a cap of 95 games played that season, Santo was in Chicago to stay.

The Pirates series was the end of a road trip, and the Cubs returned to Wrigley Field for a series against the Milwaukee Braves two days later. At long last, the field of his childhood television screen days was in his sights. Santo entered the park with both anticipation and reverence. Santo emerged from the dugout with Ernie Banks early—before the gates were opened to the public—and stole his first glimpse of the empty ballpark.

"I stepped on the grass at Wrigley Field, and I felt like I was walking on air," Santo said. "There was just something there. I knew exactly I was in the right place."

For Santo, it was coming home to a place he had never been before.

Less than a week later, Santo hit his first major-league homer against the Cincinnati Reds.

Soon enough, Wrigley Field became a second home. Between 1960 and 1973 with the Cubs, Santo led the National League in games played three times, triples once, and walks four times. Eleven times Santo hit 20 or more home runs, with a career high of 33 in 1965; and his best single-season batting average was .313 in 1964.

Like his friend and teammate Ernie Banks, who every year in spring training predicted a Cubs pennant, Santo was known for his optimism and his expectations that the Cubs would win "this year."

REFLECTING ON BASEBALL

Ron Santo retired as an active player in 1974 after playing one season with the Chicago White Sox. Even though he was still in Chicago, playing for the cross-town organization wasn't the same. Santo was too immersed in Cubs culture.

Santo never expected to find the rest-of-his-life calling in 1990, when he tried out to become a member of the Cubs' radio broadcast team. Always enthusiastic and known for his honesty, Santo was no polished professional announcer. He emerged from his audition session convinced he had botched it.

What Santo didn't realize at the time was, the Cubs wanted him because of who he was rather than who he might become. They liked his style, his delivery, his support for the team, his natural storytelling, his humor. They didn't want Santo to sound like every other broadcaster fresh from journalism school. He signed on, not knowing how it was going to go, and has remained on the job ever since, completing his 17th season behind the mike in 2006, and becoming an institution a second time around with the Cubs.

Partner Pat Hughes takes care of the fundamentals, and Santo comments on the action. With his somewhat gravelly voice, Santo carries listeners on the same emotional ride that fans in the seats take. Hughes makes sure the listeners know what the score is, and Santo takes pains to let them know what it means—even if it is painful. Hughes and Santo enjoy the type of broadcast booth chemistry that all ball clubs seek, but none can manufacture. It flows naturally, and one reason they are so successful together is that they are having fun together.

The Cubs retired Santo's No. 10 jersey near the end of 2003 season—an event that was a joyous occasion for Santo and fans.

The one cloud that has shrouded Santo's stay with the Cubs—long after his playing days—but very real nonetheless, has been his ongoing battle with diabetes. Santo beat the disease back in his youth sufficiently to excel as a player. Despite his insulin treatments, however, the dangerous side effects of the illness have plagued him. Improving medical treatments and technologies have aided Santo in his fight, and he long ago put that dispiriting early lifespan prognosis in his rearview mirror. About 10 years after his retirement, Santo had some difficulties with his vision—one common side effect.

That has hardly been Santo's only health challenge. He's had hardening of the arteries, quadruple bypass surgery. In 2001, he endured partial amputation of one leg below the knee; and in 2002, he had partial amputation of his second leg. He had to take some time out of the broadcast booth for bladder cancer treatments, too. Through the middle of the summer of 2006, Santo calculated he had had 23 operations.

Throughout all of the setbacks, Santo has persevered, sometimes philosophically, almost always with a smile. He has been the comeback announcer of the year twice, and repeatedly sets new standards for appearing in public with a good attitude. An online column referred to Santo as "the perfect antidote for pessimism."

A few years ago, Santo's son Jeff made a moving, acclaimed documentary about his father called *This Old Cub*. The film depicted Santo's daily routine, his difficulties adapting to prosthetic legs, but above all put on display his irrepressible optimism. Former teammates whom Santo does not see often, still monitor news reports of his health from afar and worry about him.

One-time Cubs pitcher Dick Ellsworth, who lives in Fresno, California, but does not attend games in Chicago, said he has tried to go out of his way get word to Santo of his concern. "When it became apparent to me that Ron Santo was having some severe health problems, I called him a few times to tell him that I was thinking of him, and wishing him the best, and that I was concerned for him."

For more than three decades, Santo has served as the celebrity chairman of the Juvenile Diabetes Research Foundation's Chicago chapter. He organizes an annual JDRF Ron Santo Walk to Cure Diabetes and has helped raise millions of dollars for the cause.

If there is one great personal baseball disappointment Santo has suffered in the years since he retired and acquired an AARP card, it is the failure of Baseball Hall of Fame voters to enshrine him in Cooperstown, New York. On the face of it, Santo has the numbers to be chosen. He was regarded as the top National League third baseman of his era. But more than 30 years into retirement, the voters who review the cases of recently elected players, as well as the Veterans Committee, have overlooked Santo.

Each time election results are about to be announced, Santo's hopes rise. Each time the results are announced, Santo is let down. His emotions have yo-yoed for years. To many, the Hall's error in not choosing Santo has been unconscionable. A writer named Joe Sheehan took up Santo's cause on ESPN.com, suggesting "the omission of Ron Santo is the most egregious mistake ever made by the Baseball Writers

Association of America. They should have inducted Santo 20 years ago."

Many Hall of Famers—including old teammates Ernie Banks, Billy Williams, and Ferguson Jenkins—have lobbied for Santo's inclusion. In 2005, Santo lost out for the 17th time, and fell only eight votes short of the 75 percent of voters needed to be selected.

Williams believes Santo's time is coming soon—perhaps in the election that would induct him in 2007.

"People from the other league (American League) are beginning to recognize what he did," said Williams, a 1987 inductee. "I'm glad that he has been exposed on WGN radio, and every now and then the camera is on him. A lot of players, a lot of Hall of Famers, believe Santo should be in there."

Santo is not one to pretend that the honor is meaningless for him. He has felt those rejections keenly. However, he is garnering more support, and it seems likely he will be chosen in 2007 or perhaps soon thereafter.

"It did make me feel good that I received an increase in the votes," he said after the 2005 vote.

The Cubs have not won a World Series since 1908, and Santo the player could not turn that tide. And no matter how closely the evidence has been sifted, the voters for the Hall have yet to be swayed. It just may be that one of the most devoted Cubs of all time will receive his biggest baseball rewards after a half-century around the game.

Hopefully, the Cubs will win a World Series championship with Santo at the microphone. Call it "fantasy baseball" if you wish, but Santo believes it's a reality.

Chapter 11

BILLY WILLIAMS

THE EARLY LIFE OF BILLY WILLIAMS

Billy Williams, star baseball player, was an all-star fisherman as a youth. He and his brothers got to know the local rivers well growing up in the tiny town of Whistler, Alabama, just outside Mobile. The Williams' took much advantage of the abundance of fish they could catch. Even today, decades removed from those carefree days, whenever Williams returns to Alabama for family reunions, he and his brothers set out for the same waters to drop a line.

Williams grew up with four brothers, and all of the guys enjoyed playing all kinds of sports outdoors. When they weren't fishing, they were playing baseball, which was the most popular sport among the kids in that neighborhood. The Mobile area had a well-deserved reputation as a hotbed of baseball. Among the sport's luminaries who got their start in the city located on the Gulf of Mexico were Satchel Paige, Hank Aaron, and his brother Tommie, Tommy Agee, and Williams.

"The streets were like a mile long," Williams said. "There were numbered streets, and you could get a team up like that. All of the guys from Sixth Street would go play the guys from Seventh or Eighth Street. It was like a road trip. We'd go there one day, and they'd come over one day. We were swimming in baseball."

During Williams' and Aaron's era, a local man named Ed Tucker cared about keeping kids out of trouble and giving them a chance to get ahead. If he came across any youngster in the Mobile area, Tucker tried to enlist him for a baseball team.

"Ed Tucker was the guy that made sure every young individual who wanted to play baseball got a chance," Williams said. "Hank Aaron was a second baseman on one of those teams. One of my brothers played with him. He was a pitcher."

As they progressed through school until their mid-teens, some of the best players were noticed and invited to play on the area semi-pro teams. By the time he was 16, Williams was playing with men.

"I was playing with guys who were maybe 25," he said. "The minute you made a mistake, they would correct the mistake, right at that time. They said if we wanted to play baseball, then you couldn't play it that way. They said, 'If you want to play, you're going to have to do it the right way.' There was a sense of them wanting the younger guys to do things the best way."

In the 1950s, scouts scoured the backwoods, hoping for an unexpected discovery. Williams was noticed, and in 1956, he hooked up with Buck O'Neil. O'Neil, a multiple Negro Leagues pennant-winning manager with the Kansas City Monarchs and a first baseman with batting titles on his resume, had just become a scout for the Cubs. In 1962, he became the first African-American coach in the majors, also for the Cubs.

O'Neil signed Williams for the Cubs organization. The 1950s were not the best time to be black in Alabama. The

NAME: Billy Leo Williams
BORN: June 15, 1938, in Whistler, Alabama
HOMETOWN: Whistler, Alabama
CURRENT RESIDENCE: Chicago, Illinois
OCCUPATION: Retired major-league baseball player; former big-league coach; current executive assistant, Chicago Cubs
POSITION: Outfielder
HEIGHT: 6-foot-1
PLAYING WEIGHT: 175 pounds
ACCOMPLISHMENTS: Eighteen-season major-league player between 1959 and 1976, 16 seasons spent with the Chicago Cubs, two seasons with the Oakland A's; lifetime batting average of .290, career total of 426 home runs, 1,475 runs batted in; led the National League in games played six times; led NL in runs (137) and hits (205) in 1970; 2,711 career hits; later served as a coach for the A's and spent three different stints with the Cubs as an on-field coach between 1980 and 1982, 1986 and 1987, and 1992 and 2001; elected to the Baseball Hall of Fame in 1987.
THE GAME: Chicago Cubs versus St. Louis Cardinals in a doubleheader—June 29, 1969

Called "Sweet Swinging Billy Williams," Williams was elected to the Baseball Hall of Fame after an 18-year career during which he swatted 426 home runs and collected 1,475 RBIs. A former Cubs coach, he remains close to the team, making appearances to promote the club. *Brace Photo*

Civil Rights Movement that would alter American society was just blossoming. Williams knew what it was like to be called nasty names. Unfortunately, some of that hatred followed him during his tour of southern minor-league franchises. During a personal crisis in San Antonio, Texas, Williams was fed up, was planning to quit the Cubs and professional baseball. Ultimately, O'Neil soothed Williams, convincing him he would receive the opportunity he coveted and would become a top player.

Williams came of age just as Negro Leagues teams went bankrupt, and Major League Baseball was broadening its reach and acceptance of black players. Still, he was in Alabama long enough to play against Paige and then in Florida with the Hall of Fame right-hander as a teammate. Paige did make it to the majors—past his prime, but when he still could be effective. The opening of the big leagues to blacks came too late for Cool Papa Bell, Buck Leonard, Josh Gibson, and many other African-American greats.

"I was right on the crest of seeing some of those old-timers play," Williams said. "And then I saw what happened to this game after 1956."

After Williams joined the Cubs organization, he followed a traditional path to the majors, working his way up through the minors; and in 1959, he took his first at-bats as a member of the big club.

THE SETTING

In 1959 and 1960, Billy Williams saw sporadic action for the Cubs; but by 1961, he was a regular and a budding star, cracking 25 home runs with 86 runs batted in. Over an eight-season period leading up to 1969, Williams never hit fewer than 22 home runs and emerged as a perennial All-Star.

Soft-spoken, steady, with a smooth cut that made lesser players jealous, "Sweet Swinging" Billy Williams became a fan favorite. In some ways, Williams played in the shadow of Ernie Banks, who had already been a two-time Most Valuable Player, but they became identified as one of the deadliest one-two punches in the league.

Williams regularly turned in remarkable, career-highlight hitting games. He was unassuming, not outsized, but you never knew when he was going to erupt. On August 21, 1968, Williams led the Cubs to a doubleheader sweep of the Milwaukee Braves, 5-4 and 13-5. During the course of the two games, Williams drove in nine runs with a home run, a double, three singles, and a sacrifice fly. Only a few weeks later, Williams slugged three homers—all three being two-run jobs—for six RBIs in an 8-1 victory over the New York Mets. The day before Williams also connected for two homers and the combined five home-run total over two consecutive games tied a major-league record. In April of 1969, Williams struck four consecutive doubles in an 11-3 triumph over the Phillies, also tying a major-league record.

The Cubs started out hot and stayed hot. With Leo Durocher at the helm, the Cubs seemed in danger of capturing their first pennant in 24 years. From opening day on, the Cubs remained in first place for 155 straight days, until they dropped behind the Mets on September 10. They also drew 1.6 million delirious fans, and the players and spectators both realized they were experiencing something special together.

"We all thought that was our year to go to the World Series," Williams said.

THE GAME OF MY LIFE

BY BILLY WILLIAMS

The Chicago organization set aside the day at Wrigley Field as Billy Williams Day. It was a doubleheader against the Cardinals.

When I left home that day, I wasn't sure we were going to play because it was cloudy and rainy, and it looked like it was going to rain hard. In the first game, I wound up hitting a double and scoring the winning run. There were more than 40,000 fans there that day, and I also broke a record by playing in my 895th and 896th straight games, ironically passing Stan Musial for the National League record.

Before the game in the ceremonies, the Cubs organization gave me a lot of stuff. They gave me a new car, a watch, a fishing boat, a trailer, a pool table, and a washer-dryer combo. I was out there sitting on the bench waiting for them to start. I didn't go into the clubhouse because I didn't want to miss the ceremony. The other players were in the locker room. Leo came out, and he saw there was no one else on the bench. They knew what time it was supposed to start, but Leo was kind of fretful. So he started hollering and yelling and getting the guys out of the clubhouse. Leo had that voice that carried.

Normally, when a team has a day for a guy he is not as good as he wants to be because he's trying too hard. Yet, in the second game, I hit a single, a double, and a triple. I needed a home run to hit for the cycle. My last time at the plate I tried so hard to hit a home run and you know, when you try so hard, you don't do it.

I wound up striking out, but fans gave me a standing ovation.

GAME RESULTS

The Cubs swept the Cardinals on Billy Williams Day by scores of 3-1 and 12-1.

"We held on to first place," Williams said. "So that was a joyous day. Doing what I did on the baseball field and staying in first place. So it was great."

Williams played in every Cub game that season, stroked 21 homers, collected 95 RBIs, and batted .293. He was at the peak of his career and ahead still lay some of Williams' greatest achievements. The 1972 season was special for Williams. It seemed he was in command at the plate from April to October. He batted a league-leading .333, swatted 37 home runs, and drove in 122.

Williams also produced his greatest single hitting day in the majors that season. For one day, at least, he was Superman in cleats. On July 11, Williams cracked eight hits in eight at-bats in a doubleheader against the Houston Astros. In the first game, Williams went 3-for-3. In the second game, Williams went 5-for-5 to cap a stunning performance at Wrigley Field.

"You go up to the plate, and you get your first hit," Williams said. "The second time up, you get a hit. The third time, you get a hit—and that's the first game. So you're swinging the bat real well. The fourth time, you get your fourth hit. You get a fifth hit, you get a sixth hit, a seventh hit, and an eighth hit. You certainly have to be in a zone.

"That has got to be one of the greatest games I've played in. That day will stick out in my memory for many, many years."

The electricity and the hope generated by Durocher's arrival eventually petered out, and the Hall of Famer departed in the middle of the 1972 season. Williams enjoyed playing for the demonstrative, sometimes abrasive Durocher.

"He was a good manager," Williams said. "He was always two or three innings ahead of the other manager. He had just been in so many games. The one trait many people talked about was his being a disciplinarian. He talked to you a lot when you were going well; but he felt bad, he felt sorry for you when you weren't, and he didn't talk to you that much. He felt you were more receptive when you were playing well, and you could hear what you did last week. He would tell you what happened three or four days before to let you know he didn't forget."

REFLECTIONS ON BASEBALL

Billy Williams has remained close to the sport since he stopped playing. He filled the better part of three decades with coaching jobs, and he helps the Cubs out with special assignments. He does some public relations appearances and attends most home games, and he is one Hall of Famer who still attends the annual induction ceremonies in Cooperstown.

In 2006, Williams was present for the induction of former Cub relief pitcher Bruce Sutter and the induction of 17 long-dead players and owners from Negro Leagues baseball. Although he was overlooked for induction and this oversight created nationwide indignation, Williams' old mentor, Buck O'Neil, delivered a heartfelt speech representing the other African-American recipients who received their due. It seemed retroactively even more fitting when O'Neil went into a Kansas City hospital citing fatigue and died at the age of 94 on October 6, 2006.

In Cooperstown at the time, O'Neil, always regarded as a magnificent ambassador for baseball, seemed healthy and was a major player in the festivities.

"It was a good recognition," said Williams, who is very conscious of the pioneering efforts of early black players who were shut out of the majors because of the color barrier. "It was a joyous time just to see the smiles on the faces of the family members. It was a great time. I wish every black ballplayer who played this game in the major leagues could have witnessed that because it was an historical moment."

Not only was Williams impressed with O'Neil's speech (he noted that O'Neil's deep-voiced delivery always contributed to his making a memorable speech), he also had the chance to share time with O'Neil once again. Williams also spent time with Monte Irvin, another Hall of

Famer who played both in the Negro Leagues and with the New York Giants' pennant-winning clubs of the early 1950s before joining the commissioner's office.

"I talked to Buck about a lot of those individuals that played in the 1930s; and I talked to Monte Irvin who played with some of those individuals," Williams said. "I think the thing we don't realize is the hotels weren't five-star hotels, and the buses weren't air conditioned. They had to travel 1,200 miles and get off a bus and play a game of baseball. They did it because they loved the game, and they wanted to perform. Plus, while I was there, they unveiled a statue of Satchel Paige."

Williams, now graying and balding, was touched by that visit to Cooperstown in several ways. Not only did it allow him to experience by proxy some of the stories and events his predecessors lived through, it reminded him of his own induction day nearly 20 years earlier.

"You play this game, you enjoy this game, you play for so many years, and you're not expecting this," Williams said of his 1987 reaction upon being told he was elected. "You get to the end and people start saying you need to be selected for the Hall of Fame, but you still don't know whether you will be or not. It took me three years after I was eligible and eight years after I retired. It's just mind-boggling when the writers feel you belong in the Hall of Fame with all of the greats."

The moment it sunk in for Williams, he was on the dais, sitting with Bob Feller, Mickey Mantle, and Ted Williams.

"That's when you really feel that you are now a member of the Hall of Fame," he said.

Chapter 12

ERNIE BANKS

THE EARLY LIFE OF ERNIE BANKS

Ernie Banks grew up in a poor area of Dallas and said his father, Eddie, worked long hours trying to keep the family fed and clothed. The earliest years of Banks' childhood came during the Depression, and he remembers his dad subsisting on Works Progress Administration jobs.

Banks' mother, Essie, took care of the cooking and washing. Many years later, Banks said the first truck he ever remembered seeing was the welfare truck that made house calls twice monthly to drop off food and clothing for families in need. He recalled his mother plucking a new pair of jeans from the clothes pile for him when he was five, and how excited he was to have his own pair of new pants. Banks said he wore them to bed. Banks was the second oldest of 12 children, and the household budget was indeed stretched tight.

The Banks' were neither richer nor poorer than their neighbors were, though. Banks' first bicycle was a hand-me-down. Throughout his youth and in his teens, Banks worked at a variety of part-time jobs to raise cash. Among other things, he shined shoes, mowed lawns, and picked cotton.

Despite not being very well off, Banks said he learned many key life lessons from his parents about a family sticking together and about bringing a positive attitude to whatever task faced him.

It was not until Banks became a student at Booker T. Washington High School that he began participating in organized sports. The school did not field a baseball team, however. It offered softball. So the future major leaguer got his start in his sport in a backwards manner, playing the similar, but slower game of softball. Banks also played basketball and football.

Banks picked up the finer points of softball, or baseball, on his own. He once encountered future major leaguer Hank Thompson in a game against another Dallas team and watched with admiration as Thompson stroked deep shots by employing a batting style that emphasized wrist movement. Banks taught himself the style and kept it for the remainder of his career, harnessing and exploding his power on contact with a wrist action that provided him with a smooth swing.

For those who knew him later and noted that Banks was a chatterbox who never shut up, his adolescent demeanor would surprise them. Shy, he would try to avoid talking to anybody at all.

"I didn't understand a lot of people," Banks said of his younger self. "I was just going out there and playing. I thought talking to human beings was just something that could make things complicated and unpleasant. So I didn't talk very much. I just watched people."

Ultimately, a scout affiliated with the Detroit Colts, a touring black ball club, observed Banks' raw talent. The summer after his sophomore year in high school, Banks was invited to a tryout and attended a clinic in Amarillo. During a game,

NAME: Ernest Banks
BORN: January 31, 1931, in Dallas, Texas
HOMETOWN: Dallas, Texas
CURRENT RESIDENCE: Marina del Ray, California
OCCUPATION: Retired major-league baseball player; former major-league coach; former bank executive
POSITION: Shortstop and first base
HEIGHT: 6-foot-1
PLAYING WEIGHT: 180 pounds
ACCOMPLISHMENTS: Nineteen-year major-league player, between 1953 and 1971, all with the Chicago Cubs; earned the nickname "Mr. Cub" for his longevity with and loyalty to the team and the organization; holder of a lifetime batting average of .274; hit 512 home runs and knocked in 1,636 runs; National League Most Valuable Player in 1958 and 1959; twice led the National League in home runs and twice led in RBIs; elected to the Baseball Hall of Fame in 1977.
THE GAME: Chicago Cubs versus Philadelphia Phillies—September 17, 1953

Famous for his upbeat attitude, belief that the Cubs would win the pennant, and his 512 career home runs, and 1,636 RBIs, Ernie Banks is known as "Mr. Cub." The superstar played his entire career with the Cubs between 1953 and 1971 and was the first African-American player to suit up for the team. A two-time National League Most Valuable Player, Banks remains beloved in Chicago. *Brace Photo*

Banks swatted a home run impressive enough to provoke the fans into passing the hat for him. He collected loose change amounting to around $6.

Banks did more than make an impression on spectators. Coolly observing the teenager was a man who didn't need either binoculars or a stopwatch to spot talent. Cool Papa Bell, perhaps the fastest ballplayer in history, discovered Banks, then recommended to his friend, Buck O'Neil, that the kid could play.

O'Neil, then managing the Kansas City Monarchs during the final days of the Negro Leagues, acted on Bell's word; and at the end of Banks' second season with the semi-pro outfit, two representatives of the Monarchs appeared at his kitchen table one day. They told Banks and his parents that when he graduated from high school he was welcome to join the Monarchs for $300 a month.

The Monarchs had a spectacular history of winning championships, of featuring pitcher Satchel Paige, of being the marquee team of the Negro Leagues. The easygoing, wise, and baseball-savvy O'Neil set the tone for the organization. He was very much a father figure to his young charges, who he knew would graduate to the majors and receive the opportunity to cross over into white baseball that he was never afforded. All of them knew in 1950 that the Monarchs were on the way out due to newly integrated major-league ball.

"Cool Papa Bell was the first one who impressed me," Banks said. "And Buck O'Neil helped me in many ways. He instilled a positive outlook in me."

O'Neil, who moved on to the Cubs as a scout after the Monarchs went under, and who became the first black coach in Major League Baseball, steered Banks towards the team, although his progress was interrupted by a stint in the Army.

On September 8, 1953, near the end of the season when he was back with the Monarchs, Banks was sold to Chicago for $35,000 and given a trial at shortstop. Almost simultaneously, Gene Baker, who had been playing with the Cubs' AAA affiliate Los Angeles Angels, was given a trial at second base.

They became the first two African-Americans to play for the Chicago Cubs, and they became the first black double-play combination in major-league history. Baker, who was six years older than Banks, came from Davenport, Iowa, and spent eight years in the majors with a .265 batting average. Technically, Baker was the first black player on the Cubs' roster, but Banks was the first black player to enter a game.

THE SETTING

Banks had stayed in touch with an old friend from his Kansas City days, Elston Howard. Howard was a catcher in the New York Yankees' system and was poised to become the first black Yankee.

"When he told me he was going to sign with the Yankees and be sent to a Class B team in Michigan, I told him to stay in touch and let me know how it was playing in organized ball," Banks said. "He did. He said it was not too different from the Negro Leagues. He said if you just played hard every day that things would be okay; and that was nice to hear."

Baseball was undergoing a revolution. The Brooklyn Dodgers introduced Jackie Robinson to the majors in 1947. That made him the first African-American to play major-league ball in the 20th Century. Robinson was the barrier breaker, and other teams followed at their own pace hiring black players. Cleveland took the lead in the American League. The New York Giants moved quickly in the National League. Some teams lagged, but several teams recognized the change and were anxious to find their own stars who could compete with Robinson, Roy Campanella, Don Newcombe, Monte Irvin, and Willie Mays.

When he got out of the service, Banks ignored tryout offers from the Dodgers and Indians and returned to the Monarchs, wherein the Cubs then benefited from Banks' O'Neil connection.

THE GAME OF MY LIFE

BY ERNIE BANKS

The first game I played in was on September 17. I came up at the end of the 1953 season. Phil Cavaretta was the player-manager. He had been the Most Valuable Player for the Cubs the last time they won the pennant. That was 1945. They still haven't won another pennant. I can't believe it to this day.

I went out to the ballpark like usual that day, and when I showed up around the batting cage, Cavaretta said, "You're playing today." He said it very quietly. I didn't think it was that big a deal. I know some people would say they were nervous, but I didn't have that much time to think about it.

I think I'm a very unusual person in that I just thought, "That is the way it is supposed to be." You just did what you were supposed to do. I mean playing was what I was supposed to do. That's why they brought me there. I'm not saying it's just because you are paid to do something, but you're there to play. I don't get overwhelmed by it.

Players always remember their first game, though; but as a player, you want to continue the journey each day. You have a whole lot of photographers, fans, writers, the media—they'll remember it for you. Each time, each inning, each game, I was trying to do something to help the team win, to turn in a performance of doing my best. That's all it was.

When I watch a game, I just look at the enjoyment that the players are having that day—not my enjoyment. I worked and lived my life each day, each moment. I have a neighbor who is a physicist. We talk about this a lot. What's the meaning of it all? The meaning of it all is what you're doing now, not what you did in the past or what you will do in the future—just what you're doing right now.

That's what I kind of center my life on.

In my first game, I went 0-for-3, and we lost. I made an error, too. We lost 15-3 or something to the Phillies.

I didn't save souvenirs from my playing time—no bats, no balls, no pictures. The true measures are a spiritual thing. True treasures are in heaven, not on earth. I don't have any memorabilia, as they call it. I see people who do, and there's nothing wrong with that. Sometimes I sign something for somebody, something they like or enjoy, and I know they're happy for that moment.

The best sport, or any sport, that brings joy to me is how you can make somebody happy doing so little. If signing a piece of paper, magazine, or book, or whatever, makes them very happy, that should remind us of the wonderful thing an athlete owns: that ability to make people happy.

If I was on a quiz show and somebody asked me what was the best game I ever played, and there was a buzzer that was going to go off, I would be able to give an answer right away.

I would say, "I haven't played my best game yet."

GAME RESULT

The Cubs actually lost to the Phillies by a score of 16-4 on the day Banks made his debut, but his memory was not far off. Although Banks does remember a little bit more about his first game, he said he almost never focuses on the snippets of detail of other games that another player might recall in minute detail forever.

During his 19 seasons with the Cubs, Banks hit 12 grand-slam homers. He also hit three home runs in a game four different times (1955, 1957, 1962, and 1963). During the 1955 season alone, Banks slugged five grand slams, burnishing his reputation as a clutch hitter whose slugging was even more dramatic when the bases were loaded.

Over the years following his debut, Banks developed into a full-fledged star who became one of the best players in baseball. He was also one of the best-liked players. Teammates, opponents, and sportswriters all liked being around Banks because he possessed an upbeat attitude and nearly always wore a welcoming smile on his face. He had also become much more outgoing than he was as a teenager.

The combination of consistent attitude and consistent performance led a Chicago sportswriter named Jim Enright to call Banks "Mr. Cub." The appellation stuck for life; and decades after his retirement, Banks is still called by the complimentary nickname, even among those too young to have seen him play.

Nearly as memorable for Banks as his first-ever major-league game was a game that took place 17 years later when he recorded his 500th home run. The 500 home-run club is still exclusive more than 35 years later, and Banks experienced a considerable amount of extra attention in the weeks leading up to the feat during the 1970 season.

"My career was winding down," Banks said. "My children were getting older. I was thinking more about family stuff. My daughter Jan said, 'Please, Daddy, get it over with.'"

On May 12, in the second inning of an eventual Cubs 4-3, 11-inning victory over Atlanta, Banks took Braves hurler Pat Jarvis deep—end of quest.

"Some of the players and some of the writers made a pretty big deal about it, but there was no big celebration," Banks said.

REFLECTIONS ON BASEBALL

Ernie Banks retired from baseball at the end of the 1971 season, and his 2,528 games remain the most anyone ever played in a Cubs uniform. He was inducted into the Baseball Hall of Fame six summers later.

Periodically, Banks has returned to Chicago to sign autographs, to lead the singing of "Take Me Out to the Ballgame" at Wrigley Field, and to appear at important Cubs events.

He eternally retains the same sunny disposition. When he answers his telephone, Banks always delivers a hearty "How are you?" His sentences are infused with enthusiasm, and if you have missed him, his answering machine will greet you with perky music. Unfailingly, Banks will ask a caller how his love life is going, or if he is married. Banks could have been the matchmaker in *Fiddler on the Roof.* That's just Ernie being Ernie, wanting everyone to be happy, and wanting everyone to feel as good about life as he does.

Banks' one regret about baseball is that the Cubs could not break their World Series drought when he was in the lineup. He ached to play in a World Series, but many of the teams he played on finished well short of the National League pennant.

"In those days," said pitcher Glen Hobbie, Banks' old teammate, "if you wanted to beat the Cubs, you just pitched around Banks. Oh, could he ever hit."

It took Banks' old friend a little bit longer to reach the majors, but the late Elston Howard did have one advantage in his career. His Yankees seemed to win the American League pennant every year and seemed so spoiled that if they didn't win the World Series the season was gauged a failure. Banks would have loved meeting Howard in just one Series.

"That would have been real nice," Banks said. "Never came close. It was always the Dodgers and the Yankees."

Banks never wanted to manage, and after two years as a Cubs coach, he retired from that profession, too. But even as he passed his 75th birthday, Banks had no intention of retiring to a rocking chair. He still has big plans on two fronts.

He has said more than once in the last couple of years that he would like to win the Nobel Peace Prize for doing something special for humanity. He would like to see the world's richest athletes band together and make contributions to a fund that would use the money to help alleviate poverty around the world.

And if contributing to world peace and prosperity is not a large enough task to tackle, Banks would also like to rescue the Cubs. As the 2008, 100th anniversary of the last time the team won the World Series approaches, Banks wants to become the owner or president of the team he loves. He wants to be the front man for a group that will lead the team out of the wilderness and into the playoffs. He wants to live to see the Chicago Cubs stand tall again on top of the baseball world.

So far the plan has not worked out. As the Cubs sank to the bottom of the National League in 2006, Banks met with Tribune Company officials to make a pitch. He was told the team was not for sale; but as summer turned to fall, he was not giving up, either.

"You've got to be patient with this stuff," Banks said. "Gotta be patient."

Chapter 13

KEN HOLTZMAN

THE EARLY LIFE OF
KEN HOLTZMAN

Ken Holtzman grew up in the St. Louis area where he became a star athlete for University City High School before graduating in 1963. His father, Henry, worked in the machinery business, and his mother, Jacqueline, was a housewife.

The southpaw was the Most Valuable Player on his high school's state championship team. Holtzman enrolled at the University of Illinois, where he became a star pitcher at a higher level.

The Cubs drafted Holtzman in the fourth round in 1965, but he very much wanted to finish college. He foresaw a career in business, and he wasn't sure he wanted to sidetrack it for years playing baseball if a sports career was not going to be financially worthwhile.

"I knew if I played baseball, I'd be behind when I entered business," Holtzman told *Sport Magazine*.

He need not have worried. The Cubs saw him as a future star and signed him for a $70,000 bonus. In the 2000s, that is nothing for a coveted draft pick, but in the 1960s that was an eye-catching amount of money. Holtzman spent only about two months and 86 innings worth of his time in Caldwell, Idaho, and Wenatchee, Washington, before he was called up to the parent club in September of 1965.

The late Buck O'Neil greeted Holtzman when he flew into Chicago.

"My biggest thrill was when Buck O'Neil picked me up at O'Hare International and brought me to Wrigley Field for the first time to meet Ernie Banks, Billy Williams, and Ron Santo," Holtzman said.

It seemed that only one thing could divert Holtzman's career. The United States was becoming more heavily involved in the war in Vietnam. Young men were being sought for what would soon be full-scale combat duty in Southeast Asia. Holtzman joined the National Guard, and guard duty periodically interfered with his baseball career.

One of the things that attracted the Cubs to Holtzman, for better or worse, is that they pictured him as the second coming of Sandy Koufax. Like Koufax, Holtzman threw from the left side. Like Koufax, Holtzman threw fastballs that could make batters blink. And like Koufax, Holtzman was Jewish. At a time when the nation was not quite as cosmopolitan, Holtzman's heritage was a frequent topic. He was a hero to young Jewish children who were sports fans. He was an anomaly for the rest of the country, a pitcher who was just a little bit different.

Although Holtzman, just as every other left-hander who ever played, was not quite of Koufax's caliber, he was definitely good enough.

Forty years after Koufax played, viewpoints have broadened in the United States, which has become more accepting of human differences from skin color to religious observation; so it is difficult for some to realize just what kind of impact Koufax made. He was the first genuine Jewish baseball superstar since Hank Greenberg; and when he refused to pitch on Jewish high holidays—which

NAME: Kenneth Dale Holtzman
BORN: November 3, 1945, in St. Louis, Missouri
HOMETOWN: University City, Missouri
CURRENT RESIDENCE: St. Louis, Missouri
OCCUPATION: Retired major-league player; former insurance salesman; former sports director at a St. Louis area Jewish community center; currently a substitute teacher in the St. Louis area
POSITION: Pitcher
HEIGHT: 6-foot-2
PLAYING WEIGHT: 175 pounds
ACCOMPLISHMENTS: Played 15 seasons in the major leagues and won 174 games; split his time between the Chicago Cubs, Oakland A's, Baltimore Orioles, and New York Yankees; pitched two no-hitters for the Cubs, but was part of the three World Series championships with Oakland and was with Yankees for another World Series.
THE GAMES: Chicago Cubs versus Atlanta Braves—August 19, 1969; Chicago Cubs versus Cincinnati Reds—June 3, 1971

Although the left-hander enjoyed championship success with other teams, Ken Holtzman was a popular figure with the Cubs between 1965 and 1971. He pitched two no-hitters for the Cubs, in 1969 and in 1971—two performances revered in team lore. *Brace Photo*

invariably arose around the time of the World Series—he became a mainstream hero among Jews who were not even sports fans.

One of those fans was Holtzman's mother, Jacqueline. In a 1966 game, when Holtzman was scheduled to face Koufax on the mound, she seemed torn about whom to root for—her son or her idol. "Maybe you can get a no-decision," she told her son. Actually, that time, Holtzman defeated the master, 2-1.

Later, when Holtzman had become a veteran of air travel with the Cubs, he said he made a point of ordering kosher food on planes. It was always better quality food, he said.

"I believe in Jewish values," he said in an interview with the publication, *Jewish Post*, "and my religion."

THE SETTING

Ken Holtzman appeared only briefly as a Cub at the end of the 1965 season, playing in three games. A year later, before his 21st birthday, he was in the rotation and compiled an 11-16 record. In 1967, Holtzman put together a 9-0 season while only competing in 12 games.

By 1968, Holtzman's National Guard obligations were becoming worrisome for the Cubs. He could muster only an 11-14 record, but there were extenuating circumstances. Holtzman's season was interrupted 10 times by the National Guard. During the late August Democratic National Convention, Holtzman's Illinois National Guard unit was activated and was part of the scene as demonstrators protested at the Conrad Hilton.

Protestors were bloodied in the streets, tear gas wafted over downtown, arrests were made, and through the looking glass of history the convention and event became regarded as an embarrassing stain on Chicago's reputation. While Holtzman was wearing another kind of uniform, his teammates were playing the Houston Astros.

By the 1969 season, things had calmed a bit. Holtzman's pitching schedule was back to normal, and he turned in an overall performance that started to live up to his and the Cubs' expectations. Holtzman finished 17-13 and was becoming an intimidator in the rotation.

On May 11, Holtzman shut out the Giants at Wrigley Field. On May 16, he shut out the Astros. He kept running up scoreless innings. On August 2, Holtzman pitched a two-hitter against the Padres.

Although even the best pitchers of all-time do not throw no-hitters, Holtzman had certainly spent the season setting up his August 19 gem. Over the years, Holtzman has repeatedly insisted that any no-hitter is a good day with a lot of luck, and he hasn't changed his tune. He frequently uses phrases involving the word luck when coaxed into discussing his no-hitters.

Ironically, Holtzman also insists he never really pitched a big game for the Cubs. That's because in his mind big games are not individual achievements revolving around no-hitters, but performances that occur in playoff and World Series games. Holtzman had the pleasure of that duty many times, but with Oakland and New York, not with the Cubs.

THE GAME OF MY LIFE, PART I: AUGUST 18, 1969

BY KEN HOLTZMAN

My first no-hitter occurred in August when we had over 40,000 people every day, and we had about a 10-game lead in the division. The wind was blowing in that day. It cost Hank Aaron a home run in the seventh inning. (Outfielder Billy Williams caught the ball leaning against the right-field ivy). Aaron also made the last out on a grounder to second baseman Glenn Beckert.

I knew I had a no-hitter every inning after the third because the fans, who sit very close to the field, kept reminding me after each inning.

GAME RESULTS

The Cubs defeated the Braves 3-1 before 37,514 fans in an afternoon game. Although Holtzman was fine enough to put the Braves down without a base hit, he did not obtain any of his 27 outs by strikeout. He walked three batters.

Chicago led throughout the game. Third baseman Ron Santo slugged a three-run homer in the first.

In an oddity, regular catcher Randy Hundley could not play because of an injured thumb, and backup Bill Heath, whose entire Cubs career lasted nine games, was also injured when he broke his hand on a foul ball and had to give way to a third backstop, Gene Oliver.

The 1969 season is one of the most special in Cubs history since the 1945 World Series appearance. The team sprinted out of the gate and stayed in first place all summer before being passed by the Miracle Mets in mid-September. Holtzman nearly got the chance he craved to pitch in a World Series for the Cubs.

Some Cubs felt that manager Leo Durocher relied too much on the regulars and not enough on his bench as the late-season lead shrunk and the Mets came on strong.

"The '69 team had a lot of stars, but was not very deep," Holtzman said. "I'm still convinced that playing all day games (in the heat and heart of the summer) and not utilizing all 25 guys was a big Cubs disadvantage versus the rest of the league."

THE SETTING

In 1970, Holtzman finished 17-11. His future looked bright in Chicago, but things went awry in 1971. He was in the midst of a poor season, en route to a 9-15 finish when he completed a second no-hitter.

The Cubs, too, had become different animals, with an 83-79 season under Durocher that was far from the 1969 joy ride. Holtzman was only 2-6 with a sad 5.40 earned run average when he pitched his second no-hitter. It was a rare feat for any pitcher not named Nolan Ryan, Cy Young, or Sandy Koufax.

THE GAME OF MY LIFE, PART II: JUNE 3, 1971

BY KEN HOLTZMAN

My second no-hitter in Cincinnati was also lucky because Johnny Bench narrowly missed getting a bunt single when it rolled foul at the last second. No-hit games are well-pitched games with a generous amount of luck thrown in.

I also lost a couple of no-hitters in the ninth inning, one on a misjudged fly ball, so obviously you have to be very fortunate to complete a game like that.

As special as those two games were, they don't compare to the many World Series games that I pitched, especially Game 7 of the 1973 World

Series. The Oakland A's of the early 1970s are one of the greatest teams of all time, and even today do not get the respect and recognition they deserve.

GAME RESULTS

This was a tense game all of the way. The Cubs won, but only 1-0, and needed Holtzman's brilliance to stay ahead. He completed the game by retiring the last 11 Reds in order.

No-hitter or not, Holtzman soured on the Cubs. He wanted to play for a pennant-contender. The Cubs soured on him after the losing season, so when Holtzman requested a trade, they shipped him to Oakland for outfielder Rick Monday.

Although Monday was a solid all-around player for the Cubs, Holtzman's best seasons were ahead of him. He won 19, 21, 19, and 18 games over his next four seasons, and the A's won three straight World Series titles.

During the 1973 American League playoffs, the A's were scheduled to play the Baltimore Orioles in Baltimore on Yom Kippur, the holiest of Jewish holidays, and Holtzman declined to take his turn in the rotation. There was no fallout from fans, and the Orioles even told Holtzman they would find him a synagogue where he could worship. The next day, a limousine showed up at his hotel and delivered him to a temple. He was guided to a seat next to a gentleman who stuck out his hand and introduced himself as Jerry Hoffberger—owner of the Orioles. The A's went on to best Baltimore in five games during the American League Championship Series before outlasting the Mets for their third consecutive Series championship.

After some additional glory with the Yankees in another World Series, Holtzman returned to the Cubs to wrap up his playing career during the 1978 and 1979 seasons.

REFLECTIONS ON BASEBALL

Holtzman maintains friendly relations with the Cubs, but it's clear that the biggest moments of his career took place while he was wearing the uniform of the Oakland A's.

"We didn't draw nearly as well as the Cubs," Holtzman said, "but more than 30 years later, we are as beloved in the Bay Area as the '69 Cubs are in Chicago."

Two of Holtzman's three daughters live in Chicago, and they own Cubs season tickets.

"They have joined me three times when the Cubs invited me to sing during the seventh-inning stretch over the last few years," he said.

That doesn't mean, however, that Holtzman always roots for his old team. He played for four major-league clubs, and that colors his perception of the standings to this day.

"I have a rooting interest in several teams," Holtzman said, "because I played with either their manager or pitching coach during my career."

Still, it would be hard to imagine the Cubs in the playoffs or World Series without Ken Holtzman in attendance. He might even throw out a first pitch that no one could hit.

Chapter 14

FERGUSON JENKINS

THE EARLY LIFE OF FERGUSON JENKINS

Hall of Fame pitcher Ferguson Jenkins is Canadian by birth. He was born in Chatham, Ontario, where he attended public school through high school, lived there during the off-season throughout his baseball career, and owned a ranch with his dad. His family lived roughly 60 miles from Detroit.

From an early age, Jenkins was enamored with the great outdoors. As a youth, he was about as active fishing and hunting as he was throwing a baseball, and he remains deeply involved in those hobbies in retirement. He caught bass, salmon, crappie, walleye, and any other species of fish he could find—mostly on trips with his father, Ferguson Holm Jenkins.

"My father was one of the first ones to introduce me to hunting and fishing," Jenkins said. "He'd rather fish, though. But there was plenty to hunt in the Chatham area, white-tail deer and pheasant."

Jenkins was seven or eight years old when his dad took him to a nearby park and taught him some basic fundamentals of baseball. The older Jenkins hit his son ground balls and fly balls to field. Although Jenkins didn't start pitching until he was 16, he played the game in organized leagues from the time he was a youngster.

"I played right through the leagues, tyke, peewee, bantam, midget, juvenile, junior, that type of thing," Jenkins said. "In Canada, we didn't have Little League or Babe Ruth. It was called by different names, and the teams were all sponsored by service clubs like the Jaycees and the Kiwanis."

Classifying himself as a "decent" hitter, Jenkins played mostly first base. Then he decided he wanted to pitch. It was an astute career change.

"I just said I wanted to do it," he said. "I thought I'd give it a try. One of our pitchers came up with a sore arm. I volunteered to pitch, and lo and behold, it became—well, not easy—but it was a position that I liked."

Whether Jenkins made throwing a 90-mph fastball look easy, the major-league scouts who surveyed northern talent believed he did. There were summer leagues in the Chatham area that scouts made pilgrimages to, where a season might last 35 games, and Detroit was so close Jenkins could moonlight there.

"There was just a lot of baseball being played in our area in the summer," Jenkins said. "When I look back over the years, the reason I got noticed was that I played in the *Detroit Free Press* tournament. There were a lot of good players in the Michigan area like Alex Johnson and Bill Freehan. I was 17 or 18 when people began looking at me as a pitcher, not a fielder."

Jenkins had not mastered a vast repertoire of pitches by any means.

"I just threw the ball relatively hard," he said. "I really didn't learn breaking balls until I signed."

Jenkins drew attention from a handful of major-league clubs and signed with the Philadelphia Phillies. His first stop in the minors in June after he finished high school

NAME: Ferguson Arthur Jenkins
BORN: December 13, 1942, in Chatham, Ontario, Canada
HOMETOWN: Chatham, Ontario
CURRENT RESIDENCE: Anthem, Arizona
OCCUPATION: Retired major-league baseball player; former major-league coach; ex-rancher
POSITION: Pitcher
HEIGHT: 6-foot-5
PLAYING WEIGHT: 210 pounds
ACCOMPLISHMENTS: Nineteen-year major-league player with the Chicago Cubs, Philadelphia Phillies, Texas Rangers, and Boston Red Sox; winner of 284 games; seven-time 20-game winner, six with the Cubs; three-time All-Star; winner of the National League Cy Young Award in 1971; member of the 3,000-strikeouts club with 3,172; elected to the Baseball Hall of Fame in 1991.
THE GAME: Chicago Cubs versus Montreal Expos—September 1, 1971

Winner of 284 career ballgames in 19 major-league campaigns, Ferguson Jenkins put together a remarkable run of six 20-victory seasons in a row for the Cubs between 1967 and 1972. He also struck out 3,192 batters in his career and was elected to the Baseball Hall of Fame. *Brace Photo*

was with the Class D Miami Marlins. The season ended after two months in Miami, and over the next few seasons Jenkins hurried through minor-league stops in Chattanooga, Little Rock, and AAA Buffalo.

"Somebody really liked what I was doing," Jenkins said. "That's why I graduated so quick, ahead of a lot of other people."

What also helped was the time Jenkins spent over two summers polishing his game in Puerto Rico. His big-league education really took place in the tropics.

"My second year of winter ball, in 1964, I really developed a good slider, and my control was excellent," Jenkins said.

That is when he first allowed himself to think he might have a shot at making it to the majors. His confidence grew, his control allowed him to stay ahead of hitters, and he displayed four pitches—fastball, slider, curveball, and change-up—that he didn't hesitate to throw.

"If somebody really was watching me play, they would know I could play," Jenkins said.

The Phillies put Jenkins into seven games in 1965, and he finished with a 2-1 record. The next season he started the year with the Phillies; but after one appearance, he was traded to the Cubs.

Cubs manager Leo Durocher pictured Jenkins as a strapping hard thrower who could go every day. In 1966, Jenkins appeared in 60 games for the Cubs and compiled a 6-8 record. It is a forgotten period in Jenkins' career, because Durocher soon realized the big man might be more useful as a starter than a reliever. By the 1967 season, Jenkins was in the rotation.

THE SETTING

Ferguson Jenkins went from a relief pitcher—at a time when they were less respected as lower men on the totem pole—to a 20-game winner in one season. In 1967, Jenkins finished 20-13. It was the beginning of a spectacular run of success for him with the Cubs.

The next several years also flaunted his durability. In 1968, Jenkins made 40 starts, pitched 308 innings, and finished 20-15. In 1969, Jenkins made 43 starts, pitched 311 ⅓ innings, and finished 21-15. In 1970, Jenkins made 40 starts pitched 313 innings and finished 22-16. In 1971, his Cy Young season, Jenkins made 39 starts, led the National

League with 325 innings, and finished 24-13. The wins also led the league.

"I was having fun," Jenkins said. "It was a fun situation to be a starting pitcher. It was three days' rest and go get 'em. I enjoyed that."

Jenkins said he never paid attention to the notorious wind at Wrigley Field, ignoring how the flags were rippling above his head. He had enough to worry about with the type of superstars populating the league when they stepped into the batter's box.

Many of those better hitters were actually in the lineup behind Jenkins, notably Ernie Banks, Ron Santo, and Billy Williams. Together, they came within cab-hailing distance of winning the 1969 pennant.

"We really came on," Jenkins said. "The people in Chicago really started to come out to watch us. We had several sellout crowds. It started in 1968; and from then on, it just never stopped."

With a core group of stars intact, the Cubs began every year after 1969 in that era with the idea of winning a championship—and 1971 was Jenkins' finest. In May, he threw a four-hit shutout at the Phillies and recorded 12 strikeouts. In July, he beat the Phillies again with 14 strikeouts. In August, Jenkins threw a two-hit shutout at the Braves, and on August 20, he won his 20th game of the season by beating the Astros. All summer long, Jenkins was an equal-opportunity destroyer.

Not only was Jenkins superb on the mound, he carried a big stick that season. Simply because no one expects them to hit well, sometimes pitchers are more boastful about what they do at the plate.

THE GAME OF MY LIFE

BY FERGUSON JENKINS

The year I won the Cy Young Award, I had about 27 RBIs on 20 hits. The game against Montreal I hit two home runs and knocked in three runs. I hit a two-run homer and a solo homer.

I hit the first home run off Bill Stoneman, and then I hit the second one off Jim Britton, who came on in relief. I drove in enough runs to win the game myself that day, and held them, too, to just six hits. It was a lot of fun sitting on the bench that day. I had pretty good success against Montreal usually, but they had a decent team back then with Mack Jones and Rusty Staub.

My teammates razzed me a little bit about being a hitter, but I had already hit a couple that season. That year I hit six home runs, so that was a phenomenal year, and I was so happy.

I hit the first home run in the fifth inning, and Johnny Callison scored on it. Stoneman also played for the Cubs. I hit another one in the seventh after Britton came in. He was their third pitcher. I ended up 2-for-3, with two runs scored. That was one of my best hitting days.

GAME RESULTS

The Cubs defeated the Expos, 5-2, that day. It was just like being back in high school, where the pitcher is usually the best athlete on the team, and he can win his own game from the batter's box. Major-league pitchers dream of such occasions, but they rarely occur. Jenkins did hit six homers in that single season, a prodigious output for a pitcher. His production equaled the Cubs' team record set by John Clarkson in 1887 and then tied by Bill Hutchinson in 1894.

Still, Jenkins made his living with his right arm, not with his Louisville Slugger. He ached for postseason play, but never played on a team that made it. During his Cubs days, he had to be content to call matchups with the other league pitching studs his "big games," and he reveled in facing the Dodgers' Don Drysdale and the Cardinals' Bob Gibson.

"There's nothing easy about pitching against somebody with the same kind of qualifications as you have," Jenkins said. "I mean, it was a real challenge."

On days when he was pitching, Jenkins got to the ballpark early, stretched, took batting practice, and asked the trainer for a rubdown before he would stretch again.

"Then you put on your game face, and you head to the bullpen," Jenkins said. "I'd sign autographs along the wall as I went. I never got into the mood where I'd turn the fans off. I'd give the ball away when I was through pitching. As soon as my warm-up was done, I threw it into the stands, usually to some kid, or whoever wanted it."

After winning 20 games in a season' six years in a row, Jenkins slumped to a 14-16 record in 1973 and found himself wearing a Texas Rangers uniform in 1974. The move worked out pretty well. Jenkins won a career-high 25 games in the American League in 1974. In some late-career quirks, Jenkins ended up going to the Boston Red Sox, back to the Rangers, and then back to the Cubs before retiring in 1983. It was as if he lived his career forward and backward. Jenkins is foremost identified as a Cub, but he is probably almost as popular in Texas.

"I got elected to the Texas Ranger Hall of Fame a few years ago," Jenkins said. "I get back to Texas to do special event days, and I'm on their alumni board."

REFLECTIONS ON BASEBALL

Ferguson Jenkins spent 10 years with the Cubs and six years with the Rangers, but Cub fans count him as one of their own. They made sure that love was if not lovelier the second time around, that Jenkins knew he was appreciated during his final two seasons as a player in 1982 and 1983.

Dallas Green, who won a World Series managing the Phillies in 1980, came over to the Cubs as general manager to build a winner. In the fall of 1981, he tracked down Jenkins and asked him if he wanted to return to Chicago.

"He was right to the point," Jenkins said. "He said, 'Can you still pitch?' I said, 'Of course.' He said, 'You know, we need some veteran pitching.' Wrigley Field was always good to me, and I came back."

Jenkins won 14 games in 1982. After he retired, Jenkins became a coach, dividing eight seasons between the Cincinnati Reds, the Rangers, and the Cubs. And then, for a while, Jenkins focused much of his attention on a 160-acre ranch in Guthrie, Oklahoma, minding horses and cattle. Two tragedies—the death of his wife, Mary-Anne, from injuries suffered in an automobile accident and the death of his three-year-old daughter, Samantha, in a murder-suicide case involving Jenkins' then-fiancée—pushed him into a change of scenery in Arizona.

Although his base is in the Southwest, Jenkins can often being found singing "Take Me Out to the Ballgame" at Wrigley Field, signing autographs in the Chicago area, playing golf in Wisconsin, hunting with old Cub friends in the West, and volunteering his services for the Make-A-Wish Foundation. He caught a 50-pound king salmon on a trip to Alaska, so Jenkins definitely has active frequent-flyer accounts.

Some of his greatest pleasures involve the same sports he grew up with: hunting and fishing. He has hunted and fished with Hall of Fame official Greg Harris, been bow hunting for deer with former Cubs Jody Davis and Keith Moreland, and hunted elk in Idaho with another ex-Cub, Bill Buckner.

"I like to hunt elk, moose, and caribou," said Jenkins. "I'd like to hunt brown bear, those bears on Kodiak Island in Alaska. Jody and I will do it."

There will be no mistaking the prey. Those are two guys who know the difference between a grown bear and a cub.

Chapter 15

RANDY HUNDLEY

THE EARLY LIFE OF RANDY HUNDLEY

When he was in elementary school, Randy Hundley wanted to be a shortstop and pitcher—with a curveball—for his Little League team. He wanted to be where the action was. When Hundley was eight years old, however, his father, Cecil, gave him some advice: Stop pitching and throwing the curve, or you'll ruin your arm.

"I loved pitching," Hundley said, "but my dad said, 'Son, you're going to hurt your arm, and then your career is going to be over with.'"

The day is imprinted on Hundley's mind. It was a hot August afternoon in steamy Virginia, and he remembers sweating "like crazy." Father and son were walking through the front door when his dad stopped them, pointed his finger at Hundley, and told him he was going to teach him how to be a catcher. That was another action position, all right. You got to handle the ball on every throw.

Cecil Hundley, a former semipro baseball player, knew the sport. He also watched catchers collect bumps and bruises on foul tips, wild pitches, passed balls, and collisions at home. It was not for nothing that catching gear was called "the tools of ignorance." Hundley's dad had a plan to elevate the intelligence of the catcher, or at least protect him better. On that humid day, his father informed Randy that he was about to become a one-handed catcher, with his left hand inside the meaty mitt. Rather than steadying it with his right hand, Hundley was ordered to hold it behind his back, safe from most danger.

Hundley reported that his father's declaration was accompanied by a threat. "He said, 'If I ever see you catch a ball with your bare hand, I am going to come take you out of the game. The coach won't have to do it—I will.'"

The reason Cecil Hundley was so adamantly in favor of one-handed catching was not simply because he had seen the amount of damage done to catchers' hands, he had experienced the injuries himself. "He had his bare hand busted time after time and wasn't able to play anymore because of it," Hundley said. "He really was ahead of his time."

Cecil Hundley had planted the idea of catching in his son, but Randy did not own a first-class catcher's mitt.

"You have to have proper equipment," Hundley said. "I went in the sporting goods store one day, and I found this catcher's mitt. I put it on my hand and smelled the leather, and you know it fit so perfectly. Every day, I would go in that sporting goods store and look at it. But shucks, even in 1950, the blooming thing was selling for almost $100. There was no way I could tell my dad about that mitt. So I'd stop by the store every day to make sure it had not been sold."

Hundley had become such a regular window-

NAME: Cecil Randolph Hundley
BORN: June 1, 1942, Martinsville, Virginia
HOMETOWN: Martinsville, Virginia
CURRENT RESIDENCE: Palatine, Illinois
OCCUPATION: Former major-league
    baseball player. Minor-league manager
    and scout; operator of baseball camps
    for kids and fantasy camps for adults
POSITION: Catcher
HEIGHT: 6-foot
PLAYING WEIGHT: 175 pounds
ACCOMPLISHMENTS: Fourteen-year major-
    league player with the Chicago Cubs,
    San Francisco Giants, and San Diego
    Padres between 1964 and 1977;
    introduced and helped popularize the
    one-handed catching style now
    commonplace in professional baseball;
    selected for 1969 National League All-
    Star team; caught 114 games or more in
    a season six times; hit career-high 19
    home runs in 1966; led National League
    catchers in fielding in 1972 with .995
    percentage; helped develop son Todd
    into a 14-year major-league catcher.
THE GAME: Chicago Cubs versus Atlanta
    Braves—May 21, 1966

Randy Hundley helped perfect and introduce the one-handed style of catching behind the plate and during his 14-year major-league career made one All-Star team. His son, Todd, also had a major-league career and played briefly for the Cubs. *Brace Photo*

shopper that eventually the sporting goods storeowner called the house and talked to his father.

"This was after about a month of me going there every day," Hundley noted, "and the owner said, 'You've got to buy this mitt for your son.' I didn't know he did that, but sure enough, he let my dad have it for like $35, and I got that mitt. I used that mitt for the longest time."

One day, the elder Hundley simply presented the glove to his boy, saying, "Here, son, I understand this is what you've been wanting.' I couldn't believe it. I had gone by every day at the store just to protect it. I tried to hide it from everybody else. It was made by Wilson. It had Hal Smith's name on it—probably the Hal Smith who played for the Cardinals. My dad was a Cardinals fan, and he just loved Stan Musial, so I probably related it to the Cardinals."

So Hundley became a catcher, and not too many years later he could afford any catcher's mitt in the house. He played high school ball in Madison, Virginia; and as soon as he graduated, Hundley signed a contract with the Giants. In one of the pivotal moments of a lifetime that are hard to forget, Hundley recalls sitting in his junior year sociology class, gazing out the window at beautiful spring weather and fantasizing about being outdoors playing baseball when he was summoned to the principal's office.

"I'm just eating my heart out because I just wanted to go and play baseball and somebody knocks on the door and says there's somebody here to see Randy Hundley," he said. "I thought, 'Oh, great, I get out of class.' I'm walking down the hall, and I see this silhouette of a huge man, about 6-foot-3, maybe 250 pounds, and I'm thinking, 'I have no idea who this is.'"

Hundley approached the man, shook hands, and the visitor said, "Randy, my name is Tim Murchison, and I'm a scout with the San Francisco Giants." He handed Hundley a card. Hundley still had his junior and senior years to play, but he was as excited as if he had won the lottery.

"Can you imagine the blooming emotion you have?" Hundley said. "I mean, I knew I was a good player, but I had no idea how good, or how I compared to everybody else. I just liked to play. All I wanted to do was win. But I remember the high I got from that visit. I didn't tell anybody about it at the school, but before you know it, the word is out all over the place that a scout had come to see me. I was just on a high for months and months and months after that."

When they parted, the scout informed Hundley that he was going to keep watching him for the next two seasons.

"I eventually signed with the Giants because of loyalty to him," Hundley said. "I had other clubs offer me more money at the time, but I wanted to show him loyalty."

THE SETTING

Randy Hundley did make it to the majors with the Giants and played two games in the 1964 season. He was playing at AAA in Tacoma, Washington, when regular Giant catcher Tom Haller was sidelined by a foul tip off his hand.

Hundley was called up just in time to be thrust into a heated Dodgers-Giants series against Los Angeles' best pitcher—a guy named Sandy Koufax. The southpaw was at the peak of his powers, every fourth day demonstrating the wicked fastball and deadly curve that would propel him into the Hall of Fame.

"Of course, the Giants mainly wanted me to catch and throw, but I had to go to bat, too," Hundley said. "After the third pitch, I stepped out of the batter's box, grabbed some dirt, and looked Koufax over. I said to myself, 'I need to find a brown paper bag and find another job because I'm overmatched here.'

"He was just incredible. A fastball, you'd think it would be low, and it rises into the strike zone. A curveball you'd think it's going to be over your head, and it's down thigh high. You couldn't pick up the location on it, either."

The next day, the second of the two games that constituted Hundley's entire major-league season, he was in the lineup against Don Drysdale, another mound genius with a supersonic fastball, who was on his way to the Hall of Fame as well. As a bonus for a rookie, Drysdale had a reputation as a brush-back artist who liked to intimidate batters by knocking them into the dust.

"The third pitch, just before he releases it, he yells, 'Look out!'" said Hundley. "And he throws this ball right at my head, and my helmet goes flying. My bat's flying. Here I am, a kid, thinking how much I respected Don Drysdale as a player and a pitcher, and I figured, 'What the heck, he's showing me respect.' He doesn't know who I am, but it made me so mad I couldn't see straight. I brushed myself off, and I was just trembling. I hit a long fly ball down the left-field line right in front of the wall, about four feet foul. The left fielder caught it, but you know what? I was so proud just to be able to make contact after that."

Hundley played just six games the next year before being transferred to the Cubs, where in 1966 he caught 149 games. He was not yet 23 when the season started, and he was still establishing himself on a veteran team that was embarking on a dismal, 53-win campaign.

THE GAME OF MY LIFE

BY RANDY HUNDLEY

We had a players-only meeting before that game, and everybody was expressing things on their minds. I was just sitting back listening. Finally, somebody says, "Randy, what do you think?" I hang back one second. It was difficult for me to say anything at the time. I thought the veterans would say what needed to be said. When they're talking, you have no idea where it's going to go. I felt I had to just try to be myself, what my convictions were in the pit of my stomach and just go with it. I didn't hold back too much.

I said that the veteran players were a little bit disappointing in that they wanted to blame things on the rookies. All I wanted to do was go out and win games. I got on some of the veteran players. I didn't like some of the things I had seen and had a tough time tolerating.

Then we went out to play the game. I had three hits that day, and I came up in the bottom of the ninth inning with two outs and won the game with a home run. The Braves had a relief pitcher in the game named Chi-Chi Olivo, and he had some kind of trick pitch that got everybody out.

I was talking to myself and saying, "You know what, he's going to try to sneak a fastball by me here." And sure enough, he threw me a fastball, and I was sitting on it and hit the home run. That was a big game.

GAME RESULT

The Cubs won the game, 7-6, in Atlanta; and Hundley not only made it clear he belonged in the starting lineup, but with his outspokenness, backed up by a clutch hit, he made it clear that he had leadership qualities and had come to win.

A few weeks later, Hundley got his revenge on Don Drysdale for the wakeup-call fastball thrown at his head his rookie year. Hundley smashed a grand slam off a Drysdale offering during the fourth inning of an 8-1 Cub victory at Wrigley Field.

"In Chicago, when I hit that grand slam, I remembered that he'd thrown at me," Hundley said. "I'm sure he didn't remember. You know, he was just doing his job and doing what he thought was best for him. I understood that. But yeah, I remember the grand slam, and I was quite proud of it."

One reason catchers burn out sooner than other position players is the strain placed on their knees from squatting day after day, plus the injuries suffered when balls somehow miss all of their protective padding. Once he assumed his position with the Cubs that season, however, Hundley was hard to move out.

In 1967, Hundley caught 152 games, and in 1968, he caught a record 160 games—followed up by 151 more games caught in 1970. He became a Chicago institution behind the plate. Hundley stayed with the Cubs through the 1973 season, then played one year with the Minnesota Twins and another with the San Diego Padres before returning to the Cubs to wrap up his playing career.

Once he retired, Hundley had hopes of working his way back up through the minors to become a major-league manager, but things didn't go smoothly.

REFLECTING ON BASEBALL

Randy Hundley was managing AAA in Des Moines for the Cubs when he was asked to take a demotion to manage in rookie-league ball and refused to do it. He felt he would be starting at the bottom of the ladder once again in 1982. Instead, Hundley geared up to run a baseball clinic for kids.

"That first year we had a great turnout, and it was a great success," Hundley said.

The Cubs changed over their administration and hired Hundley back as a scout and a fall instructional league coach, then let him go again.

"All I wanted to do was be in baseball, so I went to the winter meetings; and I just got people telling me I was overqualified for what they had," he said.

He pulled out after a day and a half, miffed by what he felt was a runaround. Refusing, as he described it, "to beg for a job," he came back to the Chicago area and developed his kids' clinics into a popular, thriving business. His first full year, he ran 10 weeks of kids camps at Harper College in the Chicago suburbs.

One of Hundley's guest speakers on the importance of education was Rich Melman, co-owner of the Lettuce Entertain You Chicago area restaurant chain, who asked Hundley if he had considered doing adult camps.

He had never thought about it until that moment, but the suggestion morphed into a lightning flash. In seconds, Hundley said he thought adults would prefer fantasy camps at spring training sites in Arizona, where they could mingle with former players and wear major-league uniforms.

"The whole shebang," Hundley said. "We could let people dream of what it was like being in the big leagues."

Someone growing up in Hundley's household had his own set of baseball dreams. Hundley's son Todd literally followed in his footsteps. He also played 14 seasons, his lifetime batting average was almost identical, and he even played briefly with the Cubs.

"It is a lot more special than my own career," Randy Hundley said. "He's such a wonderful person. He worked hard, he played hard; and you know, we both are among the few catchers who caught 150 ballgames in a season. We're both very proud of that. He had an excellent career, and I'm very proud of him."

The idea of an adult baseball camp with major leaguers was wildly popular. The first camp was conducted in January of 1983. The 25th anniversary camp was held in the winter of 2007. The usual head count is between 115 and 120 players.

Lifetime Cubs fans flock to the warm-weather getaways to live out their fantasies in Arizona sunshine. Hundley's old teammates—and later generations of Cubs—thrived on the gatherings, too, viewing the sessions like reunions.

"Through the camp we've been able to maintain friendships," Hundley said. "It's just been wonderful. We have made a lot of people happy over the years."

Chapter 16

RICK MONDAY

THE EARLY LIFE OF RICK MONDAY

Rick Monday was born in Arkansas but raised in California. His parents left the South before his first birthday to settle in Santa Monica, just outside of Los Angeles.

"My folks moved to California when the mud was still wet between my toes," Monday said. "I was only like 11 months old."

Rick's late mother, Nelva, a single parent, mainly raised him. "She taught me a great deal of what's right and what's wrong," he said.

Southern California is one of the best places in the union to be a baseball player, because the weather cooperates year round. The weather is conducive to playing catch and taking batting practice just about any time, including Christmas Day.

Monday was always a talented baseball player. He attended college at Arizona State, one of the traditional national NCAA powers, and was invited to play in the Alaska Baseball League for the Fairbanks Goldpanners, in the 1960s the elite summer college team available. While there, he encountered crusty Red Boucher, the founder of the team that has hosted more than 100 players on their way to the majors.

A gruff, joking, former Navy man with a passion for baseball, Boucher, now in his 80s, has not been forgotten by Monday. Boucher later became mayor of Fairbanks and lieutenant governor of the state of Alaska, but has said he wants to be buried in his Goldpanners uniform.

"A lot of people would have volunteered to bury him a long time ago," Monday teased.

Monday had not yet turned 21 when he made the leap into the majors with the Kansas City Athletics, playing 17 games in 1966 before becoming a regular the next season. Monday spent six years with the A's, including the first four seasons after the team moved to Oakland. He was becoming a brilliant fielder who was improving as a hitter when he was traded to the Cubs in late 1971 for pitcher Ken Holtzman.

THE SETTING

During his first several seasons in the majors, Rick Monday had not been viewed as a power hitter. He provided occasional big hits, but was more of a steady, pick-your-spots slasher. But barely a month into his first season with the Cubs, Monday produced a startling, three-shot game against the Philadelphia Phillies. In an 8-1 victory, Monday swatted homers his first three times up and added a single in the ninth inning.

The performance not only opened the eyes of observers, but also won him the night's possession of the television clicker in his hotel room—an invaluable prize. Monday and Cubs shortstop Don Kessinger were road roommates, and they adopted a little challenge game. The men decided that whoever had the best performance that day could decide what television program would be watched that night. Monday's three-homer day gave him undisputed control.

NAME: Robert James Monday
BORN: November 20, 1945, in Batesville, Arkansas
HOMETOWN: Santa Monica, California
CURRENT RESIDENCE: Vero Beach, Florida
OCCUPATION: Retired major-league baseball player; broadcaster, Los Angeles Dodgers
POSITION: Outfielder
HEIGHT: 6-foot-3
PLAYING WEIGHT: 200 pounds
ACCOMPLISHMENTS. Nineteen-season major-league baseball player with the Kansas City Athletics, Oakland Athletics, Chicago Cubs, and Los Angeles Dodgers; appeared in 1,986 games with a lifetime average of .264; led National League outfielders in fielding with a .996 percentage in 1972; clouted 241 career home runs.
THE GAME: Chicago Cubs versus Los Angeles Dodgers—April 25, 1976

Rick Monday's major-league outfield career was long and productive. He played 19 seasons and made two All-Star teams. Currently, he is a broadcaster for the Los Angeles Dodgers. He will always be remembered as the guy who saved the American flag from burning in center field.
Brace Photo

"He's one of those guys that has a great sense of humor and is not afraid to throw a little innocent barb in your direction. He's not afraid to take a barb in return, either," Monday said. "So what we ended up doing was playing King of the Room. The King of the Room also got to decide where we would eat lunch or dinner that day, but the most valuable thing was the King of the Room had control of the channel changer."

Ironically, when Monday hit three homers and a single, Kessinger went 5-for-5. Kessinger had more hits, but they were all singles. The twosome put their stats up for arbitration.

"So we had to put it to a vote," Monday said. "The team voted. I got him on a technicality, but we were all laughing. Don goes, 'I can't believe this. My gosh, I get five hits in five at-bats, and I'm not King of the Room?' We could only have hoped to have that problem on numerous occasions."

Major leaguers have not had road roommates for about 30 years, and Monday said that while the convenience of a single room is pleasant, he thinks players who never had the experience might be missing out.

"If you were lucky, it was a roommate that you enjoyed being with somewhat, someone you respected, and someone you got along with," Monday said. "That was the way it was with Don Kessinger. It was a delight—an absolutely quality human being."

Monday was new to the National League in 1972, so Kessinger tutored him on the background of many of the pitchers he was going to face.

"He was a great source," Monday said.

After a few years with the Cubs, Monday was well established in center field. In 1973, he hit 26 home runs and scored 93. In 1974, he hit 20 home runs and scored 84. In 1975, he scored 89 runs. The 1976 season was about to become the most productive of Monday's career—32 home runs, 77 runs batted in, and 107 scored—but he didn't know that, in the first month of the season, he would experience what would become his life's most memorable game. It came on the 100th anniversary of the first game played in Cubs history, the year of the United States' Bicentennial.

Thirty years later, it has reverberated in Americans'—not just baseball fans'—minds ever since.

THE GAME OF MY LIFE

BY RICK MONDAY

The biggest game—the biggest impact—I was fortunate to deliver for the Cubs was on April 25, 1976.

I hear about it almost every day.

I was playing in center; and in the fourth inning, I saw two men climb out of the stands and run towards left-center field. One man was carrying something under his arm, and I saw them spread it out on the outfield grass. I realized it was an American flag. The other guy had a can of something and was pouring liquid over the flag.

I just moved out of instinct. I began to run towards them. I ducked down and grabbed the flag away. When I picked it up, one of the two guys was putting a match to what he believes is still a flag on the ground. That's how close it came to being ignited, and my first thought was, "This flag is doused with lighter fluid." You could smell it. You could feel it on my hand. It was soaking wet. My first thought was, "Is this thing really on fire?"

I think the single most moving moment was after I took the flag away from them. When those two people were being escorted off the field, the fans were booing—and then applauding the fact that they were taken away. But then, what took place still gives me goose bumps 30 years later. In one particular area of the stadium, and then another, and then another, then all 25,000 who were there that Sunday afternoon, began to sing "God Bless America."

It was not prompted on the Diamond vision board. It was not announced. There was no music to it. It just happened, and to me, that was the single most moving moment because that was a validation that, "No, what those guys were doing, we don't like it, we don't want it to happen, and they are taking their rear ends off the field."

GAME RESULTS

The Dodgers won the game, 5-4, in 10 innings, but little attention was paid to the final score—major attention, coast to coast, was paid to Monday's deed. It became a symbol of patriotism; and despite all of his success on the field, it has overshadowed Monday's play and is the single most defining moment in his career.

Monday went to bed a baseball player that night and woke up an American hero. Probably not one in a hundred Cubs fans can tell a questioner who won the game, and even if they don't remember the date, they would likely refer to the contest as, "The game Rick Monday saved the flag."

"I was surprised that day after the ballgame," Monday said.

Somewhere over the years, Monday stopped being surprised. People, baseball fans or not, associate his name with preventing a flag from being burned in public, and he knows there are worse ways to be remembered.

"WGN had a policy, and still does, when someone runs on the field, of pulling the cameras off the field," Monday said. "So that incident was not captured by a television camera, either, or shown over and over again."

Monday's sprint to save the flag may have relied on instinctive movement, but it also reflected his beliefs. He had spent six years in the Marine Corps Reserves and supported United States military men and women then and now.

"Whether you agree or don't agree with what's happening in this country, one thing we need to agree upon is that wherever service men and women are, wherever they are sent, they get our support 100 percent," he said. "And to desecrate the flag, in my view, is basically demeaning the overall respect of the people who have given of themselves, and have given themselves, in order to protect the rights and freedoms that flag represents for all of us."

Despite putting up the best numbers of his career and becoming an overnight sensation, however, that was Monday's last season in a Cubs uniform. In January of 1977, he was traded in a five-player deal that brought Bill Buckner to Chicago. From 1977 to 1984, Monday played with the Dodgers, and even before his retirement from the baseball field, he found his way into the broadcast field.

REFLECTING ON BASEBALL

Broadcasting—Rick Monday always had the voice for it. Even as a kid, his deep voice attracted attention in the classroom when he tried to whisper behind the teacher's back. It was hopeless. He always got caught.

"If I tried to whisper to the person next to me in junior high and high school, I was always heard," he said. "It wasn't because I was loud, just because of my voice. I don't know if you remember when your voice cracked. I was in the eighth grade in a social studies class reciting the Gettysburg Address. When it cracked, I went, 'What the heck is this?'"

While Monday was playing with the Dodgers, the local ABC affiliate approached him and asked if he would be interested in broadcast work.

"I would be foolish if I told you I was not," he told his interviewers.

Monday began working for the station during the off-season in 1979 and expanded his duties there and at other outlets in Southern California after he retired. In 1993, he joined Dodgers telecasts. Monday is in his 60s now, and he has been in broadcasting longer than he played in the majors, but he still has fun being close to the game.

"I remember what it was like in the first game I played in the major leagues—all the emotion I had after dreaming about playing since I was a kid in a Little League uniform and as a kid sitting in the Los Angeles Coliseum watching the Dodgers shortly after they moved to Los Angeles," Monday said. "You're around this game, and then, physically, you're not continuing as a player. You stay in the same industry with people you know and you understand, but it is a different venue," Monday explained. "You're around a game that I feel very honored to have been able to be a part of for 19 seasons as a player and I still enjoy the excitement of the unknown and the competition and seeing how a ball club goes into a season and makes adjustments and changes. It's something I really love doing."

About seven years ago, Monday moved to Vero Beach, where the Dodgers hold spring training, so he could spend six additional weeks at home during the year. The king of Dodger broadcasters is Vin Scully, who is several years older than Monday, so there is no reason why the junior partner should consider retiring as long as the voice that bugged his hometown teachers holds up.

Monday has held almost as tightly to baseball as he has to the American flag he personally confiscated from the would-be desecraters. And although someone mentions the incident to him almost every day, Monday and his wife put the flag to more active use in 2006.

"My wife, Barbara Lee, and I have had that flag since, through the damage of two hurricanes. It's been in a safe-deposit box for the last two years for a couple of reasons," he said. "One, it's very precious to us from a symbolic standpoint. And monetarily we've been offered over a million dollars for it. This (2006) being the 30th anniversary, we have had quite a few things that we used it for that we are very active in—a lot of different charities."

Although Monday has never seen video of the attempted flag burning, a Pulitzer Prize-nominated picture was captured by James Rourke, a *Los Angeles Herald-Examiner* photographer. The Mondays have had contact with some of the people in the background. In the 30 years since the rescue, Monday also collected many, many letters from people moved by what he did.

"Letters you just read and you have to wipe away the tears about recollections of people saying where they were, what they were doing, when the flag incident took place in 1976," he said. "My wife has been in contact with some people, for lack of a better description, who want to do a coffee-table book compiling some of those letters from the 30 years with pictures."

As that idea took shape, the Mondays received an email from United States Army Sergeant Javier Vasquez of the 101st Medivac Airborne Unit in Baghdad. Vasquez, who is from Los Angeles, told the Mondays that to honor the 30th anniversary of Rick's save of the flag, his unit flew a flag over their hospital, took it down, ran missions with it on the window of a rescue helicopter, then signed pictures of it. The soldiers sent the Mondays the flag with the goal of having it forwarded to the Dodgers Dream Foundation that raises money to build fields for youth baseball.

During the summer of 2006, the original flag also came out of hibernation. Barbara Lee heard about a group called the Patriot Guard Riders.

"They are strictly volunteer and there is no political agenda," Monday said. "There is no theme that they have other than respect of the flag, to carry the flag for those that have carried the flag.

"They are comprised of former and current service men and women, people who have been in the military, and their mode of transportation is for the most part motorcycles. When a fallen soldier's body is sent back from Iraq—they post where every soldier's funeral is going to be and when that casket is arriving in the country—and they provide escorts from the airport to the funeral home, and then from the funeral home to the cemetery while providing escorts and security for the family."

Protesters who want to see the war in Iraq end and U.S. troops brought home, have sometimes held demonstrations at the funerals of soldiers.

"I've only attended one service with the Patriot Guard Riders, in Arlington National Cemetery," Monday said. "It was very respectful and extremely moving. My wife, though, has attended quite a few, and at one point, a group protesting the war has even yelled obscenities at families. I've never been so proud to be around some people in my life as I was in Arlington National Cemetery.

"Barbara Lee contacted these people and asked if they would like to get involved in some way with this flag we had been sent from Baghdad. In about a week's time, the Patriot Guard Riders volunteered to Pony Express this flag from Vero Beach to Los Angeles. The night before they were scheduled to go, Barbara Lee was thinking, 'This needs to be bigger. It needs to have more impact.'

"So she called them up and told them, 'I'm going to join you, and I'm going to bring the flag that Rick stopped those two guys from burning 30 years ago."

Monday, who was broadcasting Dodger games, was tied up with work. Barbara Lee had never been on a motorcycle, but she joined the excursion and carrying the immortalized flag itself, rode through 14 states in 14 days.

"They stopped in veterans' hospitals," Monday said. "They stopped in military installations, and every state that they went to, at the border, there was a change of the guard, and the flag was handed to the next ride captain."

And full circle, 30 years later, a flag earmarked for destruction only to be rescued on a baseball field by Rick Monday, reappeared at Chavez Ravine for a July 4 Dodgers game.

Chapter 17

MILT PAPPAS

THE EARLY LIFE OF MILT PAPPAS

Milt Pappas, son of Greek parents, first became involved in baseball not as a player, but as a batboy when he was seven or eight. He was invited to fill the role for a local semi-pro team in Detroit.

Then Pappas went out for Little League, a move that caused family disruption. His father, Steve, operated a grocery store, and his mother, Eva, said young Milt had to help out in the store instead of playing baseball after school. He said he wanted to play ball. She said, "No, it's more important to help out your dad."

When she followed through by confiscating Pappas' Little League uniform, he was furious and bitterly disappointed.

"I remember, for two days I cried, and I didn't come out of the bedroom," he said. "Finally, she realized that baseball meant a lot to me at that particular point, and she gave my uniform back."

Pappas' parents were Greek immigrants who knew little about baseball when they moved to the United States. They picked up the sport on the fly.

"They had to learn everything when they came to this country," Pappas said.

The man who would pitch one of the greatest games in Chicago Cubs history began his baseball career as a shortstop and claims he was a pretty decent hitter as a ten-year-old. One day, Pappas' team was getting clobbered, losing about 11-0, and the manager asked for fresh volunteers to pitch.

"Reluctantly, I raised my hand," Pappas said nearly six decades later, "and as they say, the rest is history."

He had definitely discovered the right position. Many years later, when Pappas was nationally known and was making a good living at the game, his mother made sure to tell him how proud she was. His dad, who had been disabled by a stroke and could not travel to watch his son pitch live, spent long hours next to the radio listening to his Baltimore Oriole son mow down batters.

"My mom would come, of course, when we played in Detroit," Pappas said. "She'd come to the games in person with my brothers. It was pretty neat."

Actually, Pappas was well known in the area before he finished Cooley High School. His pitching arm earned him attention locally and then with major-league scouts when he completed his senior year with a 7-0 record and a 0.50 earned run average. Of the 16 major-league teams in business in 1957, in an era before the player draft, 13 made contact with Pappas.

The Tigers allowed Pappas to work out at Briggs Stadium and left him tickets for games at the will call window. He had access to the clubhouse, too; so the Tigers were sure the young pitcher was going to sign with them.

However, the Orioles proved to be Pappas' favorite suitor. A scout named Lou D'Annunzio spotted him at 14 and followed him through

NAME: Milton Stephen Pappas (Miltiades Stergios Papastegios)
BORN: May 11, 1939, in Detroit, Michigan
HOMETOWN: Detroit, Michigan
CURRENT RESIDENCE: Beecher, Illinois
OCCUPATION: Retired major-league pitcher; former college baseball coach, North Central College, Illinois; former import-export business official; former liquor salesman; building products salesman
POSITION: Pitcher
HEIGHT: 6-foot-3
PLAYING WEIGHT: 190 pounds
ACCOMPLISHMENTS: Seventeen-year major-league career with the Baltimore Orioles, Cincinnati Reds, Atlanta Braves, and Chicago Cubs; winner of 209 games with a lifetime 3.40 earned run average; winner of 15 or more games seven times; lifetime winning percentage, .560; two-time American League All-Star.
THE GAME: Chicago Cubs versus San Diego Padres—September 2, 1972

The right-handed son of Greek immigrants won 209 games in a 17-year major-league career, but one stands above all others. While pitching for the Cubs in 1972, Pappas came within one batter of hurling a perfect game on a two-out walk in the ninth inning and had to settle for a no-hitter. *Brace Photo*

Babe Ruth ball, American Legion play, and high school. Pappas even bowled with the guy and played pool. Baltimore signed him for a $4,000 bonus. No team was willing to pay more than $4,000 because the era's rules required an 18-year-old bonus baby to stay on the major-league roster for two years.

Pappas' long-term relationship with D'Annunzio—he said he was like a second father—and the additional involvement of future Hall of Famer Hal Newhouser, who had been a Tigers' pitching fixture and was Baltimore's head scout, gift-wrapped him for Baltimore. When Newhouser brought Pappas to Baltimore, he made sure he bought some nice clothes.

"Four thousand dollars was the money everybody offered me," Pappas said, "but Baltimore offered me a major-league contract. I was dead set upon getting a major-league contract, because that afforded me the opportunity to go to spring training with the big team. Plus, their pitching staff was just about the oldest of all the pitching staffs, so I figured if I was to make it to the major leagues pretty quick, it would be with them."

Pappas expected to be sent to the minors in 1957, but was kept on the bench with the Orioles, wasting most of the year right out of high school. Eventually, manager Paul Richards picked a late-inning spot to use Pappas. The Orioles were getting thumped by the Yankees, and Pappas got the call to the mound.

"When they said, 'Pappas, you're in there,' I said, 'Oh, my God,'" Pappas recalled. "The first pitch I threw in warm-ups went to the backstop, and the first four hitters I faced in organized ball were Enos Slaughter, Mickey Mantle, Yogi Berra, and Bill Skowron. (Three are in the Hall of Fame.) That was my introduction to major-league baseball. Unbelievable."

Pappas was tabbed for four games of relief appearances, but when he went to spring training in 1958, it was clear something had rubbed off by osmosis. He was 19 years old, in a major-league rotation, and finished 10-10.

THE SETTING

After his rookie year, Milt Pappas put together eight consecutive winning seasons for the Orioles as a starter; but he was shipped to the

Cincinnati Reds in 1966 as part of the blockbuster trade that transferred Frank Robinson to the Orioles. Reds management proclaimed Robinson washed up, but the analysis was faulty. Robinson matched his National League superstar play with similar results in the American League. Cincinnati fans were angry at the team but took out their frustration on Pappas. He was treated as an enemy hurler.

"I wasn't very popular in Cincinnati," Pappas said. "Every time I took the mound, they just booed the living hell out of me, which made my two years there just absolutely abominable. It was the worst two years I ever spent in baseball."

About one-third of the way through Pappas' third season in Cincinnati, he was traded to Atlanta. Then, about a third of the way into the 1970 season, he ended up on the Cubs and a place where he was always appreciated. When Pappas pitched the best game of his career, he was nearing the end of a second straight 17-win season for Chicago.

"It was cold, a dreary Saturday afternoon," Pappas said. "The game didn't mean anything at that point in the season besides playing for pride. Yet, being a major-league baseball player, you do the best you can do for your team. I didn't have overly spectacular stuff, but you don't have to have particularly great stuff in the bullpen as far as I'm concerned. I tried to save as much as I could for when I walked out on the mound. Warming up was just that: getting your stuff together, getting your arm loose, and getting ready to pitch a ballgame."

Throwing a no-hitter is like being struck by lightning, but even more rare is the perfect game—the one pitching feat no hurler can expect in his major-league career.

THE GAME OF MY LIFE

BY MILT PAPPAS

I wasn't feeling all that great that day. You know, it's so funny in baseball, when you discuss pitchers and the way they feel. If a pitcher feels as good as he should, he becomes a pitcher instead of a thrower if his forte is primarily artistic stuff. That's what happened to me that day. I was blessed with great control.

It was cold, though, and I didn't feel like I had particularly good stuff. When the game started, let's put it this way: I didn't feel like I was going to go out there and pitch a no-hitter. The idea was just to go out there and do the job, hope for a win, score some runs and come out of there with a W.

When I was with Baltimore, I had a no-hitter going into the eighth inning against Minnesota, so I had been through the first six, seven innings before. I didn't pay a whole lot of attention probably until the start of the seventh inning.

Once you look at the scoreboard and see that it's true, you know what's happening. Nobody's gotten any hits. In the eighth inning, I was a little more aware because my teammates were doing the don't-talk thing, the superstition. Oh, they were horrible. Nobody said a word. When I came off the mound after the top of the eighth inning, I was walking down the dugout stairs, and I said, "Oh guys, by the way, I'm pitching a no-hitter."

Everybody just lit up. They started talking, and it loosened everybody up but me. I went down the stairs between the bathroom— below the dugout and the clubhouse—and the cops were back there; and the ushers were back there; and the walkie-talkies and the beepers were going off. They made me more nervous than the Padres did. I said, "Get out of here! Let me alone!" After I loosened my teammates up, those guys made me tight as hell. The security was driving me crazy.

It wasn't just the no-hitter. By the eighth inning, I knew I hadn't allowed a single baserunner. I knew that it was a perfect game. I had gone back in my head and said, "Hey, I don't remember anybody getting on base." I didn't say that to anybody else. Yet, when I said that about pitching the no-hitter, I'm sure they were cognizant of it at that time. I knew.

In the top of the ninth inning, I thought it was all over. John Jeter hit a medium fly ball to center, and Billy North slipped and fell. I said, "There goes the no-hitter, the perfect game. There goes everything." And Billy Williams came out of left field on his white charger. I never saw Billy run that hard or as fast in the whole time I watched him play. He came out of nowhere and caught the ball after Billy North slipped.

The next play was a ground ball, and Don Kessinger made a good play at shortstop (on Fred Kendall). Then Larry Stahl came up (pinch hitting for pitcher Al Severinson). I got it to one ball and two strikes.

Then, the next three pitches were all on the outside corner, but my little fat umpire friend Bruce Froemming called them all balls.

The last three pitches were all on the outside corner. When I walked Larry Stahl, I was just livid with Bruce Froemming. I mean, if I wouldn't have gone to jail, I'd have killed him. I just felt he had robbed me of something that is so rare. But then Ron Santo came over from third base and said, "Hey, Milt, don't forget, you've still got a no-hitter going."

When Garry Jestadt popped out to second, Santo came over and jumped into my arms. So I got the no-hitter. I think Ron Santo epitomized the whole day afterward when he said, "That's the only time I ever had a letdown after a no-hitter."

GAME RESULTS

Milt Pappas retired the first 26 batters in the game the Cubs won 8-0 before just 11,144 fans at Wrigley, but he remains bugged that he came an inch from a perfect game.

When the game ended, most of the focus was on the no-hitter, an outstanding enough feat that is usually a once-in-a-career opportunity for a major leaguer.

"I was elated," Pappas said. "In fact, that was the first time I had ever pitched a no-hitter and that included Little League or anywhere. It was the first time in my whole life, so I was feeling pretty good. Phone calls were coming in with congratulations. Relatives and friends and a couple of neighbors brought flowers and put them on my porch. When I went out to dinner with my kids and wife, people were congratulating me. I watched the ten o'clock news, and the headlines were, 'Milt Pappas pitches a no-hitter.' Once the news was over and nothing was happening anymore, I thought, 'I could have pitched a perfect game.' It wasn't until six or seven hours after the ballgame that it sunk in: I missed a perfect game. But a no-hitter is pretty special, too."

During the current era of baseball, every single game is recorded, taped, with instant replay, using sophisticated equipment. That was not true in 1972. Pappas said there was only a 16-millimeter tape of the game, and he did not see any replay of even the ninth inning until years later.

"It was shown on WGN greatest moments, or whatever," he said. "Otherwise, I would not have had anything of the no-hitter on tape at all."

REFLECTIONS ON BASEBALL

Although any fan who witnesses a perfect game and any player who played in one would never forget it, Pappas' no-hitter has the same kind of legs. It is talked about and written about more than the average no-hitter (if there is such a thing).

"I wonder even to this day," he said in 2006, "whether or not that moment would live on as much if it would have been a perfect game. The fact is it should have been a perfect game if not for a blown call by the umpire. I think that's what's made this live on for 34 years. There were 11,000 people at the game that day, but I've met about 300,000 who say they were at the game. It's got its own life. WGN is running a commercial saying if you don't go out to Wrigley Field you might miss a no-hitter like Milt Pappas' in 1972. It just goes on and on and on. It's just amazing."

Pappas earned his career 200th victory about three weeks after the no-hitter, but he played only one more season. It was a poor one, and Pappas finished with a 7-12 mark. Although he had opportunities to keep pitching, Pappas chose to retire in 1973. He was only 34 and sometimes thinks he should have stuck around longer.

When Pappas joined the Cubs in 1970, he moved to the Chicago area and loved living in the region so much he never left.

"Sometimes, in winter, I think I've got to be nuts to live here, but I do; and I think the baseball fans here in Chicago are the greatest in the world," he said, "just fantastic fans. I go to some White Sox games, two or three a year, and three or four Cubs games a year, but I watch on TV every day.

"It's still got to be the Cubs (winning the World Series) one of these years. Every morning of my lifetime, I wonder whether or not I'll ever see a championship for the Cubs."

Chapter 18

GARY MATTHEWS

THE EARLY LIFE OF GARY MATTHEWS

Gary Matthews was born in San Fernando, California, where devoted players took advantage of the ability to hone their skills year-round.

A top athlete at an early age, Matthews could hardly make a move without scouts circling overhead. He was such a pure athlete and smooth player that it was only a matter of *which* team would invest in him.

Matthews came along too late for scouts to fight over him, though, since the draft was in place when he finished high school in 1969. The Giants later won the Matthews sweepstakes by making him a No. 1 draft pick and, in a bit of foreshadowing, shipping him directly to Illinois.

Both the Giants and Matthews discovered quickly that he was too good for the caliber of ball played at Class A Decatur. In a short season of rookie ball, Matthews batted .322. That showed the Giants that he belonged in a higher classification, and in 1970 Matthews played closer to home in Fresno. He spent 1971 with Amarillo in Class AA and began the 1972 season with Phoenix. He torched AAA pitching for a .313 average, and by the end of the season, Matthews was with the Giants. His 20-game look-see produced a .290 batting average that put him in the majors for good.

Matthews hit .300 with 12 home runs and 10 triples in a flashy full rookie season in 1973 and won Rookie of the Year honors.

The young Matthews impressed longtime Giants coach Wes Westrum, who called him "an aggressive, hustling ballplayer with a great attitude."

Matthews became a dependable hitter averaging between .280 and .300 just about every season for the Giants and later the Braves when he was traded—then hit even better when he moved on to the Phillies. The Phillies won the only World Series in team history in 1980, but Matthews did not join them until 1981. Still, it was one of the most important transfers of his career. Phils manager Dallas Green got to know Matthews and his capabilities, and Green remembered his skills after he became the Cubs' general manager.

Although they did not repeat their 1980 title, the Phillies were a good ball club when Matthews was there. Future Hall of Famers like pitcher Steve Carlton, third baseman Mike Schmidt, and all-time major-league hit accumulator Pete Rose were the standouts. Rose paid Matthews one of the best compliments of his life when he bestowed the nickname "Sarge" on him.

"He dubbed me 'Sarge,' and it just stuck," Matthews said. "Someone named 'Sarge' was a pretty

NAME: Gary Nathaniel Matthews
BORN: July 5, 1950, in San Fernando, California
HOMETOWN: San Fernando, California
CURRENT RESIDENCE: Chicago, Illinois
OCCUPATION: Former major-league baseball player; former Chicago Cubs minor-league hitting coordinator; former Toronto Blue Jays coach; former Toronto Blue Jays broadcaster; former Milwaukee Brewers coach; member of former Cubs manager Dusty Baker's coaching staff through the 2006 season
POSITION: Outfielder
HEIGHT: 6-foot-3
PLAYING WEIGHT: 190 pounds
ACCOMPLISHMENTS: Sixteen-year major-league player with the San Francisco Giants, Atlanta Braves, Philadelphia Phillies, Chicago Cubs, and the Seattle Mariners; one of first players to take advantage of full free agency; was the National League Rookie of the Year in 1973; named Most Valuable Player of the 1983 National League Championship Series; member of the 1979 National League All-Star team; lifetime average of .281 in 2,033 games played; recorded 2,011 hits; father of 2006 All-Star Gary Matthews Jr.
THE GAME: Chicago Cubs versus San Diego Padres in the National League Championship Series—October 2, 1984

A lifetime .281 hitter during 16 major-league seasons, Gary Matthews not only played for the Cubs, but returned to the team as a coach for manager Dusty Baker. The outfielder was a team leader for the Cubs' 1984 playoff team, and his son, Gary Matthews Jr., became a major-league All-Star. *Brace Photo*

tough guy, and he made it sound as if he gave it to me because I was a guy who you could count on in the clutch. In Philadelphia, my last year there, I almost single-handedly got us into the playoffs, and we were able to beat Los Angeles to get into the World Series. It was all really special."

Matthews was one of the "glue" guys on whom a manager could rely. He was a smooth fielder and made things happen on the basepaths.

THE SETTING

Dallas Green had taken on the challenge of trying to rebuild the Cubs, and he knew the Phillies' personnel better than the Phillies' officials. More than once, he picked the Phils' pockets in trades. One of those occasions allowed him to add Matthews to the Cubs roster late in spring training before the 1984 season began. The Cubs sent Bill Campbell and Mike Diaz to Philadelphia for Matthews, Bob Dernier, and Porti Altamirano.

The trade was the key to solidifying the everyday lineup. Dernier became the center fielder, Matthews the left fielder, and the Cubs were off to a 96-win season and a spot in the postseason.

"I had been traded before and gone to other teams, so moving to a new team wasn't that big a deal," Matthews said. "You just want to go and hopefully make your team a winner. I had just been in the World Series (in 1983 with Philadelphia) so coming to Chicago and having a lot to do with them winning was pretty gratifying."

Matthews made himself at home—and made himself some new friends—by hitting a home run during the Wrigley Field opener, becoming a do-everything guy for the Cubs that season. He batted .291, walked a league-leading 102 times, recorded an on-base percentage of .410 that also led the league and drove in 82 runs.

"I think Gary Matthews was really the captain of that team, if there was such a thing," said Cubs pitcher Scott Sanderson. "I think he had a huge influence on the younger players, showing them how to go about being a winner."

The Cubs drew a then-record 2,104,219 fans that year, clinched their first first-place finish since 1945, and did it with five members of the starting lineup and one starting pitcher who had come over from the Phillies. The Cubs could thank Green's savvy and raiding ability.

"There were a lot of ex-Phillies," Matthews said. "We put the team together. We had a great year, and it's something to be remembered."

THE GAME OF MY LIFE

BY GARY MATTHEWS

We won the division championship in late September, I think with about a week to go. We were in Pittsburgh when we won it, and we did the whole thing with champagne.

It had been almost 40 years since the Cubs had finished in first place, and we wanted to be the team that went back to the World Series. That was a big goal for us. Being part of the team that broke the streak and won the World Series has been a big goal when I was coaching with the Cubs. The city would go crazy. They really love baseball, for sure, on the North side.

I had just been in the World Series, and I wanted to get back there and win one. The Phillies lost in 1983 to the Baltimore Orioles. With the Cubs, we had some characters on the team, and we played selflessly. It was one of the better teams I played with throughout my career. We had so much fun.

There was a lot of emotion in Chicago because the team hadn't won in such a long time. So there was a lot of excitement when the National League Championship Series opened against San Diego. Then, we went out and ended up winning handily.

It was obviously a great game. The first game of the playoffs here (in Chicago), and we won 13-0. I hit two home runs. The fans thought we had won it all right there. A player can't think that way, but we really felt good about what we did that day—and it felt good to me to do what I did.

That game stands out.

GAME RESULTS

The thrashing of the Padres gave the Cubs a 1-0 series lead and a huge boost in confidence in the best-of-five series. There were 36,282 Wrigley witnesses as Chicago stroked five home runs and soon-to-be-named Cy Young Award winner Rick Sutcliffe held San Diego scoreless on two hits over seven innings.

A festive, party atmosphere permeated the old park even before the game. Mr. Cub, Ernie Banks, threw out the ceremonial first pitch, and the team obtained a waiver to allow him to sit on the bench as an "honorary coach."

And then Bob Dernier launched the second pitch of the game from Padres starter Eric Show into the stratosphere for the Cubs' first homer.

It was more of the same the next day. Before another full house, the Cubs put the Padres away again, 4-2, behind pitcher Steve Trout. He allowed only five hits in 8 ⅓ innings.

The Cubs had three chances to win one game. They were one win from the World Series. The drought was about to end, but the Series then moved to San Diego, and everything fell apart. The Cubs lost 7-1, 7-5, and 6-3. Just like that, the miracle was aborted—once again, no World Series for the Cubs.

"The last game in San Diego stands out for me, too, where we didn't play so well," Matthews said. "It isn't as much fun to remember that one, but the fact is, being in the playoffs is fun."

One thing that made Matthews uneasy was the oddity of having to play the first four games of the NCLS with umpires from the amateur ranks. Major-league umps were on strike, and the Cubs employed umpires from the Big Ten for the games in Chicago; and the Padres hired local guys in California. The regulars returned for the fifth game.

"We just did not fare really well out there with the umpires," Matthews said. "Again, they were there for both teams, but they were from the same area, and they were making favorable calls for the Padres."

REFLECTIONS ON BASEBALL

Gary Matthews retired as an active player after the 1987 season and briefly tried his hand in the business world. He missed baseball too much, and his reputation as a hard-working, knowledgeable baseball man earned him opportunities as a broadcaster and a coach.

Matthews joined the Dusty Baker regime with the Cubs and served as first-base coach in 2005 and 2006. He marveled at how the fan energy jump-started by the 1984 team has just grown and expanded to the point where Wrigley Field is sold out every day whether the Cubs win or lose. In 2006, the Cubs attracted nearly 3.2 million people.

"It's changed since I was playing, but there is still some of the old here," Matthews said one day during the 2006 season while sitting in the Cubs dugout at the end of batting practice. "We haven't been able to put this thing together, but the fans still come out. They come out in numbers. It's changed, though: They don't particularly care for the losing, and they show their displeasure with boos. When I played, they didn't hardly do that at all."

When he played, and in the years since, Matthews raised a couple of baseball players in his own family. Son Delvon played in the Milwaukee Brewers' minor-league system in 2000 and 2001. Gary Matthews Jr. made his pop proud by making the American League All-Star team in 2006 representing the Texas Rangers. He has also played for five other teams, including the Cubs, in an ongoing seven-year major-league career.

"I'm very, very happy for him," Matthews Sr. said. "It's gratifying. He had a tough road; but he kept his head up, believed in himself, never let anybody say that he couldn't do it, played excellent defense throughout, and now he's put together his offense and a lot of people are talking about him."

Many fathers with family businesses hope their sons will follow in their footsteps, but it's far more difficult in professional sports. Matthews Sr. certainly understands the challenges his son has confronted and still confronts in the majors.

"You always hope when your son plays, or does anything that you're doing, that he does it better," the older Matthews said. "My career was longer, but he's on the road to really do some special things. I only made one All-Star team. He has the chance to make more. I only hit one grand slam. He has the chance to pass that. He just wants to be a guy who really plays hard, who thinks about his team and plays consistently. I'm happy that he's happy."

Chapter 19

BURT HOOTON

THE EARLY LIFE OF BURT HOOTON

Burt Hooton is more Texan than the Alamo. He was born in Texas, grew up in Texas, went to high school in Texas, and attended college in Texas. He is also a pitcher all of the way. He learned how to pitch young and dominated at the high school and collegiate level before he was ever labeled a prospect to play major-league baseball.

He was always one step—or fastball—ahead of the competition regardless of the level he played. Hooton graduated from King High School in Corpus Christi with a diploma, but when it came to pitching, the right-hander already seemed to have the inside track on a master's degree.

As a high school senior, Hooton compiled a 15-1 record and led his team to the Texas state championship. In 1968, it would have made perfect sense for Hooton to move directly into professional baseball, where there was demand for his services, but he preferred trying out college ball first.

"I was drafted by the Mets out of high school, but didn't sign with them," Hooton said. "We (his family) gave signing a serious thought, but we decided the money wasn't there. It was a good decision."

Hooton said he injured a knee playing basketball his senior year and because medical procedures weren't as sophisticated as they are now, he said he was "looked at as damaged goods" in some quarters. However, legendary University of Texas coach Cliff Gustafson still came through with a scholarship for Hooton.

"Coach Gus gave me a full ride," he said.

Hooton proved to be just as dominant in NCAA play as he had in high school play. Enrolling at the big school in Austin, Hooton was an immediate and enduring sensation for the Longhorns. As a collegian, he put up a 35-3 record, accompanied by a 1.14 earned run average. He also threw 13 shutouts for Texas. Among his collegiate accomplishments, Hooton threw two no-hitters. Hooton became the first pitcher in NCAA history to be named first-team All-America three straight times. He was one Horn who hooked 'em.

The Chicago Cubs, enamored by the flamethrower's potential, drafted Hooton in the secondary phase of the 1971 Major League draft, paying him a $50,000 bonus, and before the summer was finished, he made his big-league debut. The Cubs viewed Hooton as the needed replacement in their rotation after they traded Ken Holtzman to Oakland.

Within three weeks of leaving his college campus, Hooton was sharing a clubhouse and dugout with Ernie Banks, Ron Santo, Don Kessinger, Glenn Beckert, and others.

THE SETTING

The Cubs brought Hooton directly to the majors to see how he would fare. He was a bit withdrawn being thrust

NAME: Burt Carlton Hooton
BORN: February 7, 1950, Greenville, Texas
HOMETOWN: Greenville, Texas
CURRENT RESIDENCE: San Antonio, Texas
OCCUPATION: Retired major-league baseball player; former pitching coach, Salem (Oregon), Albuquerque, Houston Astros, Round Rock Express, University of Texas; current pitching coach, AA San Antonio Missions
POSITION: Pitcher
HEIGHT: 6-foot-1
PLAYING WEIGHT: 210 pounds
ACCOMPLISHMENTS: Fifteen-year major-league player with Chicago Cubs, Los Angeles Dodgers, and Texas Rangers; winner of 151 games; lifetime 3.38 earned run average; National League All-Star 1981; pitched no-hitter in 1972; chosen Most Valuable Player in the 1981 National League Championship Series for two victories and allowing zero earned runs; won a World Series game in 1981, helping Los Angeles to the World Series title.
THE GAME: Chicago Cubs versus Philadelphia Phillies—April 16, 1972

Wrigley Field fans will never forget a fire-balling right-hander who won 151 games in the big leagues before starting a long coaching career, Burt Hooton. In only his fourth major-league game in 1972, Hooton pitched a no-hitter against the Philadelphia Phillies. *Bruce Bennett/Getty Images*

onto a veteran team, though the very professional group of stars made him feel welcome.

"I was pretty much awestruck," Hooton said. "You're sitting in the clubhouse, but you've got to pinch yourself to see if you're really there. They did a good job of accepting me. Probably a couple of guys resented that I was there, but every one of those big names is a class act. They're all great guys. It was just a good group of guys."

Hooton could not only throw fast, but he possessed an unusual pitch that came to be called a "knuckle curve." Batters didn't exactly know what they were seeing, but Hooton could get men out with it.

Manager Leo Durocher gave Hooton his first start in June of that season in a game against the Cardinals; but St. Louis manhandled Hooton, and the Cubs sent him to AAA Tacoma. Settling in and making a quick adjustment, Hooton overpowered Pacific Coast League hitters, setting a new league record with 19 strikeouts in one game. In a late-season September call-up, Hooton looked like his old self from UT days. He struck out 15 batters in one game and hurled a two-hit shutout in another. Overall, in his big-league Cubs cameo in 1971, Hooton appeared in three games and finished 2-0.

It was obvious, come spring training of 1972, Hooton, then 22, was ready for regular major-league action. Less obvious was the type of gem he was capable of when April and the regular season began. In the fourth start of his career, Hooton authored some baseball history.

On an unseasonably cold day, about 40 degrees, with a strong wind, Hooton introduced another team to the knuckle curve he had experimented with and polished since he was 14 years old.

THE GAME OF MY LIFE

BY BURT HOOTON

The no-hitter came in my fourth big-league start. It was a very cold day, and we had also just finished a 13-day strike so there weren't very many people at Wrigley. I just focused on pitching the game against the Phillies.

It was a no-hitter, but I didn't even feel like I was on. I walked seven. But around the fifth inning—between innings—I realized, "Nobody has a hit yet." After that, I just thought about getting one out at a time and just throwing as hard as I could.

I always had good concentration, but I used it (the no-hitter) as kind of more of an incentive. I've always been pretty good individually with each hitter, with each pitch. Nobody said anything about it in the dugout, though. You don't say anything. It's that superstition. For me, it was more disbelief than anything.

It was also a windy day—that's one reason the weather was so nasty—but the wind was blowing in. That can help a pitcher at Wrigley Field. There was one really well hit fly ball, but the wind held it up, and it was caught. I also struck out seven batters.

So I pitched a no-hitter in my fourth big-league start. Nobody expected that, I'll tell you.

GAME RESULTS

The Cubs defeated the Phillies, 4-0, in Hooton's no-hitter. He walked seven and struck out seven; and although no reports of deaths caused by frostbite were filed among the crowd of 9,583, some in attendance may never have felt their fingertips again.

Hooton's achievement set off a commotion. In his postgame press conference, reporters wanted to know all about him and his tricky pitch. He was a bit overwhelmed by the attention.

"I had always been quiet," Hooton said. "They asked me what I would do now. I didn't know how to celebrate."

Hooton felt almost as giddy near the end of the season when he hit a grand slam off 300-game winner Tom Seaver, and the Cubs beat the Mets, 18-5. The homer, Hooton's first in the majors, shot off his bat at Wrigley during a seven-run inning. Mets pitchers compounded disaster by walking 15 hitters that day. Hooton, however, respected Seaver too much to gloat about defeating the big winner.

"It was a day that he (Seaver) didn't have it," Hooton said. "He did okay, didn't he?"

Hooton could not sustain the magic of the no-hitter moment throughout the whole summer. He finished the season 11-14, although his earned run average was a superb 2.80. By 1975, Hooton was gone, sent to the Dodgers for Geoff Zahn and Eddie Solomon. He pitched his most consistent baseball for the Dodgers, twice finishing with 18 wins and once with 19, and turned in sterling efforts in the postseason.

During his ten years pitching for Los Angeles, manager Tommy Lasorda gave Hooton the nickname "Happy." They were together on a New Year's Eve in the Dominican Republic, where Hooton was competing in winter ball, and on the stroke of midnight—while all others were celebrating—Hooton barely looked up from playing a game of solitaire. Lasorda noticed and said, "Well, ain't he happy."

Lasorda, the Dodgers' Hall of Fame skipper, was impressed by Hooton the thrower, though, and endorsed the idea of landing him for L.A. in 1975. Hooton turned in a 12-game winning streak that season.

REFLECTIONS ON BASEBALL

Burt Hooton's big-league pitching career wrapped up in 1985 with a 5-8 season playing for the Texas Rangers. He was 35 and took some time to complete the college degree he had begun at the University of Texas, majoring in broadcast journalism.

"I didn't really know what I was going to do," Hooton said.

After Hooton had been out of baseball for two years, the Dodgers telephoned and asked if he was interested in becoming the pitching coach for their Class A team in Salem, Oregon. It was a short-season league, only two and a half months long, and Hooton's wife, Ginger, and his two children could accompany him. He enjoyed the experience and returned for a second season. Then Hooton began moving up the ladder, tutoring more accomplished players in higher leagues.

Hooton always praised his Los Angeles pitching coach Red Adams as the best he worked with when he played, so he tried to emulate Adams' philosophy helping young pitchers, without trying to drastically change them.

"I told them I'd like to keep coaching," Hooton said of his conversation with the Dodgers and other teams. "I don't have any desire to manage. Being a pitching coach is kind of like being a semi-manager."

Over the years since, Hooton has taught and helped hundreds of young pitchers at his alma mater, with the Astros, and in several towns in the minors—and it has made him happy.

Chapter 20

STEVE STONE

THE EARLY LIFE OF STEVE STONE

Steve Stone grew up in the Cleveland suburb of South Euclid, where he attended high school. Stone was a medium-sized athlete and in recent decades, scouts have looked for taller, beefier pitchers who could break the radar gun with their speed. Stone's skills were more of an acquired taste. After high school, he enrolled in Kent State University, and his battery mate on the baseball team was future New York Yankee star Thurman Munson.

"Thurman Munson was my catcher; and when most of the scouts in the baseball world went to see Thurman, they coincidentally saw me pitch every now and then," Stone said.

Stone was scheduled to graduate from Kent State in the spring of 1969. Instead, he signed a contract with the San Francisco Giants, and that summer, he played minor-league ball in Fresno. After the season, he returned to Kent State, completed his student-teaching obligations and earned his degree.

He finished in March of 1970; and although Stone was not on campus at the time, he had connections to the controversial and shocking Ohio National Guard shooting of students during an anti-war protest in May of that year. During that tumultuous era in U.S. history, there was considerable campus unrest, and students regularly protested the refusal of the government to withdraw troops from Southeast Asia.

There were marches in the streets and tremendous tension between college students and authority figures—especially those in uniform if they patrolled campuses. One of the four students killed by rifle fire during the tragic May 4 incident that came to be known as the day America shot its children, was a young woman Stone knew.

"Sandy Scheur from Pittsburgh was dating a fraternity brother of mine who was in jail for breaking curfew," Stone said. "She said to my fraternity brothers, 'Let's go watch a demonstration.' They left my apartment. Another couple of my fraternity brothers were leading them; the guys saw the guns being pointed, but she didn't. She was shot through the back of the head."

THE SETTING

Steve Stone was in the majors by 1971, when he finished 5-9 for the Giants. He pitched a second year in San Francisco, going 6-8, and then spent the next six years in Chicago, bouncing between the White Sox and the Cubs.

NAME: Steven Michael Stone
BORN: July 14, 1947, in Cleveland, Ohio
HOMETOWN: Cleveland Heights and South Euclid, Ohio
CURRENT RESIDENCE: Chicago, Illinois and Phoenix, Arizona
OCCUPATION: Retired major-league baseball player; restaurant owner; sports and baseball broadcaster
POSITION: Pitcher
HEIGHT: 5-foot-10
PLAYING WEIGHT: 175 pounds
ACCOMPLISHMENTS: Eleven-year major-league player; played with the San Francisco Giants, Chicago White Sox, Chicago Cubs, and Baltimore Orioles; won 107 games; in 1980, led the American League in wins with 25, and in winning percentage at .781; was a member of the AL All-Star team that season and won the American League Cy Young Award.
THE GAME: Chicago Cubs versus San Diego Padres—July 6, 1976

Stone had a 6-11 season with the White Sox and went to the Cubs and pitched well enough to go 8-6 and then 12-8. Then he suffered through a miserable 3-6 season in 1976 with an injury, but threw a highlight game or two at the right time that resurrected his career.

"In 1976, I became the first Cub free agent ever," Stone said. "I was the first Chicago Cub to play in a season without ever signing a contract. I was reluctant. I didn't want to be a free agent,

Popular Chicago broadcaster Steve Stone jokes that younger generations of sports fans don't even realize he was a pitcher. While the best of his 11 major-league seasons were recorded elsewhere, including a Cy Young Award season with Baltimore, Stone's career was dramatically affected by his time spent with the Cubs. *Brace Photo*

but I came off a 12-8 season in 1975, and they offered me a $2,500 pay cut.

"Considering that I had gotten an $11,000 raise off an 8-6 year in 1974, it didn't seem to be a prudent business move to accept the $2,500 cut."

The worst nightmare of a player without a contract came true for Stone. He incurred an injury to his right, or throwing shoulder.

"I didn't sign a contract, and I hurt my rotator cuff that year," Stone said. "I saw a doctor named Tom Satler, a doctor of kinesiology, and he told me he thought he knew what was wrong with me. I had never heard the words 'rotator cuff' before. He said, 'Put your hand out. Turn your palm up.' He put a one-pound weight in my hand, and it fell to the floor. He said, 'You've got a rotator cuff injury.'"

Stone spent about three months rehabbing the injury, but as he improved, he couldn't convince the Cubs to put him in a game. He pitched batting practice and finally got a chance to throw in a real game again.

THE GAME OF MY LIFE

BY STEVE STONE

I had a game in July when I came back and threw six innings—Bruce Sutter came in and threw the other three innings—we shut out the Padres, 4-0, at Wrigley Field.

Up until then, after Dr. Satler's treatment, I had only been throwing batting practice. I don't think the Cubs wanted to use me at all. I was going to be a free agent. They weren't really in a rush to get me regular starts. I wasn't part of their future. I was so frustrated throwing batting practice that nobody could hit the ball out of the cage against me.

Lou Fonseca, the old hitting instructor, went up to John Holland, who was a vice president who had been general manager and was going to be again, and said, "Why isn't he pitching?" Holland said, "Oh, I don't know." And Fonseca said, "The stuff I saw today could shut out the Yankees." So they pitched me.

As was their custom, Bill Veeck, who owned the White Sox at that time, and Roland Hemond, the general manager, would come over to Wrigley Field and watch the Cubs when the White Sox were out of

town. I happened to start the game, and then our manager, Jim
Marshall, took me out of the game.

I only gave up three hits, struck out five guys, and I even had a hit.
But the most important thing it showed was that I was back and
healthy. Because Veeck and Hemond saw me pitch that day, they
drafted me and said, "Everybody says you have a bad shoulder; but we
saw you pitch, and it doesn't really look like you do."

Near the end of the season, I remember having a real interesting
conversation with Salty Saltwell, who was the general manager that year.
I said, "Salty, you know we've gone this entire season, and I'm gonna be
a free agent. From a business standpoint, losing me for nothing makes
no sense. You've got a couple of choices here. You can sign me, and you
can trade me. You can release me. You can sign me and keep me, take
me to spring training next year, and see what happens. Or if you do
nothing, you let me go, and you lose me. That seems to be the least
practical of all the decisions because you get nothing for me."

And he said, "Well, Steve, Phil Wrigley is going through a divorce.
Things are a little up in the air, but I'll get back to you." I said "Okay."
That was September of 1976, and I haven't heard from him yet.

The season came to an end, and I didn't have a contract with the
Cubs. I didn't have any contract. At that time in free agency, a team had
to draft you. It didn't cost them anything, but they had to say they were
interested in you. It was really kind of an interesting thing. This was the
first time it ever happened, so nobody really knew exactly how this was
going to work, but five teams said they were interested in me.

GAME RESULTS

The game meant nothing to the Cubs in terms of their season, but
it meant everything to Steve Stone in terms of his future. After the
season, Stone received a phone call from Danny O'Brien, the general
manager of the Texas Rangers. He asked Stone how much he wanted to
be paid and Steve said that he would be happy with a contract of
$75,000 a year for two years. Stone said O'Brien replied, "Oh no, we
can't do that."

Not because it was too much money per se, but it was too much
money for a pitcher without the type of marquee name the Rangers
wanted. Stone said O'Brien told him that Rangers owner Brad Corbett

wanted to make a statement to the fans and was going to pay $1 million to Doyle Alexander.

"I'll take a million dollars," Stone said. He predicted he would win as many games as Doyle Alexander during the coming season, but O'Brien said the fans wouldn't buy it given Stone's recent 3-6 season and an injury. That ended the negotiations with the Rangers.

Bill Veeck, the ever-popular Sox owner who later was inducted into the Baseball Hall of Fame, swung an unorthodox deal with Stone. Veeck never had deep pockets, and during that ownership stage with the Sox, he was in the rent-a-player market. He hired players for one year and then let them get rich in free agency off someone else.

Veeck gave Stone a $60,000 contract for one year.

"I don't have the money for a long-term deal, and I can't gamble that your arm is going to be okay," Veeck said. "I'll tell you what I'm going to do. If you are healthy, then someone next year is going to have to pay you. So I'll give you your free agency at the end of this one year."

Veeck was the only one who offered Stone a genuine deal. Stone accepted the terms and won 15 games. (Alexander won 17 that season.) And since Stone was doing so well, Veeck bestowed a $5,000 bonus.

At the end of the season, Stone was a free agent again, but rather than go on the market with his increased value, he cut a fresh deal with Veeck.

"'Bill, you gave me one year when nobody else would,'" Stone said. "'My father always told me that you have to balance the scales. Your young pitchers aren't ready, so I'm not going to go free agent. I will give you back one year, and at the end of the year, we'll be even. But I want my free agency at the end of that year also. Same deal we had last year.' And he doubled my salary."

Veeck doubled the $60,000, plus the bonus, for a $130,000 deal and threw in some incentives. The team wasn't as good, but Stone won 12 games for the White Sox that season and led the staff. Veeck urged Stone to test the market, but promised him that if he couldn't get a good deal he would sign Stone for one year for $200,000.

"He was a great guy," Stone said.

So Stone entered free agency with a built-up resume—27 wins in two seasons—and the Orioles offered a four-year contract. Still, Stone hesitated about leaving the White Sox and a man he considered to be a terrific boss. He went back to Veeck and offered to serve in the dual role of pitching coach-pitcher. Veeck told him to take the Baltimore offer.

"Baltimore offered you four years," Stone said Veeck told him. "Go to Baltimore. They've got a good team. It's a tremendous deal, and I can't afford anything close to it."

Stone won 25 games one year with the Orioles, was selected for an All-Star team, pitched in a World Series, and played his final three major-league seasons with Baltimore, retiring at 34 because of tendinitis.

"He (Veeck) came up to me and said, 'I couldn't be happier for anybody than I am for you,'" Stone said. "'It worked out well.' And I said, 'Yeah, thanks to you it did.' He was one of my heroes."

REFLECTIONS ON BASEBALL

"I have thought of Bill a number of times," Stone said of Veeck, who died in 1986. "Bill took a chance on me. That first year it cost them $4,000 a win."

Stone doesn't mind thinking of himself as a bargain, but as a keen follower of Chicago baseball in his sportscasting roles he marvels at how little the Cubs have received from their unlucky, injured star pitchers Kerry Wood and Mark Prior over the last couple of years. It cost the team perhaps $1 million a win.

Playing for the Cubs in the mid-1970s was quite different than it is now. Attendance at Wrigley Field didn't even hit a million; yet in 2006, it was 3.2 million with a last-place team.

"Because of going on satellite TV, bringing over Harry Caray from the White Sox to broadcast, the Cubs have become an aberration," Stone said. "It is a team that really doesn't have to win. But still the experience of going to Wrigley Field is one of the great baseball experiences there is in the country. There are a lot of people who think it was always like that.

"Playing there in 1974, 1975, and 1976, we didn't win a whole lot, and there weren't a lot of people there. But it was still a happening thing to go there. I think this generation of Cubs fans has a tendency to believe it was always packed like this. You saw a lot of empty seats."

Stone finished playing in 1981, and then he shared the broadcast booth with the fun-loving, hell-raising Harry Caray. They were partners for 15 years, and Stone worked Cubs games from 1983 to 2004. In his own outspoken way, Stone was nearly as popular with Cubs fans as the revered Caray.

"There are a couple of generations of Cubs fans who remember me as Harry's partner," Stone said. "But they have no idea that I ever played. Then there are collectors who send me cards to sign. I got sent 10,000-15,000 baseball cards a year."

That seems like a mind-boggling number for a player retired more than 25 years who is not in the Hall of Fame, either.

"I'm serious," Stone said. "When I was broadcasting for the Cubs I would get at least that many a year, maybe more. You know, there are a lot of collectors. And I had 20 cards come out, maybe more. I have a lot of them, but I'm one of the few baseball cards worth very in little value. It keeps going down in value."

Something that does not go down in value—especially in Chicago—is Steve Stone's voice. He is 60 years old, but his baseball commentary on broadcast stations remains more in demand than his baseball cards. Chicagoans like a guy who tells it like it is.

Chapter 21

SCOTT SANDERSON

THE EARLY LIFE OF
SCOTT SANDERSON

Scott Sanderson was born in Dearborn, Michigan, but his family moved to St. Louis when he was four years old. He got his start in baseball the old-fashioned way, hanging out with the neighborhood kids playing in the backyard.

"We always lived where there were a lot of kids, so we were playing whatever sport was in season—whether it was basketball, football, or baseball," Sanderson said. "We were either on the driveway or in the backyard playing. And when I say playing, I don't mean two or three of us. There were usually ten or more of us. I think in our era that's probably how most of us grew up. It certainly has changed now."

Growing up, Sanderson had posters on his bedroom walls of Cardinals pitcher Bob Gibson and A's pitcher Jim "Catfish" Hunter. Yet, the first time Sanderson ever suited up for organized baseball was in his final year of Little League eligibility.

"My dad, John, worked for Sears; and as he would be promoted somewhere between every three or four years, we would move," Sanderson said.

Sanderson was 12 years old when his family moved from Indianapolis to the Chicago suburb of Northbrook, just in time for that last year of Little League. In those days, Sanderson split his time between shortstop, third base, and catcher.

"I loved being a catcher," he said. "I just liked being where there was a lot of action. When we played street hockey, I loved playing goalie."

The best athletes normally played several sports in high school rather than specializing in the early 1970s. Just as he had on the playgrounds, Sanderson continued to play football, basketball, and baseball in season. Given his size and ability on the mound, however, the Kansas City Royals took a chance on Sanderson, drafting him coming out of high school. However, he also had a scholarship offer from Vanderbilt and chose to attend college.

"I knew at that point I was neither physically nor emotionally mature enough to be a professional anything," he said. "I got drafted again after my junior year."

By then many more baseball scouts recognized Sanderson's potential. By the end of his junior year, Sanderson had been a member of four different USA college all-star teams. He had played against teams from Japan, Venezuela, Puerto Rico, and Nicaragua—some of the top nations in the baseball world.

"It was pretty clear to me at that point that my talent had at least shown itself to the point where I thought now I was not only very ready to be a professional, but it was time to do it," Sanderson said. "My confidence level had changed a lot since high school."

Sanderson had also played in the Alaska Baseball League, certainly at the time the premier summer college league in the country. He played for the Fairbanks Goldpanners, the team that every June 21 starts a home game at 10:30 p.m.

NAME: Scott Douglas Sanderson
BORN: July 22, 1956, in Dearborn, Michigan
HOMETOWN(S): St. Louis, Missouri;
   Indianapolis; Northbrook, Illinois
CURRENT RESIDENCE: Lake Forest, Illinois
OCCUPATION: Former major-league baseball
   player; sports agent, representing
   professional athletes
POSITION: Pitcher
HEIGHT: 6-foot-5
PLAYING WEIGHT: 200 pounds
ACCOMPLISHMENTS: Nineteen-year major-
   league baseball player; played with the
   Montreal Expos, Chicago Cubs, Oakland
   Athletics, New York Yankees, California
   Angels, San Francisco Giants, Chicago
   White Sox; winner of 163 games; three-
   time winner of 16 or more games in a
   season; pitched 2,561 ⅔ big-league
   innings; started 407 games; member of
   1991 American League All-Star team.
THE GAME: Chicago Cubs versus Pittsburgh
   Pirates—April 28, 1984

With 163 victories on his resume and 19 seasons in his background, Scott Sanderson enjoyed considerable success in the majors. Although injuries limited him in Chicago, Sanderson was the rare Cub able to say he played for two National League division winners in 1984 and 1989. *Brace Photo*

without turning on the stadium lights. The event is called the Midnight Sun game.

"I tell people about the Midnight Sun game all the time, and they just laugh," Sanderson said. "Back then Alaska was *the* league and now it's good, but Cape Cod has kind of taken over. We won the national championship (National Baseball Congress in Wichita, Kansas) when I was up there. I got in there at a time when they were still THE team, which was pretty neat and somewhat unusual for someone from the Midwest. Those teams were comprised of the best players out of the West Coast.

"It was pretty unusual for me to come from Vanderbilt. Guys are going, 'Wait a minute. Where is Vanderbilt?' I had a great time. I was up there for two summers."

Sanderson broke into the majors with the Montreal Expos in 1978 and in 1980 had one of his best seasons, finishing with a 16-11 record. Sanderson came over to the Cubs in 1984, just in time to participate in one of the most exciting Cubs seasons in history.

THE SETTING

In 1983, the Cubs finished 71-91 for fifth place in their division. Manager Lee Elia was fired in August after a tirade in which he blasted Cubs fans. Charlie Fox finished the year, but that was a transitional change; and by 1984, a lot was new and refreshing.

On Pearl Harbor Day, in a three-way trade, the Cubs sent three players—Carmelo Martinez, Craig Lefferts, and Fritz Connally—to the San Diego Padres, and in return obtained Scott Sanderson from the Expos.

Jim Frey was the new manager, and the Cubs, with a new outlook, developed a new habit—winning. The team won 96 games, won the division championship, and advanced to postseason play for the first time in 39 years. Many point to 1984 as the catalyst to the current fandom phenomenon. The mix of bombastic announcer Harry Caray, nationwide cable viewing of games, and a winning club, jump-started a magic that has endured for more than 20 years.

Sanderson was a starter coming out of spring training, but the team's roster evolved during the season. The Cubs added future Hall of Famer

Dennis Eckersley and Rick Sutcliffe, who won the National League Cy Young Award after going 16-1 with the Cubs.

"I think, coming out of spring training, people were concerned about our pitching staff," Sanderson said. "By the end of the year, we had added Sutcliffe and Eckersley, so we changed 40 percent. Bringing in two guys of that caliber changes the face of the team, I think."

Sanderson had been a Cub for less than a month in the regular season when Frey handed him the ball for a start at Three Rivers Stadium in Pittsburgh on April 28.

"I think in any walk of life you're always looking just to prove your worth or value," Sanderson said. "It feels good when people respect the job you do. That was no different. In that situation, when you come over to a team, you want to show that there's a reason why a team traded for you. You want to live up to and even exceed those expectations."

THE GAME OF MY LIFE

BY SCOTT SANDERSON

Leaving the bullpen after warm-ups, you always know how you feel that day, but that has very little to do with how the game is going to turn out. There's been plenty of times where you're sick walking down to the bullpen and maybe you've even thrown up in the locker room before the game, or you've got the flu, or you just don't feel good. You feel terrible. And then eight innings later you're leaving the game, winning 4-0 or 4-1, or whatever.

There are other days where everything is on line; and when you're in the bullpen, your fastball is on, and your curveballs hit the corner, and you're feeling like, "This is great." And you know, three innings later, you're taking a shower going, "What happened here?" That game, things felt good early. Many times in good games, you can feel it right from the very beginning. Other times you know, there might be a great play. You might have the bases loaded with one out in the second inning, and your shortstop makes a diving play on a ground ball in the hole and turns a double play.

That can save you, and you've got a great game going after that. There are just so many variables in predicting a good game or a bad game. There are certain guys who have the ability to keep on grinding their way through a game; and at the end, more times than not, it turns out well. There's other guys, I think, as soon as things don't go well for them, you can see them just kind of fold.

The hardest I threw was probably 93-94 mph, but it depends on specific points during my career. Back then, radar guns were not really a part of a game—certainly not like they are now. So we didn't have a clue. There would be times when I went through a season, and I'd have no clue what the hardest pitch was I threw.

In that game, I got everybody out except Johnny Ray. He had both hits. He got a double in the first inning, so it wasn't like everyone was thinking about a no-hitter as I went along. And he got a single later (in the fourth).

Johnny Ray was a really good hitter (.312 that season). He was the kind of hitter that I still, to this day, think is the best kind of hitter in baseball. The best hitters are ones who, when you throw them a pitch on the outside corner, he's going to take it the other way; and when you throw him one on the inside, he's going to be quick enough to spin on the ball and hit it down the line. And that's what Johnny Ray was exactly. He was the only hitter in that lineup who would do that.

I thought pull hitters, power hitters were the easiest kind of hitters to pitch. They are always trying to get out in front of the ball. I think when they do that, they give you a hole in their swing to shoot for. So pitching is a whole lot easier.

Johnny Ray was like Tony Gwynn and Pete Rose, the guys who year after year had the best averages, who weren't pull hitters. Those guys were using the whole field. When Johnny Ray's name is mentioned, that's the very first thing I think of. My mind goes back to my own personal scouting report, that he would use the whole field. Those kind of guys you've got to try to just continually move the ball around and out-guess them. It's a chess game between the pitcher and hitter. It's the thing that thrilled me most about pitching. Not only the competition, but the mental aspect of the game and trying to figure out what the hitter wanted to do and what you were going to do to combat that.

That day Johnny Ray figured me out.

GAME RESULTS

The Cubs defeated the Pirates, 7-1, that day on Sanderson's two-hitter. It was a good way to introduce himself to his new teammates, and within a couple of weeks, the Cubs moved into first place.

Dallas Green had managed the Philadelphia Phillies to the 1980 World Series championship and came to the Cubs as a general manager to piece together another winner. He was astute enough to pick off several players from the Phillies organization who could play and insert them into the Cubs lineup—players like Ryne Sandberg, Larry Bowa, Gary Matthews, Bob Dernier, and Dick Ruthven.

"A lot of those guys who came over from the Phillies, Bowa, some of those guys, they already knew how to win," Sanderson said. "It's been my contention forever that, if you put together a group, a core group of players that are winners, that's very infectious. Especially if they are leaders, and they're winners, they'll teach other guys how to win. I think we had a perfect storm there with some special players who had won in the past and knew how to win."

Sanderson finished 8-5 with a 3.12 earned run average in 24 starts for the Cubs during the 1984 season and thought the Cubs were headed to the World Series, especially after they took a 2-0 lead in games over the Padres in the National League Championship Series.

"I think we were confident," Sanderson said, "but not overconfident. We had played well. We had persevered through a tough pennant race. We won the first game in kind of a blowout (13-0), and then Steve Trout came back and pitched a really good, low-scoring game (4-2). So we had reason to be confident. We were playing well."

And then the Cubs stopped playing so well and lost three straight games and the playoff. San Diego went on to the World Series instead.

REFLECTING ON BASEBALL

Being part of that Cubs team was special for Sanderson, and he watched how frenzied the fans became.

"They had waited a long time for the team to be able to get to the playoffs," he said. "I just remember the people in Chicago being absolutely wonderful and very supportive, very excited about how we were playing."

In 1989, Sanderson's last season with the Cubs, he finished 11-9 and also got a taste of the playoffs. After that he moved around to several teams. Sanderson turned in a 16-10 performance with the Yankees and was very conscious of how sometimes the tough fans "can chew you up and spit you out if you can't take it and all that stuff." He didn't want to be one of those guys remembered negatively and truly wanted to make a good first impression. He did. Sanderson pitched a one-hitter against the Detroit Tigers, giving up the safety in the ninth to Tony Phillips, a hitter not unlike Johnny Ray in style.

"One of the reasons I had as much success as I did was that I paid attention to details," Sanderson said. "One of the discussions I always had with pitchers about a catcher or manager calling the game versus the pitcher calling the game was, 'Look, if you can tell me every pitch that I threw to this guy over the last three years and what he did with them—if you have that information to take into account for each pitch—then I think we're on equal footing.'"

Sanderson wanted to decide his own fate, throwing his own way, because he did remember all of those things and saved them up for occasions when he wanted to employ them.

"There's times when you set a hitter up for an at-bat in the future that might not come into play for a long time, maybe 10 or 15 at-bats down the road," he said.

Recalling those childhood posters of Jim Hunter and Bob Gibson, Sanderson said at various points as a young pitcher he wanted to style himself after both.

"I kind of tried to fashion myself after a combination of those two," he said. "Catfish Hunter had such great control and was in control of himself and his body when he was pitching. I loved that. But I so loved the Cardinals.

"Then I fell in love with the Cincinnati Reds' Big Red Machine. Actually, in the beginning of my career, some of those guys were in the twilight of their careers. I got to pitch against them. And Tony Perez was a teammate of mine when I got to Montreal. It was a dream come true to be in the same locker room with Tony Perez. He and his wife were so good to me as a young player. I also remember being on the mound facing Johnny Bench and going, 'Are you kidding me? I'm facing Johnny Bench. Is this really true?'"

And then Sanderson got Bench out.

"It was at the end of his career," Sanderson said, "when I was this hard-throwing, brash, cocky young pitcher."

The older, more mature Scott Sanderson, the sports agent, handles the business affairs of a younger generation of players now. And although he is not on the payroll of any franchise, he is still in the game.

"I'm still very involved in baseball," he said. "It's part of my job to know what's going on."

Same as pitchers.

Chapter 22

JODY DAVIS

THE EARLY LIFE OF JODY DAVIS

Jody Davis grew up in Gainesville, Georgia, and he is still a Georgia guy. He started hunting and fishing at an early age and still enjoys those outdoor hobbies. He also began playing baseball as a youngster and was a jack-of-all-trades in the sport through high school.

"I was the kind of guy that played anywhere," Davis said. "I played whoever's position who was pitching that day in American Legion ball. If the shortstop pitched, I played short; and if the right fielder pitched the next day, I played right field. The next day, if the first baseman pitched, I played first base."

Davis' team was very good and was poised for a good run in the state American Legion playoffs. Then the team's catcher got hurt, and Davis, although he had not played the position, volunteered.

"We had about 15 days to go in the season when our catcher hurt his knee, and I didn't know any better; so I said, 'I'll try it,'" Davis said. "I ended up catching through the rest of the playoffs. And I got drafted because of it. As a catcher. I went to Middle Georgia Junior College for two quarters, and that's when (1976) they had the winter draft. I was drafted by the Mets, and I had to buy a catcher's mitt to go to spring training."

It is never easy to make the move from high school or college into professional baseball, but when the team that chooses you wants you to play a position you know almost nothing about, it is even more of a challenge.

"I spent five years in the minor leagues, really just trying to learn how to catch," Davis said. "I needed that experience. I didn't think so at the time, but I really needed it. I thought I'd just give it a go. It took me a while to get the hang of it. I was catching high school buddies that I had played with my whole life, so when I got to spring training and I was having to catch guys from AA and AAA, it took me a while to turn it up a notch."

There were times, especially when Davis went through extended spring training and bopped around the minors, where he wondered if he was ever going to get the major-league call. Davis would have been able to travel around the world if he could have redeemed frequent-flyer miles for bus trips.

"Five years in the minors," he said. "The facilities are great now compared to when I played."

THE SETTING

By 1981, Jody Davis was property of the Chicago Cubs (he had recently been left off the 40-man roster of the St. Louis Cardinals), and he got the call to attend spring training. His breakthrough finally came when he went north with the big club, and he knew it was real when he first saw Wrigley Field.

"Pretty much the whole first year," Davis said of that season, "I felt 'Wow, I'm really here.' When I went to Wrigley Field, when I walked into the first major league clubhouse I had ever seen, when I walked on the grass, when I came out of the clubhouse two days before opening day. On the

NAME: Jody Richard Davis
BORN: November 12, 1956, in Gainesville, Georgia
HOMETOWN: Gainesville, Georgia
CURRENT RESIDENCE: Gainesville, Georgia and Peoria, Illinois
OCCUPATION: Former major-league baseball player; former owner of outdoor sporting goods store; former manager of Calgary team in Canadian Baseball League; manager, Daytona Cubs
POSITION: Catcher
HEIGHT: 6-foot-3
PLAYING WEIGHT: 210 pounds
ACCOMPLISHMENTS: Ten-year major-league baseball player with the Chicago Cubs and Atlanta Braves; two-time National League All-Star; played 1,082 games with lifetime average of .245; hit 19 home runs with 94 runs batted in for 1984 Cubs division championship team; batted .359 in 1984 National League Championship Series.
THE GAME: Chicago Cubs versus New York Mets—September 14, 1984

In his 10-year career, spent mostly with the Cubs, Jody Davis was a two-time All-Star. Competing at a position where the wear and tear is the worst, he earned the reputation as a player willing to start every game. He twice led National League catchers in games played. *Brace Photo*

field, I was excited and nervous. Then, of course, it was about a month or five weeks into the season before I got to play in a game.

"But I was going from having nothing, making maybe $1,000 a month in AAA, to making the major-league minimum of $32,500. First of all, I thought that was great."

A little bit of the giddiness wore off when baseball went on strike for part of the season.

"We're on strike, and all of a sudden the money is not coming in," Davis said. "I wasn't one of the guys who had been there for two or three years, so I didn't have any money in the bank. It was trying there for a little while."

Davis appeared in 56 games his rookie year, considerable action given that the season was disrupted by the strike, and he batted .256. By 1982, he was the Cubs' regular catcher, playing in 130 games. In the following years he became one of the busiest receivers of the time, catching 151 games in 1983, 150 in 1984, 142 in 1985, and 148 in 1986. Being Davis' backup was one of the cushiest jobs in the Western Hemisphere. All you had to do was sit back and collect a check. Of course, if you actually wanted to play for your money, you might get frustrated.

Davis' steadiness and reliability wearing the shin guards and mask earned him a nickname—Iron Man. Think of the all-metal comic book character. Davis filled the role with his gear and his game-after-game schedule. Iron Man. "Believe it or not," he said.

By 1984, not only was Davis a Cubs fixture behind the plate, he was an All-Star, putting up good power numbers. The Cubs were a first-place team that season, but they were being chased to the Eastern Division finish line by the New York Mets as they marched through September.

"To me the highlight game and the most meaningful took place in that 1984 season," Davis said. "It was late in the year. We were playing the Mets and had like a five-game lead (the Cubs won the division by 6 1/2 games). They came to Wrigley for a four-game series. All the media was saying the Mets had to sweep us to get back into it."

THE GAME OF MY LIFE

BY JODY DAVIS

The Mets had a pitcher named Brent Gaff they were using. We started Rick Sutcliffe, and he had a winning streak going.

When I came to the plate in the bottom of the sixth inning, we had a three-run lead. And I hit a grand-slam home run. It put us up 7-0 with Sutcliffe, and we won.

It seemed like as I was running around the bases that the crowd just kept getting louder and louder. It was as if, all of a sudden, the fans started to believe that we were going to actually win the division. That's the highlight of my career.

I have the play on video and watching it—even now—I still get chills. The year before, I won National League player of the week after hitting a grand slam against the Cardinals. That was my first grand slam. In that series, I hit a three-run homer on Friday, a two-run homer on Saturday, and a grand slam on Sunday. That's when the fans started chanting my name, "Jo-dy!" In those days, the Cardinals fans chanted "Oz-zie! Oz-zie!" for Ozzie Smith. For the Cubs fans, my name was the easiest, so they started chanting, "Jo-dy! Jo-dy!" And when I hit that home run against the Mets the fans were chanting, "Jo-dy!"

My dad, G.W., recorded every game on WGN at home; and if I hit a home run, he rolled it over to a highlight tape. So, when I got home at the end of the year, I had two or three hours where I didn't make an out at the plate and nobody stole a base on me.

The grand slam against the Mets made the highlight tape that year.

GAME RESULTS

The final score in the Mets game was 7-1, and Rick Sutcliffe won his 13th straight decision. The next day, the Cubs defeated the Mets again, 5-4, and upped their division lead by 9 ½ games. The Mets were not getting back into the race this time.

The Cubs claimed the division crown and advanced to the National League Championship Series to play the San Diego Padres. And in early October (playing October baseball at Wrigley was a novelty) the Cubs won the first two games, then lost the next three, and were eliminated before the World Series.

"We just had to win one of the last three games and they didn't let us," Davis said. "Going to the World Series was something we pretty much felt we had, and it never happened. We were really disappointed. After the series was over, we were sitting there going, 'Well, everybody's signed. We're all coming back, so we'll just pick it up and do it again next year.' Of course, injuries and things happened, and we never did."

REFLECTIONS ON BASEBALL

The Cubs were confident entering the 1985 season, and they played well at the start of the year—but then an epidemic of injuries struck. The entire starting rotation was decimated and the team sunk to fourth place. "Things kind of fell apart," Davis said.

Wrigley Field opened for business in 1914, and from that season until 1988, nothing but day baseball was played in the park. The day finally arrived when the Cubs adopted a schedule that included their first night games. There was much hoopla and ceremony surrounding the occasion; and then a few innings into the nighttime debut, the game with the Philadelphia Phillies was rained out.

Among the Cubs pitchers making light of the moment were Greg Maddux and Les Lancaster, who went sliding through the muck. The performance was reminiscent of a scene in the movie *Bull Durham*. Davis doesn't think there was any connection to the film, but "it was a lot of fun."

Playing under the lights at home was different for the Cubs, and the players had to get used to the park's new look with artificial light on the walls instead of sunlight.

"It was just a matter of getting the lights adjusted," Davis said. "We practiced under the lights a couple of times before we played, and there were dark places. All of the lights were around the infield, so there were no lights from behind like there were in other stadiums. If you were in the outfield you were looking at the shaded side of the ball the whole time."

Davis stayed with the Cubs into the 1988 season and finished his playing career with the Atlanta Braves in 1990. He had not planned for another career in baseball to follow. Instead, he went home, spent quality time with his three children, and coached their athletic teams for some years.

In his spare time, Davis went hunting and fishing. One of his hunting buddies was Hall of Fame pitcher Ferguson Jenkins. They shot deer and ducks and traveled to North Dakota, Kansas, and other locations. In 2003, Jenkins played a critical role in the formation of the Canadian Baseball League. He called his pal, Davis, and asked him about managing. So Davis went back to the trenches, leading the Calgary team. Alas, the league went belly up before its first season was completed. Davis' team was 24-13 and in first place at the time.

The taste of managing got Davis' juices flowing, and he began exploring other opportunities. He talked to Cubs officials and told them he really wanted to work with the team—that if they had any turnover in their minor-league operations, he would try it.

Over the winter following the 2005 season, Davis got the call. He began managing the Peoria Chiefs in 2006, then moved to take the reins of the Daytona Cubs in 2007.

"I'm glad to be back," Davis said. "I want to be part of the party when it finally does happen that the Cubs win the World Series. The White Sox got the monkey off their back, and the Red Sox did the same thing; so it's our turn. I can just imagine the party there would be if the Cubs ever won the World Series.

"In 1984, when we clinched the division in Pittsburgh, they had to close off ten blocks around Wrigley because people were just streaming out of their houses and going to the park. They were turning cars over—and that was just the division."

Chapter 23

BRUCE SUTTER

THE EARLY LIFE OF BRUCE SUTTER

Bruce Sutter's hometown of Mount Joy, Pennsylvania, is located about 70 miles west of Philadelphia. One of six children of Howard and Thelma Sutter, Sutter was an all-around star athlete at Mount Donegal High School—he was captain of the football team, which he quarterbacked, the basketball team, and the top pitcher on the high school and American Legion baseball teams. The basketball and baseball teams won district championships. Sutter later became known as one of the greatest relief pitchers of all time, but when he was in school, he was a starting pitcher who almost never needed relief help on the mound.

"When I was in high school, I don't ever remember being taken out of a game. That's the way it was. You got the ball, and you throw the ball back to the manager when the game was over. A lot of times, it was the same ball," Sutter chuckled.

Sutter had shown enough as a starter to interest major-league clubs. In 1970, the Washington Senators drafted him after high school in the 21st round. He did not sign, but instead began college at Old Dominion University in Virginia. However, he did not stay in school but returned to Pennsylvania and played for a semi-pro team in the Lebanon Valley League, a team that would earn him little attention.

A Cubs scout named Ralph DiLullo discovered Sutter, though, and Chicago signed him in 1971 to one of the most low-budget contracts a future Hall of Famer ever received—at least in the modern era. Sutter was given a $500 bonus and a monthly salary to report to Bradenton (Florida) in the Gulf Coast League.

The vast majority of young players drafted or signed as free agents never progress beyond the low minor leagues. Only a small percentage will even reach Class AA. When Sutter, the fastball specialist, hurt his arm after two minor-league games, it appeared he would be one of those guys who disappeared off the baseball radar screen, left only with the prospect of telling his grandchildren he once pitched in the Cubs organization.

The damage was severe. Sutter was out the rest of the 1971 season and unable to pitch in 1972. He took job in a printing plant where cigar box labels were made and underwent surgery for a pinched nerve. He resurfaced at the Cubs' spring training camp in 1973, but had no velocity.

Once again, from all outward appearances, Sutter was finished, his potential ruined.

NAME: Howard Bruce Sutter
BORN: January 8, 1953, in Lancaster, Pennsylvania
HOMETOWN: Mount Joy, Pennsylvania
CURRENT RESIDENCE: Kennesaw, Georgia
OCCUPATION: Former major-league baseball player; stay-at-home father
POSITION: Pitcher
HEIGHT: 6-foot-2
PLAYING WEIGHT: 190 pounds
ACCOMPLISHMENTS: Twelve-year major-league player with Chicago Cubs, St. Louis Cardinals and Atlanta Braves between 1976 and 1988; winner of the National League Cy Young Award in 1979; led the National League in saves five times while amassing a career total of 300 saves; six-time All-Star; winner of *The Sporting News* Fireman of the Year four times and the National League Rolaids Relief Award four times; career record 68-71; elected to the Baseball Hall of Fame in 2006.
THE GAME: Chicago Cubs versus Montreal Expos—September 8, 1977

However, as with so many things in life, the baseball world often works in mysterious and sometimes fortuitous ways.

Sutter hooked up with Cubs roving minor-league pitching coach Fred Martin. Martin taught Sutter how to master a new pitch that could replace his bread-and-butter fastball. The so-called split-fingered fastball rescued Sutter's career. The pitch was a variation of the forkball and relied on the thumb to push the ball out from widespread fingers. Being

One of the greatest relief pitchers of all time, Bruce Sutter saved 300 games. Sutter, inducted into the Baseball Hall of Fame in 2006, got his start in Chicago; and in his five seasons with the Cubs, he was selected to four All-Star teams. Sutter was renowned for being an innovator with the split-fingered fastball.
Ronald C. Modra/Sports Imagery/Getty Images

someone with large hands helped Sutter adapt. The pitch looked like a fastball leaving the thrower's hand, but as it approached the batter, it dropped suddenly. Sutter learned how to throw it for strikes and batters hardly ever figured out how to hit it. Years later, Sutter said, "The elbow surgery was probably the best thing that ever happened to me. Because of it, I got to meet Fred Martin."

Over the next several years, Sutter pitched for the Quincy Cubs in the Midwest League, the Key West Conchs in the Florida State League, the Midland Cubs in the Texas League, and the Wichita Aeros in the American Association.

In 1976, Sutter, who also had help developing the split finger from Cubs coach Mike Roarke, made his major-league debut. He was then used in 52 games, going 6-3 with 10 saves. He was 23 years old, and he was a big leaguer—not the starting pitcher he once was, but a heavily relied upon reliever. They were the first batch of major-league games on Sutter's resume, and none of the 661 he pitched were starts, making him the only pitcher in the Hall of Fame who never started a major-league game.

Not Sutter, not Fred Martin, not Mike Roarke, nor any Cub official or fan could imagine that the split-finger fastball would become virtually unhittable to a generation of National League batsmen.

THE SETTING

Bruce Sutter made a mark as a solid reliever his first year in the majors while posting a 2.70 earned run average. Yet, in 1977, his second season, he was the talk of the league.

New players often enjoy success during their first league circuit, hitters flaunt their plate-coverage skills and pitchers discombobulate batters who haven't yet learned their repertoires. By late in the season, Sutter's split-finger fastball was driving batters crazy on a daily basis. He had filled the crucial closer role for the Cubs as their go-to guy at the end of games. Thirty years ago, closers did not enter the game with one inning or to face only a couple batters. Frequently, they pitched two or three innings.

It was a different era for relief pitchers, and appearances tested them longer. They had to have more staying power, and if they hung around for a couple of innings it gave batters more chances to look over their pitches. A second time around the order might mean a batter embarrassed by a certain type of pitch once would deduce what he needed to do.

"Pitching three innings, that doesn't happen too much anymore," Sutter said. "The game has just changed. It's the pitch count and everything. It looks to me like they're trying to prolong guys' careers.

Back then, that's the way we pitched (longer), and that's the way you did it. You know, there wasn't any other way. And if you got hurt because of it, that was the breaks of the game."

Sutter had begun his second campaign brilliantly, wowing the Cubs, but in early August, he complained of an injury to his right throwing shoulder.

"I pulled a muscle under my armpit," he said. "I didn't look at it, and nobody else did, either, as career-threatening. I don't actually know what it's called. It was just one of those things. I pitched a lot the first half of the season and just tweaked it. It took a month or so for it to come back, and then it was fine. When I came back, once it healed up, I never hurt it again, or even thought about it again."

Sutter went on the disabled list on August 3 and stayed out of the bullpen five weeks. When he returned, both he and the Cubs were anxious to see if he could sustain the magic. He truly showed his stuff on September 8.

THE GAME OF MY LIFE

BY BRUCE SUTTER

I came into the game at Wrigley Field to strike out six in a row, struck out the last three guys on nine pitches. I pitched three innings and shut them out. I had a pretty good split finger that day.

I came into the game in the eighth inning, and I struck out Warren Cromartie, Andre Dawson, and Tony Perez. That's a pretty good group of hitters. In the ninth inning, I struck out Ellis Valentine, Gary Carter, and Larry Parrish on three pitches apiece.

The game was tied so we went into extra innings, and I pitched the 10th inning, too. They didn't score; and then in the bottom of the 10th, we scored and won the game.

I was really proud of that game. The split-finger fastball saved my career. I mean I was a one-pitch pitcher. I knew some other pitches, but 95 percent of the time—and a lot of days 100 percent of the time—it was going to be split fingers.

If you try to go through the line-up and pitch to the same guy four times in one game with one pitch, the odds are you are going to start hanging a bunch of them. My repertoire wasn't built, wasn't conducive, to go through the lineup four times—but once. ... The game against Montreal was the perfect example. The split finger just took them out.

GAME RESULTS

The Cubs won the game, 3-2, and Sutter resolidified his standing as The Man in the Chicago bullpen. He finished with 31 saves that year and a sparkling 1.34 earned run average, then put up 27 more saves in 1978. And then he got hot, collecting 37 saves in 1979.

Sutter developed a major attitude on the mound, a you-can't-hit-me-so-why-try persona. He wore a thick, dark beard that added to his presence as an intimidator, and he completely banished the idea of starting a game.

"It got to the point where I wouldn't have wanted to be a starting pitcher," Sutter said. "I liked coming to the park every day knowing I might have a chance to pitch. I liked that."

Relief pitching had evolved as an art since the 1940s and even more since Larry Sherry was named the Most Valuable Player for the Los Angeles Dodgers in the 1959 World Series. Tug McGraw made an impact with the New York Mets, and Sparky Lyle starred with the New York Yankees, but Sutter thinks Rollie Fingers' multiple World Series championship runs with the Oakland A's did the most to validate the relief pitcher's role in the eyes of fans.

"He had that handlebar mustache, and the name 'Rollie Fingers' only meant everybody recognized who he was," Sutter said. "And he was a relief pitcher. I just thought he really kind of put us on the map."

Sutter occupied a prominent place on the map himself by the end of the 1970s. He was the winning pitcher for the National League in the 1978 and 1979 All-Star games; and earned saves in 1980 and 1981.

"Back then there was no home-run derby—the game was the deal," Sutter said. "It was big when you just walked into the locker room. There were several veterans like the Pete Roses, the Johnny Benches, and the Willie Stargells. We had guys who, as soon as you walked into the locker room, would say, 'We're here to win.' We didn't have interleague play, and you never played the American League except in the World Series. It was about trying to show them that we had a better league. It was pride for the National League against the American League."

REFLECTIONS ON BASEBALL

Bruce Sutter moved from the Cubs to the St. Louis Cardinals for the 1981 season and had his greatest saves year in 1984 when he garnered 45. He then finished his playing career with three seasons on the Atlanta Braves. He retired during spring training before the 1989 season.

"I needed a fourth shoulder operation," Sutter said, "and I just said that was enough."

Sutter faced far more challenges than the modern closer, who often enters the game in the top of the ninth inning with no one on base. If he were required to warm up once in a game and pitch only one inning, Sutter figured he could have competed in 100 games a year.

"It's not only just pitching the one inning," Sutter said. "It's the warming up without stress. You're not in a hurry. You know you're going to pitch the ninth inning, and that you've got time—and you're coming in with nobody on base. There were many times when I would warm up in the seventh, warm up in the eighth, and warm up in the ninth and not pitch in the game. But I still warmed up three times."

When Sutter retired, he did not attempt to stay in the professional game but wanted to spend more time with his children. He went home to coach—the baseball teams of his sons, Chad and Ben. Sutter said he does not go to many major-league games, though he watches quite a bit of baseball on television. For years, though, he has followed the fortunes of players who grew up with his sons. Major leaguers Corey Patterson, Adam Everett, Marlon Byrd, and Kris Benson are Atlanta-area players.

"There are a lot of kids from right here locally that I've watched since they were 12, 13 years old," Sutter said. "And they know me as Chad and Ben's dad. They don't know me as Bruce Sutter, the Hall of Famer. I enjoy watching these kids play. I'll run into them in the winter and get a chance to talk. It's fun for me because now they're telling me stories instead of me telling them stories. I enjoy watching these kids grow, and I love baseball."

One of Sutter's sons played in the Yankees organization, but now the Hall of Famer is ready to tutor an elementary-school-aged grandson a little bit in the finer points of hitting and fielding.

"I'm starting over," Sutter said, laughing.

When he has free time, Sutter takes hunting and fishing trips, sometimes to exotic locations like Alaska.

"I shot a grizzly bear up there around Nome, near St. Michael," Sutter said. "I love hunting. I go all over. I lease a big place in Montana and go there every year; and I hunt a lot down here in Georgia and Alabama. There's a place near Penn State University in Pennsylvania where I go; and I'm going to Canada to go deer hunting."

Lately, Sutter's involvement with baseball on a higher level has ratcheted up a bit. He is helping DHL—the overnight delivery company—choose its relief pitcher of the month (Delivery Man of the Month) by serving on a five-man panel. For every pitcher selected during the season, a donation is made in the player's name to the Major League Baseball RBI Program that works to increase inner-city kids' interest in the sport.

Sutter's achievements, his dominance as a reliever, and his split-finger fastball earned him election to the Baseball Hall of Fame in August 2006. He was inducted in a Cooperstown ceremony along with 17 deceased former African-American players whose careers predated Jackie Robinson's integration of the majors in 1947.

"Everybody just treated me really special and really made it fun for me and my family," Sutter said. "It was just an honor to be part of it. The families were just so proud of the accomplishments of their loved ones, and it was something to be part of it.

"The attention has been crazy. I hadn't thrown a pitch for 18 years. I think, if I would have got in on the first ballot and I was still younger and had some of that arrogance and cockiness I had as a player, it would have been different. Now I'm older, and I've been away from it for so long, it was more sentimental to me."

And that just may be why Bruce Sutter cried during his induction.

Chapter 24

VANCE LAW

THE EARLY LIFE OF VANCE LAW

Vance Law grew up in a baseball family. His father Vernon won 20 games and the Cy Young Award for the 1960 Pittsburgh Pirates in 1960, a team that won the World Series in a dramatic, seven-game set over the New York Yankees.

Although the last time anyone checked, there still isn't a major-league team in Boise, Idaho, where Vance was born as one of six siblings.

"I was born in Boise because that's where my dad was from," Law said. "I went to school there for a while, but we always traveled to Florida for spring training and then to Pittsburgh for the summer when he was playing for the Pirates. In between, we made the trip back to Idaho to finish school. I would go to Forbes Field with my dad all the time. We used to be able to shag balls, and that was a great time as a young kid. We were allowed on the field back then."

Law was only a toddler when his father was the best pitcher in the National League, but when Vernon Law retired, he became an assistant baseball coach for Brigham Young University. That's where Vance got his later classroom and sports education.

An all-around athlete, Vance Law competed for Provo High School and then attended BYU. He earned All-Western Athletic Conference honors as a shortstop three years and was a three-year letterman on the basketball team. In both sports, Law was selected for the conference All-Academic teams.

"I played three years of basketball, but I gave it up my senior year to concentrate on baseball and hopefully get a chance to play professionally," Law said. "If baseball didn't work out, I thought I'd go to medical school."

One summer while playing for the Cougars, Law played in the Alaska Baseball League with the Fairbanks Goldpanners. The team hosts the wackiest baseball game in the world—The Midnight Sun game—contested on June 21 each year, starts at 10:30 p.m., but the team never turns on the lights.

"That's a fond memory," Law said. "I couldn't believe it. We were playing the Midnight Sun game with no lights on at midnight. It was dusk. It was kind of cloudy. It wasn't real clear. I've got a *Sports Illustrated*, and there's a picture in the centerfold with a silhouette against the background. It shows me there against that midnight sun."

Law matriculated at BYU between 1974 and 1978—and earned a degree in health education—but when his father's old team, the Pirates, selected him in the 39th round of the amateur draft, he chose to sign and go pro.

By 1980, Law was in the majors with the Pirates. He spent two years with the White Sox before being traded to the Expos. When he became a free agent in 1987, he signed with the Cubs and returned to Chicago, a place he says he loves.

"I had been with the White Sox, and you always heard about playing on the North

NAME: Vance Aaron Law
BORN: October 1, 1956, in Boise, Idaho
HOMETOWN: Provo, Utah
CURRENT RESIDENCE: Provo, Utah
OCCUPATION: Retired major-league baseball player; high school baseball coach, Provo, Utah; assistant baseball coach Utah Valley State; aided major-league baseball with rookie training program; head coach Brigham Young University baseball team
HEIGHT: 6-foot-2
PLAYING WEIGHT: 190 pounds
ACCOMPLISHMENTS: Eleven-year major-league baseball player with the Pittsburgh Pirates, Chicago White Sox, Montreal Expos, Chicago Cubs, and Oakland Athletics; member of 1988 National League All-Star team; lifetime batting average .256; played 1,212 games; father Vernon Law starred for the Pittsburgh Pirates.
THE GAMES: Chicago Cubs versus Philadelphia Phillies and New York Mets—August 8 and 9, 1988

A second generation major leaguer as the son of former Cy Young Award winner Vernon Law, Vance was an enthusiastic infielder during parts of two seasons with the Cubs, one of which brought him his only All-Star recognition. Law played in the first night game ever staged at Wrigley Field and went on to coach the baseball team at Brigham Young, his alma mater. *AP Images*

Side, too," Law said. "I kind of wondered what that would be like; and boy, just the way the fans and everybody accepted you, it was really phenomenal."

THE SETTING

In 1988, Vance Law became the starting third baseman for the Cubs. It was his finest all-around season. His .293 average was the highest of his career, and he drove in a career-high 78 runs, good enough for his first and only All-Star Game appearance.

In mid-summer, Law had the rare experience of being plunked in the same spot twice in a span of three games. In the first game, on June 29, the Cubs were playing the Phillies, and Mike Maddux hit Law in the left triceps with a pitch. On July 2, the Cubs were playing the Los Angeles Dodgers, and Tim Leary plunked Law in the left triceps again with a pitch.

"You couldn't have walked out there and placed it any better," Law said. "The whole hand swelled up, and the entire hand and arm turned black and blue."

And then within a week, with the Cubs in San Diego, Law got a phone call from Cubs public relations man Ned Colletti—now the general manager of the Dodgers—to inform him that he had been chosen to play in the All-Star game. Colorful arm or not, Law thought he would be able to suit up against the Padres that day. To mark the occasion of this announcement, Law struck out four times.

"It was right before the All-Star break," he said, "and the whole team was all over me. And the manager, Don Zimmer, was, too. We had a lot of fun with it because we were winning the game. I was the only guy not getting any hits. I was making all the outs."

Making outs was the exception for Law that season. He had several multiple-RBI games and was making his bat felt more in the lineup than ever.

"Shawon Dunston told me, 'You've proven what a good player you are,' Law said. "When you get the respect of your teammates, that's when you feel really good."

It really was a season of memorable moments for Law, which was also the season that the Cubs played a night game at Wrigley Field for the first time, and he was in the lineup.

THE GAME OF MY LIFE

BY VANCE LAW

I never imagined they would put lights in Wrigley Field. They had started talking about it when I was with Montreal. I remember going to Chicago to play the Cubs, and they were talking about installing lights at Wrigley Field to play night games. People said, "They'll never have a chance to win unless they do that. It wears the players out by mid-August."

I never put too much stock in that because I loved playing day games. I felt like I saw the ball better. I didn't care how hot it was. As long as I got my rest at night, that didn't seem to bother me.

And then they really did it. It was like a citywide party for the first game. They had an older gentleman flip the switch to turn the lights on, and I thought that was a classy thing. He didn't have any association with the ball club at all, he was just one of the oldest fans.

It was really an honor to be part of that. I remember that the Phillies were having a rough year; and for some reason, I recall somebody saying that it was a classless deal on the Cubs' part to play their first night game against the Phillies because they felt like it was a guaranteed win. In retrospect, it was played on 08/08/88, so I think it was just because it was a memorable date. I don't think it had anything to do with us playing the Phillies.

It's probably that the lights were ready then, too. Then it rained, and it kind of spoiled the whole thing. We played a few innings, and the game was postponed after all the hoopla and celebration. They didn't think the lights over the grandstands were going to illuminate things down to the left- and right-field corners. I was at third base, and I thought they were outstanding. I thought it was really good lighting, pretty much like everywhere else.

Even though the game was postponed, with the ceremonial flipping of the switch and all of the fanfare, I looked at that as being the first night game, although it didn't turn out to be official. It was a cool thing to be part of though.

GAME RESULTS

The Cubs led 3-1 in the fourth inning when a thunderstorm struck and washed out the inaugural night game at Wrigley on August 8. The official first night game was recorded the next night, with the Cubs triumphing 6-4 over the New York Mets.

The older fan whose name Law couldn't recall was Harry Grossman. He was a 91-year-old retired tire dealer who had attended his first Cubs game in 1906. Cubs Hall of Famers Ernie Banks and Billy Williams threw out honorary first pitches, and the Chicago Symphony played.

"In my office at Brigham Young, I have an overhead picture on the wall of the first night game," Law said. "People come in and remark on it and ask, 'Did you play in that?' And I say, 'Yep. That's where I'm at, right there.' I'm a little bit larger than a spot on the field. I have a bat from the first night game, and it's engraved '08/08/88.' It should have been '08/09/88.'"

Law's Cubs career ended when he was released in January of 1990, but he played one season in Japan with the Chunichi Dragons. Law later hooked on with the A's, but was released in October of 1991, ending his major-league playing activity.

REFLECTIONS ON BASEBALL

Vance Law and his wife, Sharon, have five children, including Tim, the oldest, who also played baseball for Brigham Young. Younger son Andrew played for the Cougars in 2005 and is likely to return after serving a Mormon mission in England.

Law has spent most of his time coaching since he stopped playing baseball and won a Utah state high school championship with Provo before moving into the college ranks.

"I'm going on 15 years of coaching, which is hard to believe," Law said at the beginning of the 2006-07 school year. "This will be my eighth year at Brigham Young. I never really thought I was going to go into this, but it just kind of fell into place. It's been very gratifying to teach some of these young players how to play and not only individual skills, but in my estimation, the right way to play. How to move runners, and play team baseball, and not just sit back and wait for three-run homers."

Even though he is based in Utah, Law—who is fond of both the Cubs and White Sox organizations and considers himself a quasi-native of Chicago—said the mystique of Wrigley Field is alive in the mountains.

"We've got people who still can't wait to go to Wrigley Field for the first time," Law said. "And they ask, 'What was it like playing there?' For me, it was really a wonderful experience. It was great playing there as a visitor and a home team player. The fans know their baseball, and they always turn out. They're struggling, but those fans, they still show up. It's amazing."

Law feels a close connection to the Cubs, the major-league franchise he roots for—from 1,000 or so miles away. Not only has Law been back to Wrigley Field three or more times to lead the singing of "Take Me Out To The Ballgame," he once sang the National Anthem as well.

His family always accompanies him on the pilgrimages to Chicago.

"We bring the whole family," Law said. "One year, we took about five families. We had a caravan back to Chicago from my neighborhood. The Cubs treated us right and gave us a box up above to let everybody see the game. The Cubs played a great part in my life, and the fans treated me great."

Chapter 25

SHAWON DUNSTON

THE EARLY LIFE OF SHAWON DUNSTON

Shawon Dunston fell in love with baseball at an early age growing up in New York. He played basketball and football in the streets with his friends, but he was passionate about baseball. He played in all of the organized leagues he could, from Little League to the Police Athletic League to a youth services league. His father, Jack, encouraged him, and Dunston was nine years old when he decided he was going to become a major-league player.

Always a New York Met and National League fan instead of a New York Yankee and American League supporter, the first game Dunston attended at Shea Stadium at age 12 pitted the Mets against the Houston Astros. He and some friends bought tickets that placed them in the distant reaches of the stadium, but they slipped into the best seats behind home plate. While Dunston's friends whooped it up, he marveled at how the game looked up close.

"I just kept watching," he said. "After the game, we went to the side of the stadium where the players came out. Another game I saw was with the Phillies. Mike Schmidt was my favorite player."

A budding infielder, Dunston could have done worse than picking the future Hall of Famer as a role model. The young Dunston had a powerful arm, and the coaches of his kids' teams always tried to talk him into becoming a starting pitcher.

"I told them, 'I'm going to be an everyday player,'" Dunston said. "I said, 'Pitching is for wimps.' I wanted to play and be out there."

Admiring Schmidt, Dunston was devoted to third base until his senior year in high school. The team's regular shortstop got injured, and Dunston volunteered to fill in. After he was drafted by the Cubs and shipped to Sarasota in Class A rookie-year ball, Dunston once again tried to set down roots at third. A player twisted an ankle, though, and Dunston moved over to short and showed off his arm.

"I went in the hole, and I gunned somebody out," he said.

After that, he was a shortstop for the Cubs, too. Even if he was a New Yorker, Dunston was happy being associated with a Chicago team. He didn't want to play for the Yankees, but would have been excited to play for the Mets. Mostly, though, he just wanted to play—he wasn't that picky.

"I would have handled it," Dunston said of being in the spotlight in New York. "I was from New York. I just wanted to be a major-league player."

The Cubs definitely saw Dunston as their shortstop of the future, and they brought him to the majors in 1985 when he was 22. Dunston was sent down in May but brought back in August and played in 74 games that year. He was in the majors for good after that and said he got the first hit of his career off Montreal Expos pitcher Steve Rogers. Dunston was not in awe of the older regulars on the team but did feel like a youngster next to some. There were seasoned veterans on the Cubs that year such as Ron Cey, Larry Bowa, and Leon Durham.

"All the players were older than me," Dunston

NAME: Shawon Donnell Dunston
BORN: March 21, 1963, in Brooklyn, New York
HOMETOWN: New York City, New York
CURRENT RESIDENCE: Fremont, California
OCCUPATION: Retired major-league baseball player; stay-at-home father
POSITION: Shortstop
HEIGHT: 6-foot-1
PLAYING WEIGHT: 175 pounds
ACCOMPLISHMENTS: Eighteen seasons as a major-league baseball player with the Chicago Cubs, San Francisco Giants, Pittsburgh Pirates, Cleveland Indians, New York Mets, and St. Louis Cardinals; 12 seasons with the Cubs; played 1,814 games; two-time All-Star; lifetime batting average .269; career totals of 150 home runs and 212 stolen bases.
THE GAMES: Chicago Cubs versus New York Mets—September 3 and 4, 1993

A tremendous fielder with pop in his bat, shortstop Shawon Dunston broke in with the Cubs in 1985 and spent 18 seasons in the big leagues. He played a pivotal role on the 1989 Cubs division championship team and was an All-Star in 1990. *Brace Photo*

said. "There weren't four, five, or six guys who were 20. It wasn't like that. I learned a lot."

The more Dunston learned, the more he played.

THE SETTING

Most shortstops earn the position with their glove. A team must have a slick fielder in the slot, or it becomes a massive gap in the defense. Dunston had that aspect of the job covered, but he also turned out to be a fine hitter who periodically exploded and clubbed an opponent into submission with his bat.

Dunston opened the 1986 season as the starter; and on April 19 he produced one of the best hitting games of his career. In a 14-8 loss to the Pirates, Dunston bashed out five hits, including a home run and a double.

"That was one of my best games," Dunston said. "If you don't make an out. ..."

Another special day came along on August 12, 1989; when the Cubs outlasted the Phillies, 9-7, at Wrigley Field as Dunston drove in six runs with a homer, a double, and a single.

"The wind was blowing out," Dunston joked about his home run years later. "It had to be for me to hit one to right field."

The 1989 season was pretty special for all Cubs who lived through it. The team won the division title and came close to advancing to the World Series for the first time 44 years. On September 15, Dunston smashed a grand slam in a 7-2 win over the Pirates, pushing the Cubs' divisional lead to 5 1/2 games. Eleven days later, the Cubs topped the Expos, 3-2, in Montreal to clinch the division crown.

"That was my greatest team moment with the Cubs," Dunston said.

Dunston became a Cubs fixture at shortstop and the player who seemed likely to hold down the fort for years—a player who seemed likely to spend most, if not all of his career as a Cub, joining the likes of Ernie Banks, Billy Williams, and Ron Santo as players always identified with the franchise. The Cubs wanted Dunston locked up long-term. Dunston wanted to be a Cub long-term. In November of 1991, Dunston signed a four-year, $12-million contract—and then things went haywire.

THE GAME OF MY LIFE

BY SHAWON DUNSTON

I had just signed my contract. I was out shopping with my daughter, Jasmine, and I bent down to pick her up in her car seat to put her into the car, and my back went out. I knew something was wrong right away because the pain was running down my leg. The pain in my right calf was killing me.

I was on my knees. I managed to get myself up and drove home, and I called the Cubs doctor. When he examined me, he said, "Shawon, this is a very serious injury. It may be career-threatening." It was a herniated disc.

I was just thinking, "I will do whatever they say, and it will get better." But he said that again (about it being career-threatening), and I was tripping. He asked me to stay in Chicago for six weeks. I was going to have to go into the hospital for five days and then rehab. I spent the next six weeks there, and I only went home to Fremont, California, for three days before spring training.

Everything was going beautifully at spring training. I felt good, except whenever I fielded ground balls I got stiff. But I started the season, and in May, I had a 14-game hitting streak going. I was in the batting cage, hitting them well, but every time I bent over for a grounder, my back hurt. I told the Cubs I couldn't play. They didn't really believe me. I played, went 0-for-5, and went back to the doctor.

This time he looked at me and said, "Shawon, you're going to have to have back surgery. You're going to be out for the year."

I had the surgery and did the rehab, so I tried to come back in August. I played two or three games, and my back locked up. I rested over the winter and came back for spring training in 1993, and I had the same problem. I was getting really scared. I asked the doctor, "What is going on with my body?" He said, "You will feel better 15 or 16 months after the surgery."

I went to another doctor for a second opinion, and he said the same thing. Well, that made me feel better. The doctors agreed. But the Cubs just hammered me. They were saying, "You just don't want to play." I could take batting practice, and I was hitting them out of the park, but I couldn't bend. I couldn't field. They thought I was just sitting on my money. There were a lot of articles saying I was just scared to play. That hurt my feelings.

I wanted to play. I was sad. I was frustrated. It got to the end of the year; and on September 3, the Cubs put me in to pinch hit against the Mets. When they announced my name coming out of the dugout, the fans gave me a standing ovation. I was not expecting that. We all got cheers, but only Andre Dawson and Ryne Sandberg and players like that got standing ovations.

The fans knew I wanted to play. I grounded out to third base. And when I went back to the dugout, the fans gave me another standing ovation. I felt like I was the best player in Major League Baseball at that moment.

The next day, I pinch hit again, and I got a single against the Mets. That was my first hit in 16 months. I was just happy to be playing. There was one play after that where I slid headfirst. I wasn't supposed to do that, but I was just playing again.

My greatest moment, though, was the day before when I made the out—the standing ovations. I will never forget that.

GAME RESULTS

To make the moment a little bit sweeter, Dunston's eighth-inning pinch-hit double tied the game at 8-8, and the Cubs later won 9-8.

"I was back," Dunston said.

Shawon Dunston played the better part of two more seasons with the Cubs before shifting between several other teams and retiring after the 2002 season. He hit well for the Cubs during those campaigns, averaging .278 in 1994 and .296 in 1995. He is just glad he didn't have to face certain pitchers more often. Most hitters seem to be like Dunston, often recalling the pitchers who gave them the most trouble instead of those they performed best against.

"The two I didn't like to hit were Nolan Ryan and Dwight Gooden," Dunston said. "I wish I could have taken a day off when they pitched. I'm not gonna lie, my whole body ached thinking of hitting against them."

Dunston has a head for dates and said, "I remember every game I played." He also studies baseball history and the eras before he started playing. "I'm good at forgetting things quickly, but some 20 years ago,

I remember. I am getting old, but I remember how special it was to be a Cub."

It was also pretty special to be a member of the 2002 San Francisco Giants when they took the World Series to seven games under Dusty Baker. Dunston played in 72 games that season, averaging just two at-bats per game while batting .231. He sensed the end of his career was coming. Even though the Giants did not win the title, Dunston ended his career on a high note. His last game was Game 6 of the World Series against the Anaheim Angels, and he hit a home run in the fifth inning.

"My son, Shawon Jr., was the bat boy," Dunston said. "I'll always remember my last game."

REFLECTIONS ON BASEBALL

If it was up to Shawon Dunston's heart he would still be playing in the majors. He would play forever, if he could, still studying books like Charlie Lau's guide to hitting and George Brett's suggestions about batting. He still has the same passion and love for the sport he discovered as a little kid.

"I've still got it," Dunston said four years into retirement. "I wish I could play. I really respect the game of baseball and the history."

Given that interest, Dunston surprisingly doesn't attend many games, mostly keeping up with the sport via television. He has no desire to manage, nor has he sought an off-field baseball job with one of his old teams. He is too busy spending as much quality time as possible with his four children, three girls and a boy.

Once in a while, the other kids tease Jasmine, reminding her that Daddy once got injured and couldn't play because he trying to pick her up—a running family joke. But Dunston spends considerable time driving them all around and watching them participate in their own favorite activities. Shawon Jr., his father said, is a solid junior high baseball player.

One day, the four Dunston kids will be all grown up and out on their own. When that day comes, Dunston might well seek to embrace his original love again. He can see himself back wearing a big-league uniform again—maybe coaching at first or third, or in the dugout.

"I would like to," Dunston said. "I wouldn't mind at all."

If that day ever comes with the Cubs, it would be no surprise if Shawon Dunston were greeted with yet another standing ovation at Wrigley Field.

Chapter 26

LUIS GONZALEZ

THE EARLY LIFE OF LUIS GONZALEZ

Luis Gonzalez grew up in Tampa, Florida, in a family of Cuban immigrants. Baseball figures prominently in both the heritage of Cuba and Tampa. Among the top major leaguers to emerge from Tampa are Lou Piniella, Dwight Gooden, and Wade Boggs.

"I grew up primarily in an Hispanic area," Gonzalez said. "Cubans, my family, thought baseball was the primary sport. It wasn't basketball, or football, or anything like that. I think in many Latin families, the players aren't very big in stature, not 6-foot-10 or weighing 280 or 290 pounds. Everybody's smaller, average looking. I think that's why most Latinos you see end up playing baseball."

Gonzalez got his start in the local Little League program, but was influenced by the passion for baseball on display in the Tampa Bay area.

"It's a hotbed for baseball, and I was glad just to be part of it and associated with a lot of great players who have come out of that area," he said.

Gonzalez excelled and was heavily recruited out of Tampa's Jefferson High School by colleges with a baseball tradition. He was wooed by Florida State and Oklahoma, but chose the University of South Alabama, where he could jump directly into the lineup without redshirting.

"I'm a people person," Gonzalez said. "I liked the other schools. I had a good time, but I wasn't a physically big person. A lot of schools wanted me to redshirt. I didn't want to waste a year. I wanted to play somewhere, and my nature has always been to be in the lineup and play every day. I was like that even at a young age. I never wanted a day off. I'm still that way today."

Gonzalez liked the attitude at South Alabama. He was told he would be given every opportunity to make the team; and if he showed his stuff, he would play. "I never missed a game in three years," said Gonzalez, who exhibited the same conscientious routine in the majors later. "I started my freshman year every game and played all the way through till my last year."

Gonzalez also benefited from playing two seasons of summer ball in the Alaska Baseball League in 1986 and 1987 with such other future major leaguers such as Mark Grace. Their team—now defunct—was called the North Pole Nicks. The small community of North Pole is located on the outskirts of Fairbanks and among the most prominent businesses in town is a Santa Claus House. Souvenir T-shirts picturing Santa Claus swinging a bat were once featured team items.

"That was a fun time," Gonzalez said. "I still keep in very close touch with the families there. It was great. It was a good experience that I'll never forget. I had fun playing with great players, some from the Pac 10 and California teams. It was a big challenge to go there and see if you could compete with those guys from the other side of the country."

Gonzalez had a tough time convincing friends and family in Alabama and Florida that he really was going to the Far North to play for a

NAME: Luis Emilio Gonzalez
BORN: September 3, 1967, in Tampa, Florida
HOMETOWN: Tampa, Florida
CURRENT RESIDENCE: Scottsdale, Arizona
OCCUPATION: Major-league baseball player
POSITION: Outfielder
HEIGHT: 6-foot-2
PLAYING WEIGHT: 185 pounds
ACCOMPLISHMENTS: Sixteen-year major-league baseball player with the Houston Astros, Detroit Tigers, Chicago Cubs, and Arizona Diamondbacks; lifetime average .285; hit 57 home runs and drove in 142 runs in 2001 as a member of the Diamondbacks World Series championship team; led the National League with 206 hits in 1999; played in all 162 games in 2000 and 2001; fielding percentage of 1.000 in 2001; five-time All-Star.
THE GAME: Chicago Cubs versus Colorado Rockies—August 18, 1995

The long and successful outfield career of Luis Gonzalez continued into 2007, but when he was much younger, in 1995 and 1996, Gonzalez spent one and a half seasons with the Cubs. He figured prominently in one of the Cubs' wildest games of all time, a 26-7 victory over the Colorado Rockies in Denver. *Brace Photo*

baseball team located in a place called North Pole, as opposed to playing AT the North Pole.

"It draws a lot of laughs," Gonzalez said. "And then you tell them that your team mascot is Santa Claus and that they hand out candy canes at the games. I actually lived right around the corner from the Santa Claus House in North Pole."

Gonzalez did put aside some North Pole Nicks souvenirs for his private collection, emblematic of his stay in Alaska.

"I always give my grandmother everything," Gonzalez said. "She saves everything for me. I think she still has my uniform and little mementoes. I remember Hallmark made an ornament of Santa Claus at the North Pole, and I thought that was pretty cool because I was playing at the time the ornament came out."

The North Pole club performed well when Gonzalez was playing and qualified for the National Baseball Congress championships held each year in Wichita, where the Alaska teams are always popular.

"Our most popular player was Santa Claus in the stands, believe it or not," Gonzalez said. "He was fully dressed and handing out candy canes to the kids in Wichita. He was an unidentified source as far as name goes, but everybody knew him as Santa Claus."

Gonzalez left South Alabama when he was drafted in the fourth round by the Houston Astros in 1988. He spent the rest of the summer in the low minors, but by 1990, he was an all-star in the Southern League. He had a September call-up and played 12 games, then became a regular for the Astros in 1991.

A solid player for the first several years of his career, Gonzalez played just one and a half seasons with the Cubs. Although Gonzalez's greatest success and many of his best baseball memories were manufactured later, he was the star of one unbelievable Cubs game.

THE SETTING

Luis Gonzalez began the 1995 season with the Astros, but on June 28, he was traded along with Scott Servais to Chicago for Rick Wilkins. Gonzalez appeared in 77 games for the Cubs that season while hitting .290. In 1996, he cranked 15 home runs, drove in 79 runs, and batted .271.

And then he returned to Houston as a free agent.

Those years were some of the Cubs' doldrums, the not-so-special, not-so-awful years. They finished 73-71 and 76-86 with Gonzalez. The 1995 season began late because of a players' strike, and despite the lackluster record just squeaking in over .500, the Cubs created some excitement as they stayed within sniffing distance of a wild-card playoff berth until the final few days of the season.

That meant every late-season game mattered for the Cubs' position and their devoted fans. Cub fans want to win the World Series. They want to win the pennant. They just want to make it into the playoffs. Period. If the team's record is so-so, so be it—so long as the team still gets the opportunity to play in October.

"It's just an exciting and fun place to play," Gonzalez said.

On one particular day in August of 1995, the Cubs crushed the Colorado Rockies, 26-7. Wrigley Field has been the site of many high-scoring games, where deep fly balls transformed into home runs because of high winds. On this day, however, the Cubs were playing in Denver in the thin, mile-high air against the Rockies.

THE GAME OF MY LIFE

BY LUIS GONZALEZ

Ooh, 26-7. You know what? After a while and so many games, they all start to run together. But there aren't too many games in your life where a team scores in the 20s—especially at this level in the big leagues.

You don't get too many games like that. I had a home run, a double, and a single, and I drove in six runs. Anytime a player is doing something very special for that day, there's a certain buzz when he's coming to the plate; or if he's the pitcher, as he's coming to the mound. You can feel a different sense in the air.

Twenty-six runs—I was glad I was part of it. I don't remember being in any game that was higher scoring. Not like that. I had good games with the Cubs, but that was probably the best one. I loved it when it happened in Chicago, at Wrigley Field. I loved playing there for a year and a half. I still love coming to Chicago as a visitor. The fans are very knowledgeable about what's going on.

GAME RESULTS

Managers will tell you that it doesn't matter how badly you beat the other team as long as the game goes into the win column. But being part of a 26-7 rout for Cubs players meant being part of history.

The 26 runs scored equaled the most ever tallied by the Cubs after 1900. Previously, the Cubs scored 26 runs in a 1922 triumph over the Philadelphia Phillies that played out much differently. The final score of that one? 26-23. One of the weirdest aspects of the Colorado victory was the rain delay that struck when the Cubs were already ahead 9-1 in the third inning. The umpires stopped play for two hours and 45 minutes, prolonging the agony for Colorado. The Rockies were humiliated and wet.

In late September of 1995, the Cubs spurted into the pennant picture with an eight-game winning streak. As the final weekend of the regular season began, a combination of circumstances existed whereby Chicago could still sneak into the playoffs. Instead, the Cubs lost two games, and their dream collapsed.

REFLECTIONS ON BASEBALL

Luis Gonzalez was a late-blooming star, having his best seasons after he left the Cubs.

In 1998, Gonzalez and his wife, Christine, had triplets. Always committed to community involvement and generous with his free time, Gonzalez has been active in programs emphasizing the importance of school for kids, the need for organ donors, the Make-A-Wish Foundation, and Phoenix General Hospital, among several others.

A $10 million-a-year player in recent seasons with the Diamondbacks, the future of Gonzalez's baseball career was uncertain at the end of the 2006 season. His contract with the Diamondbacks was up, and he became a free agent. Gonzalez worked as a guest television commentator during the postseason, but whether that was the beginning of a new career or he would continue to play ball at 40 years old was not yet clear.

Despite his fondness for North Pole and Alaska, Gonzalez has never had the time or opportunity to visit over the last two decades. He has always been playing baseball during the summer. When he does retire, Gonzalez said he wants to take a north country vacation.

"I'm actually waiting for my kids to get a little bit older," Gonzalez said, "and take them back, because I keep promising. We'll just go fishing and see the family I lived with and where I lived and the field. I'm sure it's grown so much there. It's just amazing the way things develop and change. I'm sure it will be very foreign to me when I get there."

Chapter 27

MARK GRACE

THE EARLY LIFE OF
MARK GRACE

Mark Grace was born in North Carolina, but his family moved often throughout his formative years. Many of his elementary-school years were spent in Tennessee and Arkansas, where he played Little League, but he also lived in St. Louis. There he became a Cardinals fan and particularly fond of first baseman Keith Hernandez, whom he adopted as a role model in the field.

By his high school years, Grace's family was living in Southern California, near Los Angeles, and he graduated from Tustin High School. Besides baseball, he excelled in basketball. The left-handed swinger went on to Saddleback Junior College and then to San Diego State.

In San Diego, Grace played for coach Jim Dietz, who doubled as the manager of the Fairbanks Goldpanners, and got Grace chance to play on a premier summer league team in Alaska. Dietz was an influential figure in Grace's life, and the two became close friends.

Like many of the Californians who make a summer appearance in the Alaska Baseball League, Grace was captivated by his surroundings and by competing for a team called the North Pole Nicks.

"Jim Dietz placed me," Grace said. "He sent me and a couple of other guys from San Diego State to the North Pole Nicks, and we had

229

a great team. We won the Alaska League and finished runner-up that year in the National Baseball Congress tournament in Wichita."

Grace had little time to explain to his family and friends that he was headed north—Dietz told him that he was leaving in three days. After moving around incessantly as a kid though, Grace was prepared.

"You get off the plane in Fairbanks, Alaska," Grace said, "and you drive 20 minutes to North Pole, Alaska; it's like, 'Toto, we're not in Kansas anymore.' You know, in what they call the Lower 48, you drive down the street, and a dog or a cat or some kind of varmint might cross in front of you. Up there, it's a moose or a fox, or something that you don't see very often down here. I had a great time. I just had to dodge mosquitoes all summer, that's all."

Soon Grace had improved from a player overlooked by major colleges to a guy garnering interest from major-league scouts. In 1984, the Minnesota Twins drafted Grace in the 15th round. He chose not to sign, but a year later—when the Cubs picked him with their 24th choice in the draft—he autographed a contract for them.

THE SETTING

Mark Grace made it to the majors. He showed he belonged, playing 134 games and batting .296. That set him up to play a key role on one of the Cubs' most popular teams of the second half of the 20th century, the 1989 team that won 93 games and captured its division title.

NAME: Mark Eugene Grace
BORN: June 28, 1964, in Winston-Salem, North Carolina
HOMETOWN: (Family moved often) North Carolina, Tennessee, Arkansas, Missouri, California
CURRENT RESIDENCE: Paradise Valley, Arizona
OCCUPATION: Retired major-league baseball player; television broadcaster
POSITION: First base
HEIGHT: 6-foot-2
PLAYING WEIGHT: 190 pounds
ACCOMPLISHMENTS: Sixteen-year major-league baseball player with the Chicago Cubs and Arizona Diamondbacks; lifetime .303 hitter; batted over .300 nine times with a high of .331 in 1996; played 2,245 games and drove in 1,146 runs; led National League with 51 doubles in 1995; three-time National League All-Star; winner of four Gold Glove awards; member of 2001 Diamondbacks World Series champions.
THE GAME: Chicago Cubs versus San Francisco Giants—September 28, 1998

A three-time National League All-Star with a lifetime .303 batting average, Mark Grace lived up to his name with his graceful fielding around the first-base bag. Although he won a world championship with the Arizona Diamondbacks, Grace spent all but three of his 16 years in the majors with the Cubs. *Tom Hauck/Getty Images*

The club was young, exciting, and the newcomers thought they had entered on the ground floor of something that was building and would continue to get better. The World Series just had to be around the corner.

"We had the Rookie of the Year in Jerome Walton," Grace said. "I was in my second year. The runner-up for Rookie of the Year was Dwight Smith. Andre Dawson was still playing well. Rick Sutcliffe was still throwing the ball well. Greg Maddux was there. We thought we were going to be good for years to come. The next thing we know, there's a whole new regime, and they go in a totally new direction. Jim Frey gets fired. Don Zimmer gets fired. Greg Maddux walks, and then it's a whole different era of baseball and unfortunately, losing baseball began."

Grace was one solid component, a reliable piece in the lineup during those painful years. Starry-eyed and expecting to be on a team that was a playoff threat every year, Grace was dismayed by the Cubs' sour turn.

"It was tough," he said. "There were a lot of tough years. There were a lot of losing seasons."

Still, a feeling never existed among the young guys who broke in during the late 1980s that they would have to wait nearly a decade for another crack at the playoffs. Of course, by the time the next opportunity came around, most of the original guys were gone. Grace was one of the holdovers.

The 1998 team was a far cry from the '89 squad. For one thing, basher Sammy Sosa was at the peak of his prowess, clubbing 66 homers during an incredibly captivating race with Mark McGwire to break Roger Maris' all-time single-season record, rejuvenating baseball after a debilitating labor strike. All of Sosa's teammates were in the middle of the hubbub.

When the regular season ended, the Cubs and the San Francisco Giants were deadlocked for the National League wild-card playoff spot, and they had to play a bonus playoff game just to advance to the post-season.

The Cubs lived with daily tension for the last stretch of the season as they sought a long-elusive pennant.

"This team," Grace said at the time, "makes your ulcers have a baby."

THE GAME OF MY LIFE

BY MARK GRACE

Winning the wild card in 1998 was the biggest game of my life. We had to beat the Giants to go to the playoffs. That was a huge moment in Cubs baseball history, and that game stands out.

The last time I had been in the playoffs was 1989, so it was a nine-year drought. There had been a lot of bad years between those two bookends.

Chicago is the greatest city in the world, and I've been fortunate to be in a business where I can travel all over the world. There's not a better city than Chicago. The people are great, the city is great, and they love their Cubs. There is so much hunger in those fans to win a World Series; and each time you make it to the playoffs, they think you're going to do it and end the wait.

The only ones who could compare to Cubs fans were White Sox and Red Sox fans, and they've taken care of their business. That wild-card game—to that point in my career—was the biggest game I had ever played in. The World Series with Arizona came later.

Rod Beck was pitching for us in relief. The Giants had a man on in a close game in the ninth inning, and Joe Carter was at the plate. He popped it up right to me. I caught the last out, and then it was bedlam. It was just an unbelievable feeling—we were in the playoffs.

GAME RESULTS

The Cubs won the game 5-3 after taking a 5-0 lead. Gary Gaetti's two-run homer early was a critical blow. Starting pitcher Steve Trachsel gave up only one hit in 6 ⅓ innings. Of course, Wrigley Field was packed with nearly 40,000 fans.

The joy was short-lived. The Cubs ran into a top-notch Atlanta Braves team and were swept, 3-0, in the playoffs. At that time, former teammate Greg Maddux was on the other side and was the winning pitcher.

That was Grace's last chance to play in the postseason with the Cubs, but he did produce many other memorable moments on the field with his dazzling fielding and consistent, high-level hitting. Grace was never the free-swinging, big-slugger Sosa type, who cracked a lot of home runs. But the ones Grace got seemed to come at opportune times, and Grace's bat was a significant presence in the lineup at all times.

In a May 1999 game, Grace slugged a three-run homer to beat the Florida Marlins in the 11th inning. He swatted his 2,000th career hit in August 1999, against the Expos, and in a July 2000 game against the Phillies, Grace collected three singles, a grand-slam homer, and drove in six runs. Only ten days later, he enjoyed a five-hit game against the San Diego Padres.

Perhaps Grace's favorite hitting performance occurred in a May 1993 game against the Padres. Grace hit for the cycle, including a two-run homer in the ninth inning, but he didn't derive full pleasure from the feat since the Cubs lost, 5-4.

Few fans recognize just how rare it is to hit for the cycle. Over the course of baseball history, only a few more batters have hit for the cycle than pitchers have thrown no-hitters.

"The players really appreciate it," Grace said. "They really understand how difficult it is. Unfortunately, mine was in a losing effort. You've done something remarkable. You've done something that not many guys have done in the history of the game. You're gonna get a lot of accolades if your cycle comes in a win; but if it comes in a loss, it's clearly not enough. And that's the way I felt about it.

"Yeah, I had a great game, but maybe I should have done more. Maybe it would have been better if I had hit three doubles and a home run. So it was kind of a bittersweet moment for me."

Grace departed from Chicago as a free agent in 2000, which left a bad taste in his mouth. For several years, he was estranged from the Cubs, but a rapprochement was effected in 2006 when Grace returned to town, and he led the singing of "Take Me Out To The Ballgame" at Wrigley Field. Grace pumped his fist to the crowd and said, "It's a day I'm glad finally happened."

However, Grace did appreciate earning a World Series ring with the Diamondbacks. That triumph provided an emotional high.

"If you only understood how great this is for me," Grace said after his team won. "It was better than anything I could imagine. It is better than sex. But then again, I'm kind of lousy at that."

After Grace retired, he quickly became a member of Arizona's broadcast team.

REFLECTIONS ON BASEBALL

Grace had not made plans for retirement. He loved baseball and wanted to stay close to the game, but he didn't know what he was going to do when he hung up his glove at the end of the 2003 season. There was no pressure to go to work and, indeed, Grace had the perfect opportunity to just hang out and go fishing for a summer. Grace, his old college coach Jim Dietz, and Tony Gwynn, another of Dietz's disciples at San Diego State, invested in a cabin in Alaska on the Kenai River, about 150 miles south of Anchorage.

For years, Dietz was the cabin's primary tenant. As still-active players, Gwynn and Grace were never able to break away during the summer to go fishing. When Gwynn retired, he ended up succeeding Dietz as coach in San Diego.

"It's a great place," said Grace, who must have been talking from viewing pictures because, in 2006, he admitted never visiting. "I've never been up there, but I'm going to. If I get a week off, I'm going to fly up there for a vacation. Alaska is a beautiful place."

Before Grace could become a fishing bum, a solution to his desire to stay in baseball presented itself. The Diamondbacks offered him the chance to handle color commentary for the team's television-broadcast team.

"They handed it to me," Grace said. "I didn't have to audition for it. I didn't have to do anything. I'm thankful they did, and I'm getting better and better every year. I've still got some improving to do. I know how to listen."

So even if he is wearing street clothes, Mark Grace is still in the big leagues.

"It keeps you around the major leagues," Grace said. "It's a game I love and a game I know like the back of my hand. I know all these players, and I share my knowledge with a watching audience."

When he was playing, sportswriters considered Grace to be a major-league talker who spoke his mind. Now he's getting paid for it.

Chapter 28

RYNE SANDBERG

THE EARLY LIFE OF RYNE SANDBERG

Born into a family that loved baseball, Ryne Sandberg was named after former New York Yankees relief pitcher Ryne Duren. Sandberg's earliest influence in the sport was older brother Del, who was named after Philadelphia Phillies outfielder Del Ennis.

Sandberg's father, Derwent, was a mortician, and his mother, Elizabeth, was a nurse. They were watching a baseball game on television when they heard Ryne Duren's name mentioned, and they wrote it down. Sandberg met the retired pitcher during his own career and received an autographed baseball—"To Ryne Sandberg, from the first Ryne, Ryne Duren"—a cool inscription and a neat souvenir.

Sandberg was a superb all-around athlete from an early age. Despite his success as an all-state baseball player and an all-city basketball player in Spokane, Washington, in high school his best sport was probably football. Sandberg was a *Parade* All-America quarterback who major colleges heavily recruited.

Feeling pressured by the process, Sandberg signed a letter of intent to attend nearby Washington State to play football and baseball. It made the local fans happy. However, at the end of his last year at North Central High, Sandberg was drafted by the Phillies. When he decided to sign instead of going to college, Washington State and many area fans were disappointed. But at age 18, Sandberg was a professional.

Sandberg made his minor-league debut in Helena, Montana, a rookie-league team. He also played in the Phillies chain in Spartanburg, South Carolina; Reading, Pennsylvania; and Oklahoma City. In addition, he played two seasons of winter ball in Venezuela.

In 1981, Sandberg got a September call-up with the Phillies, appeared in 13 games and got his first major-league hit—at Wrigley Field. He seemed a good bet to make the big club for the 1982 season. But Dallas Green, the previous Phillies manager, had moved on to become general manager of the Cubs and began raiding Philadelphia for so-called expendable talent.

The key components in a pending trade were Cubs shortstop Ivan DeJesus and Phillies shortstop Larry Bowa. And Green said, "Oh, why don't you throw in Ryne Sandberg, too." The Phillies thought they were set at second base with Manny Trillo and Julio Franco.

It may be the best trade the Cubs ever made.

As Ryno puts it, "Dallas Green remembered me."

THE SETTING

Ryne Sandberg was the Cubs' starting second baseman—on his way to a Hall of Fame career and recognition as one of the best ever to play the position—immediately. In 1982, his first year with the Cubs, he played 156 games and batted .271.

Instantly evaluated as a good glove man, Sandberg carried a reliable stick. He had never exhibited terrific power in the minors; but as he grew

---

NAME: Ryne Dee Sandberg
BORN: September 18, 1959, in Spokane, Washington
HOMETOWN: Spokane, Washington
CURRENT RESIDENCE: Phoenix, Arizona and Chicago, Illinois
OCCUPATION: Retired major-league baseball player; former Chicago baseball broadcaster; manager, Peoria Chiefs
POSITION: Second base
HEIGHT: 6-foot-2
PLAYING WEIGHT: 180 pounds
ACCOMPLISHMENTS: Played 16 seasons, one with the Philadelphia Phillies, 15 with the Chicago Cubs; final statistics include 2,164 games played, .285 batting average, 282 home runs, 1,061 runs batted in; 1984 National League Most Valuable Player; 10-time National League All-Star; nine-time Gold Glove winner; led the National League in home runs in 1990; led the National League in runs scored three times; elected to the Baseball Hall of Fame in 2005.
THE GAME: Chicago Cubs versus St. Louis Cardinals—June 23, 1984

Considered one of the best second basemen of all-time, Ryne Sandberg was inducted into the Baseball Hall of Fame in 2005 after a 16-year big-league career, 15 of them spent with the Cubs. Sandberg was a Most Valuable Player Award winner, was chosen for 10 All-Star teams, and won nine Gold Glove Awards. *Brace Photo*

more comfortable in a new organization, with new teammates, and in the majors overall, he began hitting the long ball more frequently.

By 1984, his third season with Chicago, Sandberg was ready to bust out. In a memorable Cubs campaign that led to a division title and a dramatic playoff series, Sandberg exploded into stardom. Sandberg led the National League in runs scored with 114. He led the league with 19 triples and added 19 homers and also batted .314. He was chosen for his first All-Star team and was named MVP at the end of the season.

In the middle of Sandberg's spectacular stretch, as the Cubs were starting to flex muscles and assert themselves, he produced a game that is one of the most famous regular-season games in club history. He turned in a performance that left fans in awe and indelibly etched itself in witnesses' minds. Many fans can't remember what team the Cubs were playing and simply refer to the contest as "The Ryne Sandberg Game." Many fans, of course, do remember that the opponent was the St. Louis Cardinals, the Cubs' chief rival, and that the pitcher Sandberg recorded his heroics against was future Hall of Famer Bruce Sutter.

The monumental game featured Sandberg smashing two home runs, three singles, and driving in seven runs at Wrigley Field as he rallied the Cubs twice in a close game before a captivated national television audience.

The pivotal moments were the ninth inning—when Sandberg hit a solo home run off Sutter to tie the game 9-9 and send it into extra innings—and in the 10th inning, when Sandberg homered again for an 11-11 tie, rescuing the Cubs after the Cardinals scored two runs.

THE GAME OF MY LIFE

BY RYNE SANDBERG

I've heard that phrase, "The Ryne Sandberg Game" about a million times. It absolutely is a memorable game. Ever since 1984, when I'm approached by fans, they've all mentioned it. They say, "Hey, Ryne, do you remember the game against Bruce Sutter?" My response is, "Absolutely." That was a game that changed me as a player, for one, and also gave our team a huge boost.

What's kind of funny about it is people call that the "Sandberg Game." I think I'm the only one who's ever called it "The Bruce Sutter Game." That's the way that I look at it.

That was my first year where I was asked by my manager, Jim Frey, to on occasion look for a pitch if I was ahead in the count and look to drive it. He wanted, hopefully, for some of my line drives to leave the park for home runs. He was very explicit.

He had just come from the American League. He loved the home runs, and he was a mentor of Earl Weaver of the Orioles, who was saying there was nothing better than a three-run home run. So that was the mind-set of Jim Frey when he came over to the Cubs. Early that season, he taught me about turning on balls, looking for fastballs in fastball situations, and being aggressive on those counts and hitting the ball hard. I really hadn't had that approach up to that point.

The way the game went, I had already had a good game with three singles, and a few RBIs. It was one of those days with the wind blowing out slightly, and I remember we had fallen behind 6-0 or 7-0 early in the game. We just chipped away; and as it turned out, I came up in the ninth inning against who I thought was the best reliever in the game at the time.

Bruce Sutter was a notorious ground-ball pitcher. At best, you might hit a hard grounder off of him. But I looked at a pitch down and in. I got underneath it, hit it for a home run in the ninth; and then I hit another one off him again in the tenth. He was still in there pitching for a third inning—in those days, the relievers or closers would go two or three innings if they had to.

I just remember running around the bases at Wrigley Field—the place was going bananas.

GAME RESULTS

The Cubs won the game, 12-11, in 11 innings. Chicago had taken a 36-31 record into the game but had lost six of its previous eight games. The victory helped point the Cubs back toward the top of the standings.

"I think we were about two games out of first place," Sandberg said, "and that was a momentum game for the whole team. I felt like it was telling all of us that, 'Hey, maybe we can do something special this year.'"

Having the awesome showing nationally telecast likely paid immediate dividends. Sandberg had been trailing Steve Sax in the All-Star voting, but the vote pattern changed after Sandberg's monumental effort. "I was trailing Steve Sax by quite a few votes," Sandberg said, "and then the next two weeks or so, I picked up a ton of votes. I credit that game with a lot of that. That exposure."

More than 20 years later, Sandberg said he is constantly asked about the game when he bumps into fans.

"People still come up to me today and ask me about that game," he said. "They tell me where they were. Many of them were at the game. Many of them were in the bleachers. Many were called by relatives who said, 'You've got to turn on this game and watch.' Many were listening to it on the radio while driving. They all have a story for me, and they just have a certain look about them when they talk about that game and talk to me about it.

"It seems like everybody was at that game. I guess they were, one way or another, in person, watching on TV, or listening on the radio."

Dennis Eckersley, still another future Hall of Famer, had just been traded to the Cubs and seemed dumbfounded by the intensity and the atmosphere. Sandberg said he had a pretty funny moment with Eckersley.

"He just sat there and watched," Sandberg said, "and after the game I remember him saying, 'Wow, Ryne, is every game like this in Wrigley Field?' He just couldn't believe what he saw, the excitement of the crowd and everything happening."

REFLECTIONS ON BASEBALL

Ryne Sandberg was a Cubs player in another notable game in team history. It was special more for the way it transformed Cub tradition than for meaning in the standings. He was on the field for the first game ever played under the lights at Wrigley in August of 1988.

"It was a big deal," Sandberg said. "It had the feeling of a playoff atmosphere, almost like everybody is watching. It was strange to take the field for the first time and see the lights and look into home plate and see the lights on the concourse. It was incredible. There was light everywhere at Wrigley Field.

"It was a whole different look, and what comes to mind is my first at-bat. They introduced me, 'Now batting, Ryne Sandberg,' and I started to walk up to the plate, and there was a huge roar from the crowd. I thought, 'Wow, this is pretty neat.' Only what happened is that Morganna the Kissing Bandit was running in from the right-field corner right at me. That's what everybody was reacting to. I thought, 'You've got to be kidding me. My first bat under the lights, and now I've got to deal with this?' But she was running so slowly that, when she got to first base, security caught up and walked her out through the visitors' dugout. Everybody booed. She never got to me. I hit the second pitch off Kevin Gross for a two-run homer, and we took the lead, 2-1, after one inning."

But the rain came and washed away all of the statistics, so the home run didn't count. Sandberg and Morganna both were washed out.

"It was a fun time," he said, "and a lot of people consider that the first night game. Though I remember hearing Harry Caray say (of the rain), 'Holy cow, even God doesn't want Wrigley to have lights.'"

Sandberg remained the Cubs' second baseman until 1997, with the exception of the 1995 season when he abruptly retired, saying he had lost his fire. He made a comeback and played two more seasons after that, however, adding to his tremendous lifetime statistical total.

The Cubs retired Sandberg's No. 23 uniform in 2005, raising the flag to the rafters of the park. In the same season, he was elected to the Baseball Hall of Fame and delivered a passionate, surprisingly dramatic acceptance speech on the state of the game.

The headline on the front page of the *Chicago Tribune* dated August 1, 2005 read, "Sandberg takes swing at selfish superstars." Sandberg was always a self-effacing superstar who played hard and let his skills do his talking more than any flamboyance. His speech touched a nerve when he lectured current stars of the game to be less self-centered and self-promoting and to show more respect to the game known as the National Pastime. He said he wanted to see more "we" than "I" in modern-day baseball.

In a memorable comment contained in Sandberg's 23-minute speech in Cooperstown, New York, as thousands listened, he said, "They tell me I played the game the way it was meant to be played. I don't know about that. I just know I had too much respect for the game to play it any other way."

Despite the seriousness of his content, Sandberg, who attends about 25 Wrigley Field games a season, ended his speech with a simple, light, exhortation that came from the heart. "Go Cubs!" he proclaimed.

Chapter 29

KERRY WOOD

THE EARLY LIFE OF KERRY WOOD

Kerry, born to Terry and Garry (really) Wood, grew up with a baseball in his hands. His father had been a talented amateur player, and from the start, Kerry and brother Donny were always on the field. Born in Irving, Texas (between Dallas and Fort Worth), Kerry grew up in the area and idolized the Rangers—especially Nolan Ryan.

Though he began his high school career as a shortstop, Wood soon moved to pitching, where he showed an overpowering fastball and a "give me the ball" mentality.

At South Grand Prairie high, Wood began to fill out and soon sparked interest from scouts. In his senior year, he finished 14-0, striking out 151 hitters in just over 81 innings. For this, he earned High School All-America honors and was taken fourth in the first round of the 1995 draft by the Chicago Cubs. He elected to skip college and sign.

Two days before the draft, however, Wood was used in both games of a doubleheader as South Grand Prairie was trying to reach its conference playoffs. Wood threw 175 pitches on the day, causing the Cubs to lash out at South Grand Prairie's coach for endangering the young righty's health.

Wood pocketed his $1.2 million signing bonus and headed for the low minors. He made three starts, pitching just 7⅓ innings, as the Cubs looked over what they'd just bought. What they found was a strong, tall young man with a high-90s fastball and a devastating curve.

During 1996, his first full season, at high Class A Daytona, Wood immediately showed why he was a first-rounder—and an uncertain quantity. He was 10-2, overpowering Florida State League hitters with 136 strikeouts in 114 innings, but also walked 70, threw ten wild pitches, hit 14 batters, and committed 12 balks.

Wood split the following season between Double- and Triple-A, where he again blew away hitters but again struggled with control. The Cubs, however, loved that he kept the ball low—he allowed only four home runs in 152 combined innings—and after one start at Triple-A Iowa in April 1998 (where he fanned 11 in five innings), the Cubs called him up.

THE SETTING

NAME: Kerry Lee Wood
BORN: June 16, 1977 in Irving, Texas
HOMETOWN: Grand Prairie, Texas
CURRENT RESIDENCE: Chicago, Illinois
OCCUPATION: Pitcher, Chicago Cubs
POSITION: Pitcher
HEIGHT: 6-foot-5
PLAYING WEIGHT: 210 pounds
ACCOMPLISHMENTS: Has played 14 seasons between 1998 and 2012, 12 with the Chicago Cubs; has won 86 major-league games; led National League in strikeouts, 2003; led National League in strikeouts per nine innings, 1998 and 2003; National League Rookie of the Year, 1998; two-time National League All-Star; currently rates second all-time among pitchers in strikeouts per nine innings
THE GAME: Chicago Cubs versus Houston Astros—May 6, 1998

Chicago manager Jim Riggleman needed someone to add fire to its pitching staff; the team had opened the season with finesse righties Kevin Tapani, Mark Clark, and Steve Trachsel as the top three starters. Wood threw much harder than any of them (some joked that he threw harder than all of them combined).

In his first four big-league starts, Wood was alternately awful and superb. He was bombed off the hill twice and in his other two starts allowed one run in 12 innings, giving him a 2-2 record and a 5.89 ERA with 25 strikeouts in his first 18⅓ frames.

Already known as "Kid K," Wood missed the plate often, but was what baseball people call "effectively wild"—i.e. his lack of control could be a benefit, because it kept hitters uncomfortable. Unfortunately, that kind of wildness meant that he was racking up a lot of 3-2 counts and throwing a lot of pitches.

On May 6, 1998, at a dark, warm, and cloudy Wrigley Field, Kerry Wood would make his fifth big-league start, facing the Houston Astros.

THE GAME OF MY LIFE

The sun was barely in evidence on May 6, but 70-degree temperatures brought out 15,758 to see the first-place Astros battle the third-place Cubs. Young Sandy Martinez was behind the plate, working with Wood for the first time.

Wood began with a statement, wiping out Craig Biggio, Derek Bell, and Jeff Bagwell on strikes, taking just 14 pitches to get through the inning. Houston's Shane Reynolds answered by fanning the Cubs' 1-2-3 hitters in the home half.

Houston's Jack Howell and Moises Alou went down swinging before Dave Clark flied out to end the second. In their half, the Cubs scored when Mark Grace doubled, went to third on Clark's error, and scampered home on Henry Rodriguez' sacrifice fly.

Houston's Ricky Gutierrez led off the third with a grounder in the hole. Third baseman Kevin Orie reached to his left and saw the ball bounce off his glove. "Base hit," intoned official scorer Don Friske, and nobody grumbled.

That was the only hit that the Astros would collect all day.

From the start, Wood was absolutely dominant. Not only did the Astros not put the ball in play often, they rarely even got the bat on the ball. Of his 122 pitches, only 30 of them were hit, either in fair or foul territory.

As the game progressed, Wood began to break out his hard, sharp breaking ball even more, and the strikeouts began to pile up. Five in a row in the fourth and fifth. Three men swinging on 16 pitches in the seventh. At this point, Wood had struck out 15 and hadn't walked a batter, much less allowed a run.

Steve Carlton, Tom Seaver, and David Cone had each fanned 19 men in game to share the NL record. Wood would have to fan four of the six remaining Astros outs to top the mark.

"I wasn't really worried about the strikeouts," Wood said later. "I knew it was getting up there. It was just one of those days where everything you throw is crossing the plate. It just felt like I was playing catch."

Rain began to fall in the seventh inning, making it even harder for Houston hitters to see and, therefore, have a chance to connect with what Wood was throwing.

Some of the Astros grumbled later that home plate umpire Jerry Meals was generous with his strike-zone calls. Houston starter Shane Reynolds struck out ten in his eight innings, lending some credence to this theory. But in truth the Astros batters were simply baffled and overpowered by a pitcher none of them had faced.

Dave Clark led off the eighth and went to a full count, but went down swinging. Gutierrez strode to the plate and strode back to the dugout four pitches later, having waved at strike three. The fans on hand were apoplectic, and went even nuttier when Wood got Brad Ausmus looking. Eighteen strikeouts. Hands clicked on keyboards furiously in the press box, sending out to the world the news of this incredible work in progress.

Almost forgotten was that the Cubs were clinging to a 1-0 lead. But in the home eighth, Chicago tacked on another run against Reynolds on two singles and a force out.

Wood strode to the hill in the ninth. At no point did manager Riggleman consider lifting his young flamethrower, nor did he keep him in to break any records.

"The focus of the day was trying to win the game. Their guy, Shane Reynolds, threw a very good game. Somewhere around the seventh or eighth inning, someone brought it to my attention that Kerry had 16 or 17 strikeouts. You are not counting them along the way. What he was doing at that point was secondary to the game."

And was Wood ever focused. Billy Spiers, a smart veteran hitter, pinch-hit for Reynolds and slapped four fouls in five pitches, sitting on Wood's fastball. Wood and Martinez, therefore, broke out the curve, and Spiers had no shot. Swing and a miss! One out, 19 strikeouts.

When Craig Biggio followed by taking a ball, then hitting a soft grounder to shortstop, the fans actually booed, because they wanted

Wood to have a chance to break the all-time record. But Wood was happy to get the second out.

What else remained but to finish with a flourish? Wood threw Derek Bell ball one, then whooshed three straight strikes past the right fielder's futile bat. Game over. Twenty strikeouts. A 2-0 victory, and a place in the record books.

GAME RESULTS

In winning 2-0, Kerry Wood threw a 20-strikeout, no-walk, one-hit shutout, something nobody had ever done in the history of baseball.

"I couldn't imagine ever doing this," Wood said after the game. "It's going to be special to strike out that many, regardless of who has done it. It hasn't settled in, and I'm still in awe a little bit.

"I'm going to give most of the credit to the fans. They were in it the whole game. Every time I got two strikes they were on their feet. You can't ask for anything more than that."

As the years have rolled by, many more claimed to have seen it than actually did. "I think I've met everybody who was at the game," Wood said years later. "Fifteeen thousand? I've met about 26,000. Every now and then people say, 'I was there.' I've met every last one."

Roger Clemens, another of Wood's idols, twice fanned 20 men in a game, but in those instances threw a three-hitter and a five-hitter. Wood's game was one of the most dominating performances in major league history.

Wood held the Astros' 3-4-5 hitters, Jeff Bagwell, Jack Howell, and Moises Alou, to an 0-for-9—all of them strikeouts. Only two Astros even got a ball out of the infield.

Had he not hit a man with a pitch and ceded Orie's infield hit, Wood would have touched perfection. As it is, he threw a 20-strikeout, one-hit shutout against a team that would win 102 games during the regular season.

Some years later, Riggleman recalled, "It was just electrifying, the way he was throwing that day. I only had five years at Wrigley Field, but to me, I would guess that he probably pitched the greatest game ever there.

"His talent indicated that on any given day, something similar could happen, but nobody could expect something like *that*. It was a combination of extraordinary performance against a very good offense. He was outstanding from the first inning on."

The fans and assembled press corps were dazed at what they had seen. After the game, Cubs first baseman Mark Grace stood in the Cubs clubhouse, puffing a cigarette, and summed it all up for the media. "That's without a doubt the best performance I've ever seen." After a short pause, he added, "And it's the best performance YOU'VE ever seen."

REFLECTIONS ON BASEBALL

Kerry Wood is a lesson in the fleeting nature of glory. Despite great gifts and a strong work ethic, he never achieved the stardom predicted for him.

He went 13-6 in 1998 and netted NL Rookie of the Year honors even though he sat out the last month of the season due to a strained right elbow. Wood had been overused all the way back to high school, and the stress of those constant full counts quickly took a toll.

But what really hurt him was a decision that came that October. The Cubs, down 2-0 in their best-of-five playoff series against Atlanta, were hoping for a miracle, and GM Jim Hendry and manager Jim Riggleman decided to pitch Wood—who hadn't taken the mound in weeks—on a cool autumn night at Wrigley Field.

While Wood pitched five gutsy innings, allowing one run on three hits, the Cubs lost, and worse, their young pitcher, already burdened with the expectation of being a franchise savior, did more damage to his elbow.

During spring training in 1999, Wood did not feel right, and was found to have a torn ulnar collateral ligament in his right elbow. He underwent "Tommy John" reconstructive surgery April 8 and missed the entire season, not returning to the active roster until May 2000.

For many pitchers, such surgery, when done early in their careers, has actually strengthened the elbow. And Wood's elbow *has* remained healthy, although he continued to have control problems as he worked his way back into the Cubs' rotation.

During 2000 and 2001, Wood took his turn every fifth day and fashioned 8-7 and 12-6 marks, but still walked far too many men for comfort. He threw more than 100 pitches in most of his starts. In 2001, a sore shoulder shelved him for a couple of weeks.

Following that injury, Wood rehabbed and enjoyed his best years. In 2002 (12-11, 3.66) and 2003 (14-11, 3.20) he was one of the league's top hurlers. In '03, he topped the NL with 266 strikeouts as the Cubs won the Central Division title.

He won two games in the NLDS over Atlanta and pitched well in his first NLCS start against the Marlins, but Game Seven of the League Championship Series was essentially the beginning of Wood's fall.

Florida scored three off Wood in the first inning, but the Cubs came back with five runs (two of them on Wood's homer). In the fifth, though, the visitors took a 6-5 lead and tacked on another in the sixth. The disappointing 9-6 loss, in which Wood allowed seven runs, ended Chicago's playoff hopes.

It was a harbinger of further miseries. In 2004, he was suspended twice for arguing with umpires, and what's worse, he sat out two months with a strained triceps. In 2005, the shoulder began barking, and shelved him three separate times. The following season, it all came crashing down as he suffered a torn rotator cuff that kept him out until August 2007.

From a peak of near-dominance, he had fallen far. From 2004-07 he won just 13 games. There are some who claim that Wood refused to change his delivery to ease strain on his arm and shoulder, and the results certainly leave room for blame on all sides.

By this time, the Cubs had recognized the inevitable truth—that Wood would never again be a reliable starter. He took over closing duties in 2008, theoretically to maximize his ability and minimize injury risk, and notched 34 saves in 65 games, fanning 84 and walking 18 in 66 innings.

Having seen their former #1 reduced to relief work, and mindful of his 12 DL trips in less than a decade, Chicago made it clear that if Wood wanted to explore the market, make some real money, and join a better team, they wouldn't mind.

So Wood left the Cubs that winter to sign a two-year deal with the Cleveland Indians. While he saved 20 games of the Tribe in 2009, he didn't pitch that well and lost the closer's job. A July 2010 trade to the Yankees gave Wood a chance to shine under the brightest light, and he was spectacular, allowing just two runs in 26 innings and registering 31 strikeouts while setting up Mariano Rivera.

Following that campaign, Wood—always a Cub at heart—expressed a desire to "come home," and he inked a one-year, $1.5 million deal. The plan was for Wood to serve as an eighth-inning setup man to Carlos Marmol, put up some good numbers, and—he hoped—convince another club that he could be a ninth-inning man again.

Unfortunately, while Wood pitched okay, the Cubs belly-flopped to a 71-91 mark. Nobody called to ask Wood to close games for them, so he chose to stay in the Windy City, inking a two-year, $6 million contract to again serve as a setup man and veteran presence.

While his career has hardly gone as planned—he probably will not even win 100 big-league games—Wood remains extremely popular in Chicago.

He remains approachable, held by both fans and media to be a genuinely decent guy and—as much as a pitcher can—has been a strong voice of leadership in the Cubs clubhouse over the years. It is believed that Wood wielded the bat that shattered Sammy Sosa's boom box after the declining slugger quit the team on the last day of the 2004 season.

Some fans believe that Dusty Baker, who managed the Cubs from 2003 through 2006, helped overwork and destroy Wood's shoulder, along with that of fellow phenom Mark Prior. In fact, both were damaged before either ever pitched in Chicago, but "Wood" and "Prior" remain cautionary words among baseball people when the talk turns to how NOT to protect valuable pitching arms.

But rather than mourn what could have been, most Chicago fans tend to remember how overpowering Wood was at his best. They remember the 2003 season, they remember his blazing fastball, and they remember that cool day in 1998 when a calm 20-year-old right-hander showed stuff as good as anyone had seen in decades.

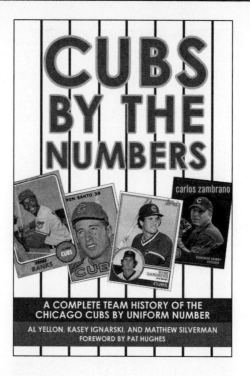

Cubs by the Numbers

A Complete Team History of the Chicago Cubs by Uniform Number

by Kasey Ignarski, Matthew Silverman, and Al Yellon

Foreword by Foreword by Pat Hughes

What do Dizzy Dean, Catfish Metkovich, John Boccabella, Bill Buckner, Mark Prior, and Kevin Hart all have in common? They all wore number 22 for the Chicago Cubs, even though seven decades have passed between the last time Dizzy Dean buttoned up a Cubs uniform with that number and the first time reliever Kevin Hart performed the same routine.

Since the Chicago Cubs first adopted uniform numbers in 1932, the team has handed out only 71 numbers to more than 1,100 players. That's a lot of overlap. It also makes for a lot of good stories. *Cubs by the Numbers* tells those stories for every Cub since '32, from 1930s outfielder Ethan Allen to current ace Carlos Zambrano. This book lists the players alphabetically and by number, but the biographies help trace the history of baseball's most beloved team in a new way.

$14.95 Paperback

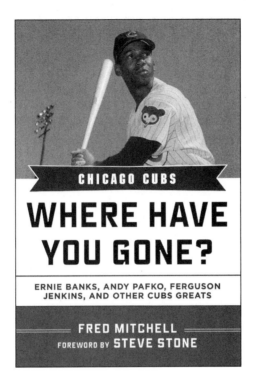

Chicago Cubs: Where Have You Gone?

Ernie Banks, Andy Pafko, Ferguson Jenkins,
and Other Cubs Greats

by Fred Mitchell

Foreword by Steve Stone

In *Chicago Cubs: Where Have You Gone?*, Chicago sportswriter Fred Mitchell catches up with more than fifty former Cubs players—some of them famous, some of them obscure, all of them unforgettable. From Mr. Cub, Ernie Banks, to lesser-known players such as Pete LaCock, avid fans of this long-suffering team will remember them for every heartbreak, every costly error, and yes, every glorious moment. Find out what happened after the lights went down and the gloves came off with such Cubs greats as Ferguson Jenkins, Andy Pafko, Dickie Noles, Gary Matthews, Billy Williams, Milt Pappas, Bobby Dernier, Lee Smith, Scott Sanderson, Jim Frey, Shawon Dunston, Ed Lynch, Don Zimmer, Steve Trout, Ron Santo, Steve Stone, Dallas Green, and so many more.

$24.95 Hardcover

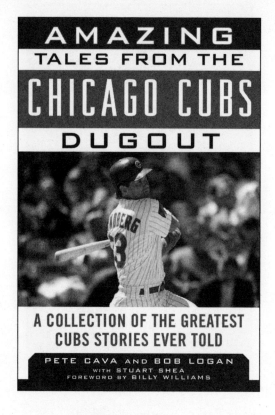

Amazing Tales from the Chicago Cubs Dugout

A Collection of the Greatest Cubs Stories Ever Told

by Bob Logan and Pete Cava with Stuart Shea

Foreword by Billy Williams

Amazing Stories From the Cubs Dugout is crammed with stories, quotes, and anecdotes about the greatest Cubs players of past and present. The story of the Cubs is part legend, part pathos; heroic and, on occasion, hilarious. Enjoy the heartbreak and joy of unforgettable afternoons at Wrigley Field. Without a doubt Amazing Stories From the Cubs Dugout is a must for any Chicago Cubs fan.

$24.95 Hardcover